School of American Research
Advanced Seminar Series

DOUGLAS W. SCHWARTZ, GENERAL EDITOR

SCHOOL OF AMERICAN RESEARCH
ADVANCED SEMINAR SERIES

The Dying Community

Grateful acknowledgment is made to
JAMES P. DUNIGAN
for his creative role
in the development of the
Advanced Seminar Series
and the general program of the
School of American Research

THE DYING COMMUNITY

EDITED BY
ART GALLAHER, JR.
AND
HARLAND PADFIELD

A SCHOOL OF AMERICAN RESEARCH BOOK
UNIVERSITY OF NEW MEXICO PRESS • Albuquerque

Library of Congress Cataloging in Publication Data

Main entry under title:

The Dying Community.

(School of American Research advanced seminar series)
Based on a seminar held in September 1976 at the School
of American Research, Santa Fe.
"A School of American Research book."
Bibliography: p. 288
Includes index.
1. Community—Congresses. 2. Community life—
Congresses. 3. Cities and towns—United States—
Congresses. I. Gallaher, Art, 1925– II. Padfield,
Harland. III. Series: Santa Fe, N.M. School of
American Research. Advanced seminar series.
HM131.D98   307   79-56814
ISBN 0-8263-0535-0

Foreword

The history of human settlement has included a persistent movement of people from smaller to larger communities, a process accelerated with the birth of civilization and its great urban centers. Our species, with astonishing steadfastness, has viewed cities as filled with action, glamour, variety, opporunity, and the promise of an easier life, as can be seen dramatically when flying over any Third World capital, where shantytown suburbs are crammed with emigrants from outlying areas. Each new arrival is hopeful of making his fortune within the "lights of the city" and confident he will escape the backbreaking labor that has traditionally been his way of life. Even modern countries reflect this movement; the United States, for decades, has experienced population growth, yet over this same period nearly half of its counties have regularly lost population, the shift clearly one from rural settlements to growing urban centers.

But the magnetic attraction of the city is only one cause of settlement decline. Some communities have come to an end swiftly by a military blow of the type the Romans dealt Carthage or by the kind of volcanic burial Vesuvius gave Pompeii and Herculaneum. More frequently, communities have perished slowly, sometimes hanging onto life for centuries. It was a deterioration of the environment that caused the abandonment of hundreds of pueblos in America's Southwest. The gradual exhaustion of natural resources, like the depletion of mineral veins, produced ghost towns throughout the mining belts of the world. And cultural changes such as the move of a political capital or the decline of a religious center have been just as effective in bringing to an end the life of a community.

Scattered over the world are thousands of such settlements that have lost population and cultural vitality, represented both by archaeological ruins where the process has been complete and by communities still in the throes of death, waiting either for the end or for revitalization. Yet, with our philosophical orientation toward progress and growth, our emphasis on bigness and success, we have tended to ignore the human component of the dying community. We have overlooked the inhabitants who remain behind, less mindful of the effect of living in a community where the end is imaginable. This volume is concerned with an understanding of these people and their communities.

The seminar that addressed these objectives utilized a variety of disciplinary and methodological approaches in a cross-cultural examination of components of the dying community, and each approach is represented in this volume. William Adams provides an archaeological perspective on community death and its symptoms. Resource economist Marion Clawson utilizes community natural resources as a point of departure. Art Gallaher, from his own anthropological work in Ireland and the American Midwest, examines the impact of external authority on the little community. Arthur Vidich considers the intrusive impact of the industrialized world on the realm of traditional settlements and the curious idealization of each by the other. Wayne Rohrer and Diane Quantic use literary and sociological data to examine the lingering impact of resource scarcity on the lives of the people. Harland Padfield probes the vulnerability of the rural community to national and global economic institutions. Alvin Bertrand, a rural sociologist, focuses on minorities and their extreme dependence on successful community leadership. David Looff describes child-rearing practices in the dying settlements of Appalachia and their resultant dependent, nonverbal, impulsive, and undisciplined adult personalities. Mary Wylie's essay on the elderly describes the positive benefits of living in a dying community with little pressure for economic growth and no orientation to youth culture. In the final chapter, psychologist Hannah Levin discusses individual adaptive and maladaptive responses within the dying community environment and the frequently strong desire to restore the past, which for survival must be overcome by the will to change.

From these divergent approaches, the reader begins to understand how the process of community decay may be a normal and complementary side of growth. While the intimate community has served human needs for thousands of years and is still celebrated in the midst of its destruction, nevertheless the life of each community, as Cicero said of man, perhaps should include preparations for its own death. What this volume has accomplished, as Gallaher and Padfield have clearly shown in their excellent integrative introductory chapter, is not only a description of the elements of the dying community but, through the volume's multidisciplinary variety, a thoughtful understanding and deep empathy for the inhabitants of these communities, a result rarely attained in an analytical work of social science.

Douglas W. Schwartz
School of American Research

Preface

This book is based on a seminar that had its inception in the fall of 1965. I was doing research at the time in County Clare, western Ireland, living in a small village that traced its ancestry through some six hundred years. This community—rising as it does above the debris of Bronze Age forts and the remains of villages racked by nineteenth-century famine and two hundred years of emigration to the New World—long felt that it would follow the demise of its neighbors. In 1965, however, the mood was one of some optimism for the future, a belief that the course of history might be taking a turn for the better. This set me to thinking about the sociocultural forces responsible for this turn, and to comparing this experience to that I had known growing up in a dying, frontier community in western Oklahoma, and to that I had while studying a small community in the northern Ozarks that felt its future irreversibly doomed.

I was visited that fall by a long-time friend and colleague from the University of Kentucky, Douglas Schwartz, who was then working on migration and abandoned settlement problems in the Grand Canyon. On a trip we made into the Connemara region of County Galway—an area that even more dramatically than Clare conveys the awesome feel of widespread community death—we speculated on and discussed the notion of *dying communities* and the need to explore more formally what lay behind them. We talked then of a seminar or symposium as an appropriate vehicle for doing this.

In 1971 I was back in Ireland on the second stage of my research there, and again I was visited briefly by Douglas Schwartz, who by now was director of the School of American Research in Santa Fe. We picked up again on our earlier discussion of dying communities, but this time in the context of the Advanced Seminar series that he had implemented recently at the School of American Research. He encouraged the development of a seminar on the subject and I agreed that on my return to the States I would set to work on it. I want to take this opportunity thus to thank Douglas Schwartz personally for his continued encouragement—no matter what other project I happened to be involved in at the time—of my interest in dying communities.

Early in 1972 I met Harland Padfield, who at the time was organizing the Western Rural Development Center at Oregon State University. I was intrigued particularly with the work he was doing on *social marginalization,* and as a result of our early discussions we decided to work together to develop a seminar on the dying community. We soon expanded our discussions to include Paul Barkley, an agricultural resource economist from Washington State University, who was visiting at the Western Rural Development Center during 1973–74.

During 1974 Gallaher, Padfield, and Barkley met for several "mini-seminars" in which we exchanged ideas, argued, and in the end agreed upon the approach to the dying community seminar reported in this book. Our discussions during this period turned mainly on the substantive thrust of the seminar and on how broadly we should pitch our ultimate objectives. While we accepted early on the need to develop a conceptual and theoretical framework for examining the decline and dissolution of community—a subject of too little attention as compared to concerns for community growth and development—we were not sure whether to focus also on the implications of community death for development policy. The social action and intervention orientations shared by the three of us made it difficult to give on this point, but in the end we decided to restrict our objectives to clarification of the basic elements in community decline, and to examine what this means for the people who live in such communities. For personal reasons, Paul Barkley had to withdraw from our team before the seminar was held. Both Padfield and I, however, want to express our appreciation for his contribution to the overall effort.

The dying community seminar met for six days at the School of American Research in Santa Fe in mid-September 1976. Essays from each of the participants were distributed well ahead of our arrival in Santa Fe. Seminar time—formal sessions during the day and discussions continuing informally into every night—thus was confined to an intensive, hard-hitting examination and refinement of the issues raised by each of the contributors. On all counts, the seminar was an intellectually stimulating and rewarding experience. Padfield and I both wish to take this opportunity, therefore, to convey again to the participants our appreciation of the contributions made by each. We wish to note further that you have responded to our queries, suggested revisions of your essays, and delays with exemplary patience and cooperation.

The advanced seminar model developed by the School of American Research is indeed exemplary—it bends all effort to insure that seminar participants sustain a focus on the intellectual issues at hand. Crucial to this enterprise is the School's excellent support staff, whose attention to detail removes all excuses for not getting the work of a seminar done. On behalf of all participants, we want to express our appreciation to the School of American Research, and especially to its director, Douglas Schwartz, for sponsoring our seminar and the publication of this volume. We wish to thank, too, the staff of the School for helping to make the seminar so productive and the completion of this volume such a pleasant task.

Finally, I wish to acknowledge the University of Kentucky's generous support for time and travel during various stages of the seminar effort, and for clerical assistance at various stages of manuscript preparation. Harland Padfield wishes to acknowledge support from the Oregon State University Agricultural Experiment Station, the Western Rural Development Center, Grant GA SS 7404 from the Rockefeller Foundation, and Grants 516–15–44, 616–15–58, and 701–15–77 from the U.S.D.A. Cooperative State Research Service.

Art Gallaher, Jr.

Contents

1
Theory of the Dying Community

ART GALLAHER, JR.
Department of Anthropology
University of Kentucky

HARLAND PADFIELD
Department of Anthropology
Oregon State University

Broadly speaking, the concept of *community* refers to social organization common to, and characteristic of, the human species. Some form of community is necessary for human survival. More specifically, the social bases for community are those shared, socioculturally derived sentiments that enable humankind to organize social relationships in unique ways. In the grand sweep of human history, *community*, as defined here, is, then, part of the very nature of man. It is the essence of that social condition necessary for human survival, and it is not necessarily place-specific. Community in this sense has existed as long as those qualities we have come to label *human*.

The seminar reported in this volume is concerned, however, with community at a lower level of abstraction, that is, with *the community*. By the latter we mean simply *a social unit existing for a purpose in a particular place*. According to this definition, there have been communities in one form or other through all of human history. Social units resembling the model of pre-Neolithic hunters-gatherers-fishermen, in which community, society, and culture must have been virtually

1

coterminous entities, survived to modern times among such peoples as the Naskapi of northern North America (Speck 1935), the Arunta of Australia (Spencer and Gillen 1927), and the nomadic Yahgan of Tierra del Fuego (Cooper 1946), to name only a few well-known examples. Though all evoke in our minds the notion of community, it is not the same image that we get when we think of the Neolithic Swiss farmer-fishermen who built their wooden houses set on piles out in lakes, or of modern farmers who identify with a village in the Ozarks (Gallaher 1961). In turn, our conception of community among the latter is not the same as that we associate with the high degree of elaboration and technical development typically attributed to the civilizations of Mesopotamian, Palestinian, and Egyptian Bronze Age cities (Childe 1946), or with more recent refinements in contemporary urban adaptation.

All associational forms share what we believe to be the most basic of all purposes—the development of collective solutions to meet the needs of group survival. If these needs cannot be met in a specific case, the psychological sense of community diminishes and a community begins to die. Projecting from this very simple premise, it is obvious that a mere assemblage of people—even if they wish to establish a community—does not a community make. Both resources and the decision-making prerogatives for the allocation of those resources must be present.

Our concern here is with that form of association generally referred to as the little community. As Redfield (1960:3) notes, it "has been the very predominant form of human living throughout the history of mankind." And Tocqueville (1947:56), referring to the village, saw it as "the only association . . . so perfectly natural that wherever a number of men are collected it seems to constitute itself." Universal in distribution, the little community has served human needs well in specific times and places for thousands of years. Its legacy, which is strong, typically evokes widespread nostalgia and commitment, and has developed a host of advocates who value its social solidarity. This solidarity is seen as the product of primary group ties, cooperative social interaction, and Gemeinschaft-type social relationships. It is seen by many, in fact, as embodying the essence of the idealized, perfect form of human adaptation, as the model against which to evaluate contemporary society (Bernard 1973:106–7).

We wish to emphasize that our conception of the community is

2

more focused than that commonly found in the social science literature. Even a casual examination reveals that the concept has spawned
a great deal of conjecture and research. Jessie Bernard (1973:33–120)
cuts through this massive literature, noting that it projects paradigms
around the ecological, class, power, and interpersonal-relations aspects
of community life. While we do not think it profitable to review these
paradigms here, it is worth noting that much that is learned from them
reveals more about how social scientists view community than about
what is happening in communities. Not to disparage the rich conceptual imagination of our colleagues in this area—community may well
be one of the most overly conceptualized areas in the social sciences—
we feel that our needs can be satisfied best with the simplest possible
approach.

We reiterate, therefore, our belief that a community exists when the
group seeks to ensure its survival through collective solutions to problems. This is not intended as a definition of community, but a way of
making operational the basic concerns that make the death of a social
unit important. Working from this base, we can say that those who
make up a community can be expected to realize and value their
distinctiveness, and that an observer can know something of a community other than his own. Our concern is not to become mired in the
frequent academic argument about what community is in the abstract,
apart from those who value such identity. Rather, we hold seriously to
the premise that both views—the inside and the outside—are important. As anthropologists, we stress the need for objectivity in the latter
and knowledge of the values and sentiments that give rise to the former. If our biases run toward an insider perspective, we are, of course,
following the familiar pathway of cultural analysis; the most important
knowledge to have of a culture is knowledge of the sentiments, ideas,
and judgments held by those who share that culture. In this sense, the
editors have had pressed on them in their own field experience the fact
that it is important to most people whether they perceive their community as holding promise for the future, as dying, or as likely to die.

A number of conditions call into question the viability of the little
community as a form of association for the collective solutions to
problems. That these conditions are not new is indicated in George
Homans's observation some time ago that "civilization has fed on the
rot of the village" (Homans 1950:367). Over the past several thousand

years the net flow of population has been mainly from the village to the city. Despite the longevity of some of the processes subsumed under the rubric of civilization, however, it may be that these processes are now more intense, and the potential for dissolution of the little community therefore greater.

Briefly, the many studies done in and of little communities document clearly that sociocultural change is a persistent phenomenon impacting all of them. The physical and social isolation of small communities throughout the world increasingly is in sharp decline because of the advance of urbanization, industrialization, and bureaucratization. Significantly, all of these processes modify not only the objective relationships, but also the quality of the subjective relationships of those who live in little communities. These quantitative and qualitative dimensions of sociocultural change, and the rate at which they occur, have led to increased interest everywhere in social planning and in centralizing the allocation and distribution of resources.

The substance of most of the changes noted above focus on modern technology, transportation, and communication. Developments in each of these areas, especially when controlled by agents external to the little community, place constraints on a local group's ability to manage the solutions to its own problems. We are not talking here about people losing their sense of community in the broader meaning of that concept, the concern raised by theoreticians like Robert Nisbet in his *Quest for Community* (1953). Rather, we are talking about their surrender of problem definition and solution to external forces. In this process the controls of the local group over the behavior of its members weaken and member loyalties shift to larger frames of reference. As is often the case, the "community" may still have a name, may still recognize geographical boundaries, and may still have people living within those boundaries. Their shared adaptive patterns, however, are no longer locale-specific or collectively addressed.

It is apparent that in some instances it is possible to say that such and such a community is dying. Further, no matter how we classify them— folk or urban, sacred or secular, literate or nonliterate, homogeneous or heterogeneous, Gemeinschaft or Gesellschaft—all little communities are influenced by the processes indicated. Each process thus has the effect of decreasing the character and intensity of psychocultural identification that the residents of a particular community feel for it. The direction seems always toward proliferation of locale-independent rela-

4

tionships, toward an outward extension of social networks, and toward classes, coalitions, and special interest associations that expand and contract, form and re-form, in amoebalike fashion. Given the kind of pressures indicated, some small communities grow, expand, and change, while others stagnate, decline, and even disappear (French 1969:chpt. 6).

It is in this spirit that the seminar on dying communities was conceived—to understand those conditions that cause some little communities to lose their capacity for survival. Our belief is that, though there is increasing awareness of the conditions noted above, much of social science and policy making proceeds as though (1) the death of community does not occur, and (2) should decline be detected the process is one that could, and should, be reversed. We feel the need therefore to explore some of the important issues bearing on the resources necessary to sustain the little community, populations in said community, and factors that influence decision-making prerogatives in it. This exploration should reveal some understanding of the processes of community decline, enable us to examine what life is like for those who live in dying communities, and provide insight into theory of the dying community. Our views on the dying community determined the selection of contributors and essays for this seminar, and the order in which they are presented.

In organizing the seminar we felt that we should dispense empirically with the question of whether communities do, in fact, die. The best evidence on this point, it seemed to us, should be that derived from culture history. Hence we set the first paper to examine the evidence from prehistory bearing on whether communities disappear, and, if they do, under what conditions.

We begin therefore with an essay by archaeologist William Y. Adams. Professor Adams's essay is appropriate as a beginning because it clearly demonstrates, from the perspective of archaeology and history at least, that communities can and do die. But while Adams's piece serves as closure to the premise of the seminar and of this book, it is an appropriate start for other reasons as well. It provides a firm philosophical basis for thinking about dying-community phenomena. As Adams's lucid analysis and vivid illustrations clearly show, not one but at least two concepts of dying community can be inferred from archaeological and historical data: dying community as a place being abandoned; and dying community as the collapse of an entire sociocultural system as exemplified by a regional, city-state, or empire system. Adams illustrates each phenomenon on the basis of both written and archaeological records.

After an extensive discussion of theories of causes of community death, Adams compels us to think about the phenomenon in terms of a dialectic between two contemporaneous but opposing processes—decay and repair. He reiterates this theme again and again: it is not the fact of destruction but the failure to rebuild, not the presence of decay but the lack of the presence of revitalization, that requires explanation. He also points out that only when an entire region is abandoned at one time do archaeologists think in terms of small, local communities *dying*. He leaves us with a conceptually simplifying but emotionally disquieting conclusion: the decay of individual communities and the decay of larger sociocultural systems are interrelated phenomena.

Adams identifies, defines, and links, then, two fundamental concepts of community death and decay—the abandonment of a natural region and the collapse of a sociocultural system. Although Adams's paper appropriately does not address it, there is yet a third archconcept of dying community that should be mentioned at this point—death of community as the extinction on a global scale of a *form* of association and social environment. Although this concept is emphasized in Chapter 5 by Arthur Vidich, it is necessary to identify it now because it surfaces repeatedly in intervening chapters, intermingling with the other two concepts of dying community. In Vidich's words, "In this fundamental sense one can speak of the death of the spatially isolated community and its distinctive cultural, organizational, ritual and ceremonial forms."

With the help of Adams and Vidich then, we identify not two but three overarching and somewhat interrelated concepts of dying community: *the abandonment of a natural region; the collapse of a sociocultural system; the global extinction of a heretofore universal form of association*. We shall come back to these three key concepts repeatedly as we attempt to place each chapter, retroactive to the learning experience of this seminar, into a coherent theoretical framework.

The general processes identified by Adams are delineated in greater detail by shifting from a historical and archaeological overview of dying communities in past civilizations to an analysis of the interrelationships between natural resources and dying communities in con-

6

temporary societies. Basic to group survival, of course, are natural resources broadly defined. Resource economist Marion Clawson defines such resources as "any quality of nature that the culture knows how to use economically to an end that is sought." His definition includes not only extractive and renewable resources, but climatic, locational, and cultural resources as well. He further points out that when or where any of these resources exist on a significant scale, human communities will develop; and in every case where the resource base shrinks, the community will also shrink.

Clawson's analysis shows how a community's culture, location, size, and rapidity of growth and decline are all determined in part by the kind of natural resource giving rise to it. Extractive or exhaustible resource bases tend to have short life cycles; renewable-resource-based towns, such as agricultural and lumber communities, tend to have longer lives; and cultural and administrative centers still longer. Dr. Clawson provides a brief summary of population decline in the United States from 1880 to 1970, most of which is resource dominated— hence regionally specific—and then discusses the policy and social philosophy of reversing decline.

Quite clearly Clawson's essay dwells on issues and aspects of the first concept of dying community—*regional abandonment*. He states: "If an inducement was necessary to draw people to an area, because of the costs of moving, those same costs serve as a barrier against their outward movement. Typically, a declining community takes a long time dying, if it ever dies completely." But he counters with this philosophical observation: "one can only say, as one surveys long periods of history and large scopes of space, that impermanence of settlements is more striking than permanence."

Clawson seems to be saying that community death in the sense of place abandonment is a function of time. He points out the contradiction of emphasis in social science research on economic growth in the midst of decay and concludes poetically, "Communities are born, grow, and sometimes prosper; many also decline, and some actually die. Is community death as inevitable as individual death, and as unpredictable?"

A regional settlement's ties to a finite resource base are but one threat to community life. In Chapter 4, social anthropologist Art Gallaher, Jr., focuses attention on the threat to the small community posed by the political order surrounding it. In this essay, Professor Gallaher addresses the third concept of community—*the small community as a universal form of association.* He talks about the dissolution of the small community caused by the loss of local autonomy—sometimes violent, sometimes subtle—to external authority. He analyzes in particular the subtle interactive processes set in motion by the giving and receiving of help, in which the local community operates as both effect and cause. The surrender or obsolescing of local statuses, dependence for goods, services, and jobs outside the local setting, population transience, and shift from local and regional cultural identity to national common denominators are some of the processes that threaten the survival of the small community.

Although "dependence on external authority" may seem to be ancillary to phenomena discussed in other essays, Gallaher zeros in on this phenomenon and explains how it assumes a momentum of its own, which becomes difficult if not impossible to reverse. Thus Gallaher's analysis rounds out the beginning of our inquiry and helps complete a coherent conceptual foundation. His core thesis suggests that Clawson's definition should be carried one step further; Clawson's concept of natural resources vis-à-vis the small community makes it explicit that they are instrumental to social ends. Gallaher's concept of authority vis-à-vis the small community makes it clear that ends do not simply emerge, dealt by an invisible hand, but that they are determined by specific political and economic bodies. And it is crucial to the existence of the small community, in both the particular and generic sense, whether these political and economic bodies in whom authority is vested are internal or external. Thus adding another base to the paradigm suggested by Clawson, and inverting the steps to make them consistent with the logic of our conceptual system (as opposed to sequences of English sentence building), natural resources are:

(5) any quality of nature
(4) the culture knows how to use
(3) economically
(2) to (an) end(s) which is/are sought
(1) by (a) decision-making authority(ies)

Therefore, if natural resources constitute the *base* of a community, then, quite simply, the small community is a function of authority. Thus the paradigm:

(6) community
(5) natural resources
(4) technology

(3) systems of benefit/cost distribution

(2) political goals and cultural "needs"

(1) political and cultural authority

In terms of William Adams's essay, a paradigm based upon the concept of *decision-making authority* enables us to attach broad significance to Adams's assertion that, from an archaeological and historical perspective, it is not the presence of decay that requires explanation, but the failure of repair and replacement to keep pace. Failure to rebuild signals the point at which a community's resource base in the broad, politically paradigmatic sense has become inaccessible. This happens only when its base of authority dissolves, or has been absent from the start.

In terms of the death of community as a *universal form of association*, secular trends in the evolution of human systems of authority are crucial to the existence of the small community in the generic sense. As they become increasingly more remote and centralized, it is inevitable that the small community will become extinct. This view is reinforced in Chapter 5 by cultural sociologist Arthur Vidich. Professor Vidich dwells upon the global impacts of 300 years of what he terms "penetration of industrial civilization." He enumerates six interrelated processes impacting upon the social organization of *all* humans *everywhere*:

1. the enormous growth of industrial and trade-centered cities
2. the development of machine technology and separation of economic activity from family and community relationships
3. the growth of centralized government
4. the development of bureaucracy as the chief means of societal administration
5. the development of mass communications and universal literacy
6. the evolution of uniform, worldwide division of labor.

Vidich goes on to say that "these processes will continue unabated until such time as the isolated, primitive, rural community will have no existence *in reality* even in the remote areas of the world" (italics added).

We italicize the phrase *in reality* because Professor Vidich insightfully reminds us at the beginning of his essay that the evolution of the concept of the homogeneous, spatially isolated community derived from an intellectual tradition that was itself part of the process of the rural-urban transition. That is, the concept did not emerge from the discovery of small, self-contained communities. It evolved instead out of social criticism of contemporary economic practices, particularly of capitalism, and an emerging consciousness of social and psychic loss—if not in an empirical, at least in an ideological sense. This theme of the dialectic between subjective and objective community surfaces again at the conclusion of Vidich's essay when he discusses the social and psychological consequences of industrial penetration. We shall return to this part of Vidich's chapter in our discussion of the book's concluding essay, Chapter 11, by Hannah Levin.

Vidich's detailed analysis of the subtle processes by means of which colonial political institutions transform primitive communities into "economic resources" also adds emphasis to Gallaher's concept of the surrender (and cooptation) of decision-making authority. Vidich then discusses emerging community structures in urbanizing society, underscoring Clawson's concept of the role that the economics of natural resources plays in the florescence, decay, and/or transformation of communities—in the social order of capitalism. Invariably, communities based on less capital-intensive methods tend to give way to those based on more capital-intensive systems. Hence instability, rather than being a rare circumstance, is an inherent characteristic of small towns and rural communities. This characteristic is fundamental to Padfield's discussion in Chapter 7 of the denial of powerlessness. Vidich goes on to state, "Each economic period in American history has left behind its dying and dead communities upon which, however, in archaeological fashion, new economic and social forms have been superimposed."

In Chapter 6, Wayne Rohrer and Diane Quantic discuss the sociological and cultural impacts on the rural Midwest of three sequential economic periods in American history. Each period impacted demographically upon rural community life: population surges occurred when people, first, acquired land; second, obtained urban jobs; finally, found suitable (rural) residences. Rohrer and Quantic develop their discussion by reviewing the major works on this topic from the early 1900s through the present.

In their concluding section, they consider and expand upon a theme gleaned from David Potter's *People of Plenty* (1954) concerning the general social-psychological effect of the continuous experience of economic scarcity, which is to produce submissive, deferential, obedient, undemocratic citizens. As Rohrer and Quantic observe, "Farmers

10

and small town Midwesterners have known relative scarcity for half of this century. Even so, although smaller places decline, few disappear." Hence they become persisting life structures having continuous cultural and psychological inputs.

The Rohrer and Quantic emphasis upon the lingering impacts of resource scarcity is well-timed. Their essay reminds us of an important fact, frequently forgotten, or overlooked, because of the very terms we use to describe the phenomenon. The experience of the dying community may constitute, for some, the only reality known throughout an entire human life-span. Although it is valid in certain contexts to consider a human life-span but a second, it is also valid to observe that in the space of a "mere" human life-span, institutions are spawned that endure for many generations. There will therefore be an operational legacy that conditions perception and structures action long after the conditions that gave rise to it have passed.

In another sense as well, it is appropriate to think of dying not as a dynamic process but as a continuous state—a form of social equilibrium. As the reader will note, each writer feels it necessary to recognize the lingering aspect—almost endlessness—of community persistence in the midst of decay. To a community, as to a terminally ill patient in a modern intensive care ward, dying seems to be an endless process. Therefore the phrase *permanence of impermanence* is no mere Shakespearian expression used to evoke a fleeting awareness of reality. It becomes an explicit attempt through juxtaposition in language to solve a paradox created in part by language. It prepares us conceptually to think of the *dying* small community as perhaps *the* secular phenomenon of the industrial age. It has been occurring for two centuries at least, and must be regarded as a permanent human condition, a *persisting form of association* in its own right.

With the groundwork laid by Adams, Clawson, Gallaher, Vidich, and Rohrer and Quantic, one is prepared mentally to enter the social environment of the dying community. Chapter 7 discusses human processes of adaptation in this habitat. Chapters 8, 9, and 10, respectively, convey in terms of human experience what it means to racial minorities, the young, and the aged to be who they are in a dying community. We reiterate three key concepts of this habitat, which combine to make up the concept of the dying community: *regional (place) abandonment; extinction of a form of association* (because any other small community the inhabitants can move to is ceasing to exist);

11

and finally, persistence through time and social legacy of the dying community—hence the *dying community state,* in terms of both objective experience and subjective, intellectual concern.

In Chapter 7, Harland Padfield, a cultural anthropologist, discusses the small community in the rural context as both an instrument and object of exploitation. His essay begins with the premise that a community's life cycle does not occur in a natural environment, but rather in a specific political-economic environment—one controlled and manipulated, in capitalist societies, by economic institutions national and global in scope. Therefore, a community's reason for being is incidental to profit making. In this sense the dying community in the rural frontier context is not the end of a form of association but a form of association in its own right—one Padfield calls the "expendable rural community." He further argues that the rural community is especially vulnerable to the manipulation of its political-economic environment; and that despite this vulnerability, even while suffering the persisting effects of exploitation, rural political culture is geared not to manipulate reality but to manipulate the *cognition* of reality.

The lack of reality-based political consciousness among rural inhabitants, Professor Padfield contends, stems from the fact that, historically, rural communities arose from a collection of individuals seeking opportunity in frontier environments. In other words, the very strategies used historically to cope with their life situations operate to mystify the political and economic realities of their circumstances and negate a politically meaningful class consciousness. Ironically, the more precarious their situations, the more ideologically sensitive the issue of individual and community powerlessness becomes.

Padfield argues that the denial of powerlessness and loss of autonomy is not simply a stage a community passes through. Denial is a studied cultural strategy. The price the inhabitants pay for blaming themselves instead of the social system for economic failure secures a vital part of their cultural and class identity. But in the final analysis, the denial of powerlessness has value because it is indispensable to a more important symbolic quest—the quest for the past.

Padfield concludes that the quest for the past in the midst of economic decay is leading to the rise of a kind of rural proletariat. Moreover, the influx of culturally different people into the rural environment, without increased job opportunity for the natives, produces an experience not unlike the Indian experience with white invaders. Immigra-

12

tion is especially threatening in the case of newcomers with radical political views and liberal mores. Ideological reaction is inevitable. This reaction includes displaying symbols of a potent past depicting the supercowboy, the superlogger, the super patriot and the super individualist. It also includes local political (frequently vigilante) action.

Because it deals explicitly with institutions both external and internal to the expendable and dying rural community, the Padfield essay is an appropriate transition point for the volume. Although mention is made in succeeding essays of the macroeconomics and sociology of the dying community state, explicit analysis shifts to institutions internal to the dying community, and the decisive cast these instutions give to the experiences of those living in such circumstances.

Whereas Padfield talks about the institution of the boom community still dominating the social perspectives and political culture of the dying community, in Chapter 8, Alvin Bertrand, a rural sociologist, analyzes the persisting ramifications of the American caste and class system in small communities and identifies distinctive class and ethnic institutions that differentiate the effects of living in a dying community.

While Bertrand identifies certain racist practices, such as housing discrimination, which impact economic stress disproportionately upon lower-class nonwhites, he argues that ethnic identity makes minorities less susceptible to psychological oppression (self-blame) than whites. In part this stems from the historic consciousness of themselves as racially oppressed people. Such ideological defenses are not available to the lower-class majority. Other minority institutions developed over generations of coping with political oppression and economic stress are strong family and brotherhood associations and compatibility of welfare dependence with their political consciousness. In Bertrand's words,

> the poor and the disadvantaged always appear in greater relief during times of growth and prosperity than they do in times of depression. To acknowledge this is not to condone the difficult lot of minorities in dying communities. It is simply to suggest they may be better prepared to cope with the inherent lack of opportunity because such is indigenous to their stations.

In essence, then, Bertrand is saying that there are basic environmental features of dying communities identical to those experienced by

13

minorities for generations. Hence ethnic minority identity and culture are more adaptive to the dying community state than are the identity and culture of the white majority. To paraphrase Pogo, racial minorities can say in effect, "We have met the dying community and they are us!"

Internalizing our focus again in Chapter 9, David Looff, child psychiatrist and physician, discusses the effects on children's lives of growing up in a dying community. Although he cautions the reader that his impressions do not derive from a "scientific data base," they are based in part upon the life circumstances of his own patients. The gist of Dr. Looff's thinking is as follows: (1) there are stages in growth and development more critical than others in terms of sensitivity to community environment; (2) the adolescent and adult stages of human development seem to be the most susceptible to impairment by a socially constricting and decadent environment.

Beyond these brief reflections, however, Dr. Looff's essay is not centrally concerned with the effects of a dying community as such. Rather, his essay is concerned with institutionalized patterns of child rearing as independent and critical variables in how individual adolescents and adults cope with a dying community environment. Virtually all of Looff's clinical experience has been with child development in a variety of regional and ethnic cultures, and in the context of social and economic stress. Therefore, his method of approaching the topic is appropriate to his scientific vantage point.

Quite simply, Looff's analysis deals with the community and wider social environment as a common denominator and begins with the premise that an offspring's family environment and cultural life-style predispose the developing child to experience and cope with his or her community and life circumstances in resilient or self-defeating ways. Looff comparatively analyzes the child-rearing institutions of three distinctive cultures—Thlingit Indian, Eskimo Indian, and Southern Appalachian white. He concludes that in the main, Thlingit culture and adult personality, in the face of generations of harsh living circumstances, has tended to turn inward upon itself and become nonverbal, brooding, distance-promoting, and sullen. This style translates to frustrated and irritable mothering in which babies are at best burdensome, and at worst bitterly resented. Looff's observations were that Thlingit children, neglected and frequently abused, developed self-defeating attitudes and behavior and grew into chronically depressed and defeated adults and inadequate parents.

In Southern Appalachia, although children are loved and indulged as infants, in later stages they are ignored in terms of supervised socialization. No positive models or training limits are set on impulsive behavior, no disciplinary controls are established, and no preparation is given for age-appropriate expression. As a result, developing adults tend to be family- and community-dependent, nonverbal, impulsive, and undisciplined—in short, able to fit in and reinforce regional Appalachian dying community culture, but socially incapacitated to cope in the wider world.

Eskimo culture personality, by contrast, Looff found to be warm, outgoing, friendly, and trusting of strangers as equals. Children were welcomed into their lives and trained through succeeding stages of growth in ways insuring that they would function well as adults.

In conclusion, Looff returns to the complex issue of the role of the dying community environment. While reiterating the dangers of generalizing from one dying community to all others, he reminds us that child rearing does not become institutionalized in a vacuum and cannot be understood apart from the syndrome of historical geographic and socioeconomic characteristics and physical and social pathologies. These include poverty, disease, substandard housing, inadequate education, broken homes, and chronic unemployment. He goes on to say that what general statistics cannot reveal are the suffering, despair, and apathy. Nor can they reveal the powerful, corrosive effect this has on family life, structure, and functioning as a child-rearing environment. In other words, what Looff seems to be saying is that although patterns of child rearing are important variables in the ultimate effects dying community environments have on adult lives, the dying community environment and the political-economic forces at large impact upon the family units in ways that impair their child-rearing functions.

Looff insists however that *"the most important factor accounting for their relative successes or failures in coping as families within their beleaguered communities was their varying regional [or cultural] lifestyles."* Summarizing the effects of the three cultures he examined vis-à-vis the dying community, Looff observes that impoverished Eskimo adults and children living under conditions of severe environmental stress have a life-style that equipped them to be psychologically mobile, forward looking, optimistic, and growth oriented. By contrast, Thlingit Indian and very poor Appalachian families faced handicaps beyond the severe stresses imposed by their environments. They faced handicaps imposed by culture personality patterns.

Adults in the two groups shared inner-directed traits of pessimism, fatalism, stoicism, and individualism, which, from generation to generation, locked in their inner forces and led them to perpetuate self-defeating attitudes among their children.

. . . the interacting, reinforcing factors of physical, mental, and cultural isolation operate to hold them in disadvantaged areas, frequently resisting changes that would bring them into effective contact with the outside world.

Progressing in Chapter 10 from cultural life-styles for those growing up in a dying community, social gerontologist Mary Wylie discusses growing old in a dying community. She cautions that, as in the case of the experience of growing up, there is little systematic empirical evidence to support a hypothesized relationship between community environment and the experience of growing old. Despite this caveat, however, Dr. Wylie provides a lucid theoretical answer to the question of how living in a dying community affects old people's lives. She does this first by examining what answers are suggested by the three major theories of aging: disengagement or developmental theory; continuity theory; and accommodation theory.

Developmental theory is an outgrowth of physiological concepts of aging. In essence, it views old age as simply a next-to-final sequence in the human life cycle—a stage succeeding middle age and preceding the final state, death. Central to development theory is the concept of stage-specific psychosocial tasks. Although developmental theory provided the conceptual basis for the theory of disengagement, which Wylie describes as the first specific gerontological theory of aging, the architects of developmental theory were not concerned with aging as such, but with the human life cycle as a whole. The disengagement concept of old age is like any other developmental concept of a stage of human development: the stage is considered part of an intrinsic universal process that every individual goes through from birth to death. Implicit in developmental theory is the proposition that age-related social institutions derive from these intrinsic biopsychosocial processes rather than the other way around. Accordingly, the disengagement theory of old age in Wylie's words, "posits a mutual and synchronized disengagement between the individual and society, a necessary prelude to an individual's and society's preparation for the individual's death." In this sense an old-age home is a dying community.

The key element in continuity theory, Wylie tells us, is life-style.

16

Appropriate old-age adjustment is achieved by maintaining maximum continuity and minimum discontinuity of life-style between middle and old age. Says Wylie, "The accommodation perspective diverts attention to *how* continuity is maintained in the face of dramatic role losses." Accommodation—the redefinition of self and the development of a new series of roles—is achieved by rehearsing transitions, by observing others going through crises. In Wylie's words:

> Taken together, the three major theoretical models suggest that the dying community . . . may indeed provide a compatible environment for growing old. The desired withdrawal suggested by disengagement theory may be enhanced in an environment that is itself withdrawing from society. Continuity may be more easily achieved in a familiar environment, an environment in which one's roots run very deeply and with itself is besieged with terminal decline. Finally, the dying community provides considerable opportunity to rehearse the major crises of human existence—loss of family and friends through out-migration, depletion of financial resources as economically productive opportunities dwindle, and a diminished vigor in community life.

As Wylie reminds us, this is all hypothetical. To counterbalance pure deduction, Dr. Wylie's essay presents empirical data gathered from interviews with a sample of elderly residents living in a contemporary, small, rural, dying community in the midwestern United States. Their life satisfaction scores were higher than those of peers living in three other types of communities—*growing* small, larger metropolitan, and middle-class suburban. The affective responses of the dying community residents also revealed an awareness of an environment that offered an easy pace, a preoccupation with retirement and leisure activities as opposed to gainful employment, and opportunities and incentives to form networks of acquaintanceship and self-help. Finally, Wylie reasons, "If the community has properties that reinforce or complement the social-psychological and biological changes that occur with growing old, then it would seem that that community could provide the continuity, values, and personal friendships cherished by the aging."

Our concluding essay, Chapter 11, is by psychologist Hannah Levin. In contrast to Padfield, Bertrand, Looff, and Wylie, Professor Levin deals with the ecological context that comprises neighborhoods in dying inner cities, in which 7 to 10 million underclass Americans—mostly black and Spanish-speaking people—live *(Time,* August 29, 1977). Professor Levin analyzes the functions of community, and describes maladaptive and adaptive responses to dying community environments. Levin draws a distinction between objective and subjective images of community and emphasizes that her discussion focuses "on the process by which the individual internalizes and experiences community subjectively." Although the subjective sense of community includes objective elements, it is "not isomorphic with an objective community."

Professor Levin's definitions are quite simply and directly derived from people's responses to the question of how they experience community. Three basic concepts emerged: sense of place, origin, and collective interest. But sense of loss also emerges in the descriptions people give. Consistent with her theory of community, Levin conceptualizes the dying community in terms of "destructive forces attacking the subjective sense of community." The most pernicious destructive force, Levin argues, is the economic system, which forces some 10 million Americans to be unemployed—uprooted geographically, displaced from their community of work, and thereby denied access to the full benefits of society. Levin encapsulates their experience:

> They describe how life has lost its meaning and how they feel superfluous and unwanted. Their basic connectedness to the community of work has been severed. Sometimes the nostalgia for what has been lost is expressed when an unemployed person returns to the diner across the street from the factory that laid him off. He has a cup of coffee and talks with whomever—to recall the ties that locate him in a community now denied.

Perhaps the most striking manifestation of loss of community is the impulse to reestablish community. Drawing on examples of Jewish experiences in Nazi concentration camps, Levin illustrates the powerful psychological significance of the deliberate and ritualistic practice of community and in so doing creates a compelling thought: that the community as an institution is internalized universally in all humans and the drive for community is synonymous with survival. This theme—that the struggle to preserve the inner sense of community is the human criterion of life and, by inference, civilization—is paramount in Levin's essay and surfaces repeatedly.

The functions of community are to provide structure and value for individual effort and a balanced tension between communal obligations and individual autonomy. She cites contrasting examples of Japanese society, which has a completely communalized approach, and the

18

United States, which is the opposite extreme. Here the society does not blame itself for failing to provide a supportive developmental environment but holds the individual responsible "and thus in the dying community each individual is made to feel his own inadequacy."

Maladaptive responses to loss of community include drug addiction, lawlessness, and defensive reactions similar to those of grief evoked by the death of a loved one. As Levin observes, loss of community, like death, marks a disruption in the structure and predictability of life. Grief reactions represent the struggle to retrieve this lost sense of meaning, and "the will to adapt to change has to overcome the equally strong desire to restore the past." Defensive responses range from simple cultural conservatism, to political withdrawal, and to such forms of extremism as vigilante action. Significantly, all writers dealing with life in dying community environments, including Padfield, Bertrand, Looff, and Wylie, have emphasized this tendency.

The responses of institutions in dying communities (banks, hospitals, law enforcement agencies) also tend to be defeating. Another maladaptive response to the sense of loss of community is the growth of pseudo-communities. Levin cites people's collective identification of themselves as consumers of and believers in mass-produced and distributed products (cars, clothes, television personalities, and political slogans) as pseudo-communities.

Levin characterizes adaptive responses to loss of community as not ceasing to care for what was good and meaningful in past associations, but selecting what was fundamentally important in the lost community and reintegrating it to meet the needs of the present and the future. She gives examples of people mobilizing politically to regain control of their lives in neighborhoods, factories, and schools. She also describes collective responses, which are not place-specific, such as ideologies, which counter the social forces destroying people's sense of community. Arthur Vidich cautions us at the conclusion of his chapter (5), however, that even though analysts can describe these new forms of association emerging in industrial society in the same objective terms they use to describe communities in primitive societies, this does not mean the respective participants in these societies will experience these structures the same subjectively.

The closing pages of the closing chapter by Levin take us full circle, to the beginning, to a paramount theme in the essay by Adams. But first, we feel it important to recapitulate the institutions that influence how living in a dying community environment affects people's lives. Padfield identifies the rural frontier community. Bertrand outlines caste and class structures. Looff describes culture-personality life-styles and child-rearing practices. Wylie explores institutions of aging. And finally, Levin embroiders for us the institution of *the* community internalized in the human psyche. Each writer recognizes the consciousness of loss as pervasive and fundamental to the dying community experience. The essays taken together as a whole make it clear that the community and the individual are both effect and cause.

We identified at the beginning of this chapter three concepts— *abandonment of a natural region, decay of a sociocultural system or civilization,* and *extinction of a form of association.* We shall first put in philosophical perspective the small, spatially isolated community. Has it ever existed? Our answer is: as a natural form of association and in social philosophy, yes; in empirical science, no. On the latter score, we are dealing with a theoretical construct. It is like the model of a planet's orbit in space. The latter is not meant to approximate the planet's each and every revolution until its orbit collapses and the planet collides with another world or vaporizes into its star. The model is meant instead to represent the forces creating it. It derives from a mathematical equation. Similarly, the model of the small, spatially isolated, preindustrial community philosophically derives—albeit in a much less precise manner—from the secular forces destroying it. The intellectual impulse to idealize the preindustrial community arose, as Vidich suggests, from a pervasive disenchantment, now global in scope, with industrial civilization. The death of what Vidich calls "the spatially isolated community and its distinctive cultural, organizational, ritual, and ceremonial forms," is, more than anything, the death of an ideal model, of a culturally remembered rather than a real form of association.

This brings us to the central issue of this book—community and the health of a given social order. How necessary is the little community, or, more accurately, how close to the model of this form must new forms of association be for people to learn the *sense* of community? Are the new forms of community emerging in the metropolitan and urban contexts described by Vidich and Levin adequate to sustain the psychological sense of community so fundamental to human civilization, or is the experience of loss of community so deep and pervasive as to be crippling? Clawson, Gallaher, Rohrer, Quantic, Padfield, and Looff develop and elaborate upon the ties between the dying regional small community and the death of a society or social order. The relationships are objective, concrete, economic, and political erosions of the collective ability and will to sustain group survival. This is what is involved in the death of Thlingit and rural American frontier culture.

Levin also talks about the corrosive, debilitating effects of objective inner-city decay. Her paramount theme, however, which equates the struggle to preserve and reestablish community with human social order, takes us beyond the issue of the power of a specific community or any form of association to exist objectively. It brings us instead to the issue of the existence of a social will in the psyche of the individual. Levin's point is that this will, this struggle to preserve community, is independent of the existence of a previous objective community. She argues in fact that when an objective community is threatened, the inner sense of communtiy may be quickened. This brings us to reflect again upon Professor Adams's observation in the beginning of this book, that from a historical-archaeological perspective, the cessation of the process of rebuilding and repair signals the death of a community. Levin's argument would regard the absence of signs of rebuilding as the archaeological manifestations of the waning of the psychological vitality and sense of community of its inhabitants. A physical community is but an expression, an objective indication of this sense. Therefore, as important as specific communities are, it is the waxing or waning of this vital psychological sense of community that determines the florescence and decay of a social order.

Ending our theoretical discussion with yet another reflection upon Adams's thought-provoking observation enables us, the editors, to develop an important point of our own. Initially, drawing upon themes in earlier papers, our reflection came from an external, objective vantage point (as opposed to a psychologically subjective vantage point) and, like the earlier essays themselves, had a strong political cast to it. The point we wish to make is that each frame of reference adds different and logically defensible meanings to the same thing. It is an appropriate reminder that with respect to so-called empirical data, every conceptual system is to a certain extent self-validating, hence limited in its ability to reflect reality. The discovery of divergent explanations for the same reality is one of the prime values of a multidisciplinary seminar such as this.

These essays, taken collectively, make us mindful of the philosophical basis as opposed to the empirical basis of reality—especially of social reality. They tell us that a person, a community, indeed, an entire sociocultural system is not an entity or thing. They are processes, interacting sequences of both cause and effect. Accordingly, the dying community state can be appropriately perceived and attacked in terms of political ideology, political consciousness, and political action. The dying community state is also subjective reality. The definition of our experiences within this environment can derive from the life-styles and cultural predisposition we carry within us. Accordingly, this life experience can be attacked through the redefinition of community, ethnic, and indeed, self-identity. The example of the Jewish response to threat to their community today, contrasted with their response in World War II, rather dramatically illustrates what we are saying. Both responses are valid, both are effective, and both can be mutually reinforcing.

Finally, it appears in retrospect that the underlying, coherent theme of this volume of papers, which began as a seminar on the phenomenon of dying communities, is about the decay of our own sociocultural system.

We close with this thought by Levin:

> . . . We must . . . mobilize ourselves and struggle to preserve the remembered sense of community and integrate it into future attempts at change.
> . . . for the survival of mankind we must not capitulate to the concept that the sense of community is dead. The most binding, vital, and healthy sense of community may be generated through this struggle.

2

The Dead Community: Perspectives from the Past

WILLIAM Y. ADAMS

Department of Anthropology
University of Kentucky

Whether the metaphor of death can appropriately be applied to communities is a question that sociologists and economists may want to debate, but few archaeologists or historians will have any reservations on this score. The death of communities, no less than that of empires and of civilizations, is one of the commonplaces of their work. Indeed, in the broadest sense, every archaeological habitation site may be regarded as the skeleton of a dead community. This is, of course, an oversimplification: not all archaeological sites can be equated with communities, and not all of them died in the conventional sense of the term. Some have simply migrated en bloc to more favored localities, so that their abandoned dwellings may be likened to the discarded shells of still-living organisms rather than to the bones of dead ones. Even when the metaphor of death is appropriate, moreover, we have to distinguish between communities that were "killed," so to speak, by the violence of man or nature, and those that died a more lingering, "natural" death.

Making every allowance for migration and for "sudden death," the archaeological and historical records are nevertheless replete with evi-

23

dence of once-flourishing communities that have crumbled to dust without benefit of outside destructive agents. The names of Babylon and Memphis have long been evocative of faded and forgotten glory, and in our own time the names of such places as Teotihuacán and Tikal in Mesoamerica, Tiahuanaco in the Andes, Meroë and Zimbabwe in Africa, Mohenjo-Daro and Harappa in India are becoming equally familiar, at least to scholars. And for each of these dead metropolises there are scores of village sites that perished just as completely and far more anonymously.

It seems unnecessary to recite a further list of abandoned towns and cities as proof that communities can and do die. I shall turn instead to a consideration of two more interesting and pertinent questions, from the standpoint of this seminar: why communities die (causes of death) and how they die (symptoms of death). Archaeology and history have something to say on both these subjects; how much of their message is relevant to the circumstances of today's world remains for us to decide. Before considering the questions themselves, however, a word must be said about the nature of the available evidence.

Throughout this analysis I shall use two avenues of approach to the past: those of archaeology and of recorded history. They do not always run closely parallel, or even lead in the same direction, as the ensuing discussion will show. Indeed, in discussing many theories of community death I shall have to use the evidence of archaeology and of history in a kind of contrapuntal fashion, allowing each to stand as a corrective to the other.

To the archaeologist, prima facie evidence of community death is an abandoned settlement. As I have already suggested, this evidence must be treated with some reserve, for a community can migrate as a unit without serious disruption of its interaction networks (see Schwartz 1970). On the other side, it must also be said that habitation sites can be totally abandoned and then reoccupied by newcomers, so that continued or renewed occupation is not necessarily indicative of community survival. I shall return to these questions in later pages, in discussing the evidence relating specifically to small communities. Meanwhile it must be borne in mind that most of the archaeological theories I shall be discussing are theories of site abandonment, and not of community death as such.

Archaeological evidence of site abandonment consists of all the material remains left behind by the departed inhabitants: their houses and furnishings; the streets, plazas, and open living spaces beyond their walls, their workshops and market stalls; their places of recreation and of worship; and sometimes, also, their places of burial. All these things can tell us a good deal about *how* communities died—particularly when they can provide us with a contrast between living conditions in the last days and living conditions in earlier and presumably happier times. Not surprisingly, then, our best evidence comes from long-occupied sites, and above all from stratified sites, which permit a detailed comparison between the remains of earlier and later levels. In these sites it is of course the uppermost level that gives us our "snapshot" of the community in its dying days.

If the archaeological record has much to say about the symptoms of community death, it is more ambiguous about causes. Here in most cases we are forced to go beyond the evidence found in individual sites, and to examine them in the context of broad natural and social environments. Very seldom are we able to advance any single, conclusive explanation for site abandonment unless we have the supplementary evidence of recorded history to fall back on. Prehistoric archaeologists have nevertheless not been backward in suggesting reasons why this or that site was abandoned, and their suggestions will furnish us with considerable food for thought in succeeding pages.

Recorded history—which is plentiful for the Old World but not for the New—in one sense complements the archaeological record, for it is often emphatic as to why towns and cities were abandoned, but has little to say about the symptoms of decay. At first glance, then, the evidence of written history would seem to be strongest where that of archaeology is weakest. Closer inspection will show, however, that this is not universally the case: history no less than archaeology is capable of deceiving the unwary and the uncritical (see Bloch 1953). It is precisely for this reason that archaeological and historical evidence are both necessary in any effort to reconstruct a believable past.

One further word of prefatory explanation may be desirable here. Archaeology per se is not a profession but a technology: that is, a collection of strategies and procedures for recovering material evidence from the ground. These techniques are utilized by a number of quite diverse scholarly disciplines that share a common interest in the past, but that may, nevertheless, view it from quite different perspectives. Broadly speaking, there exists a dichotomy between archaeologists whose schooling is primarily in anthropology, and who draw their explanatory paradigms mostly from latter-day primitives and peasants, and archaeologists schooled in a number of historical and philological disciplines (Classics, Egyptology, Assyriology, Sinology, and so forth), whose explanatory paradigms derive from the historical records of the civilizations they study. As we shall see, there are consistent differences in the ways these different scholars interpret the same or similar evidence. In cases where it is necessary to emphasize the distinction I shall refer to the first group as anthropologists or anthropologist-archaeologists, and to the second group as historians or historian-archaeologists.

THE CAUSES OF COMMUNITY DEATH

Some Conventional Theories

As a starting point for this discussion I have compiled, in Table 2.1, a list of explanations that have been put forward both by archaeologists and by historians to account for the abandonment of particular sites, in cases where the causes were not historically known.[1] Even a cursory glance at the table will reveal that three explanations have consistently been preferred: invasion or war, natural disaster, and environmental deterioration. Even more remarkable is the fact that among historical archaeologists catastrophic theories (war or natural disaster) are overwhelmingly preferred, while archaeologists trained in the anthropological field show an equally strong predilection for environmental explanations. (To underscore this dichotomy I have marked with an asterisk, in Table 2.1, all of the explanations put forward by anthropologist-archaeologists; lack of an asterisk indicates the theories of nonanthropologists.[2]) Here is one more clear-cut demonstration—if one were needed—that we carry most of our explanatory baggage with us into the past; we do not find it in our sites (see W. Adams 1968a).

The three theories of site abandonment that have been most consistently offered seem to me almost equally useless for the purposes of this seminar. The theories of historians are so uniformly apocalyptic as to almost rule out any consideration of "natural" death, while the theories of anthropologists are so grandly systemic as to deny to the community any possiblity of an individual history.[3] Fortunately, however, I think it is possible for us to steer a middle course between the Scylla

TABLE 2.1
THEORIES OF ABANDONMENT IN SELECTED SITES**

		EXPLANATION FOR ABANDONMENT									
AREA	SITES AND PERIODS	Invasion or war	Natural disaster	Disease or famine	Demograph. change	Environ. change	Depleted nat. res.	Maladaptation	Economic change	Polit. or mil. change	Religious change
Mississippi Valley	CAHOKIA	?				31*		28	28		
Southwest	(Pueblo III sites***)	44*		39		44*					
Mexico	TEOTIHUACAN (Classic)	23*	42*	42*	23*	23*					
	TULA (Classic)	7*				7*			42*		7*
Yucatán	(Classic Maya cities***)	1*		1*	9*	1*	1*	1*			1*
	MAYAPAN (Post-Clas.)	32									
Peru	TIAHUANACO, HUARI, etc.					17*					
	CHAN CHAN	18									
Germany	HEUNEBURG (Iron Age)	8									
Italy	SYBARIS (Hellenic)	11	34			34					
Greece	LEFKANDI (Iron Age)	35									
Aegean	(Late Minoan cities***)	13	12						22		
	(Mycenaean cities***)	27				5			36		
	TROY	4	4								
Nubia	MEROE (Meroitic)	38								3*	
	KAWA (Meroitic)	19								3*	
Anatolia	HACILAR (Neolithic)	21									
	KANESH (Assyrian)	25	25								
	HATTUSAS (Hittite)	20									
	TESHEBANI (Urartian)	29									

TABLE 2.1 (continued)
THEORIES OF ABANDONMENT IN SELECTED SITES**

AREA	SITES AND PERIODS	Invasion or war	Natural disaster	Disease or famine	Demograph. change	Environ. change	Depleted nat. res.	Maladap-tation	Economic change	Polit. or mil. change	Religious change
	ALTINTEPE (Urartian)	26								26	
Syria	UGARIT (Ugaritic)	15	15								
Palestine	BEIDHA (Neolithic)					34					
	JERICHO	14	14								
	(Judacan cities***)	8									
Arabia	(Sabaean cities***)								40		
Mesopotamia	(Babylonian cities***)	8									
	(Many small towns***)						2*				
	UR (Seleucid)					43					
Persia	BASTAM (Urartian)	16									
	DEH LURAN PL. (Medieval)									24*	
Indus Valley	MOHENJO-DARO (Indus Civ.)	41	34			41	41				
	(Punjab sites***)	30							10		
Ceylon	ANURADHAPURA (Early Med.)	8									
Cambodia	SIEMREAP (Late Med.)	33					37*		33		33
China	ANYANG (Shang Dyn.)	6									

  *Single asterisk identifies theories of anthropologist-archaeolgists.
 **Numbers in the table refer to numbered references listed immediately following the table. For
   full citations see Reference list at end of volume.
***Several sites grouped on a single line means that a common explanation has been offered for
   the abandonment of all.

References cited by number in Table 2.1

For complete documentation see the Bibliography at the end of the volume.

1. Richard Adams 1973.
2. Robert Adams 1965:62–63.
3. William Adams 1976:12–14.
4. Blegen 1963: 110, 144, 153, 161–62.
5. Carpenter 1968:67.
6. Cheng 1960:1.
7. Coe 1962:138.
8. Cottrell 1960:218.
9. Cowgill and Hutchinson 1963.
10. Dales 1966.
11. Devambez et al. 1967:448.
12. Hood 1967:109.
13. Hutchinson 1962:300–303.
14. Kenyon 1960:60, 134, 137, 197, 208–9.
15. Kenyon 1971:583–84.
16. Kroll 1972:297.
17. Lanning 1967:140.
18. Larco Hoyle 1966:168.
19. Macadam 1955:27.
20. Macqueen 1975:51.
21. Mellaart 1965:112.
22. Mellersh 1967:136.
23. Millon 1967.
24. Neely 1974:38–41.
25. ˝Ozgüc 1963:245–47.
26. ˝Ozgüc 1967:57.
27. Palmer 1965:143–60, 173.
28. Pfeiffer 1974:62.
29. Phillips 1963:249.
30. Piggott 1952:238–41.
31. Porter 1969:160.
32. Proskouriakoff 1955.
33. Pym 1963:132–38.
34. Raikes 1967:153–64, 173–80.
35. Sackett and Popham 1972:19.
36. Samuel 1966:140–41.
37. Shimkin 1973:291–95.
38. Shinnie 1967:56.
39. Titiev 1944:96–99.
40. Van Beek 1969.
41. Wheeler 1968:126–33.
42. Wolf 1959:104–10.
43. Woolley 1954:245–48.
44. Wormington 1947:107.

and Charybdis offered by conventional explanations. For one thing, we need not accept the theories of others as the last word; we can take another look at the evidence and form our own conclusions as to why sites were abandoned. Second, we (or more properly, I) can introduce additional, unpublished evidence from recent excavations that bears on the question of site abandonment. Finally, we can look at some historically documented cases of abandonment in which neither the facts nor their interpretation are in dispute. Using these three lines of attack I will proceed, in the next pages, to reconsider some of the cases listed in Table 2.1, as well as some others. The discussion will proceed on a cause-by-cause rather than on a case-by-case basis.

Reconsiderations

Invasion and *war* have probably been suggested as causes for community abandonment more often than all other explanations combined (see Table 2.1). Much less commonly, internal strife is envisioned (Larco Hoyle 1966:168; Millon 1967; Proskouriakoff 1955). As I have suggested elsewhere (W. Adams 1968a:207–8; 1973:24–25), this can result from a simple misreading of the evidence. Habitation sites after their abandonment are subject to all kinds of destructive processes, and with the passage of time it becomes increasingly difficult to distinguish the handiwork of man from the handiwork of nature. The dramatically inclined will have no trouble seeing the hand of the conqueror wherever walls have tumbled down and roofs have caved in or burned, but in fact a troop of passing schoolboys are, on the evidence of history, just as likely culprits.

If we turn from archaeology to the evidence of recorded history, we seem at first glance to find abundant instances of military destruction. Indeed, there are enough pillages, burnings, and devastations recorded in the Old Testament alone to account for the popularity of these theories among Near Eastern scholars (see Table 2.1, headings under Syria, Palestine, and Mesopotamia). If we look a second time, however, we are more likely than not to find that the supposedly devastated cities are flourishing again within a matter of generations or even of years. Kenyon (1960:60, 134, 197, 208–9) has postulated at least four violent destructions of Jericho, and Schliemann and his successors have envisioned an equal number at Troy (Blegen 1963:110, 144, 153, 161–62, 172; Finley 1970: 62–63); in each case, however, we soon find the town rebuilt on the same site. Carthage, according to tradition, was destroyed by the Romans so thoroughly that they levelled its remains and sowed salt upon them; hardly more than a century later it was described by Strabo as one of the most flourishing cities of the empire (Encyclopaedia Britannica 1929a:946). The apogee of military destruction in preindustrial times is surely marked by the Mongol devastation of the Persian city of Merv, in which over 700,000 citizens are believed to have lost their lives (Sykes 1930: 2: 80). "Those places are effaced from off the earth as lines of writing are effaced from paper, and those abodes became a dwelling for the owl and the raven," lamented a Persian chronicler of the event (Sykes 1930:2:80). Two hundred years later Merv was again flourishing, having been restored by the Mongols themselves (Sykes 1930:2:137). Tenochtitlán, the Aztec capital, was devastated by the troops of Cortés but thrives today as Mexico City, one of the world's four largest cities. We can take the cases of Hiroshima and of Dresden as further and perhaps final evidence that cities are hard to kill. I shall return in a moment to consider why this is so.

Natural disaster ranks next to war as a popular theory of site abandonment among nonanthropologists. Specific factors that have been suggested include earthquakes, volcanic eruptions, fires, floods, and various combinations of these. For obvious reasons earthquake and eruption theories have been especially popular in the Aegean (Hood 1967:109; Hutchison 1962:300–303), while flooding has been suggested most often in the Tigris-Euphrates and Indus valleys (Dales 1966; Raikes 1964, 1965, 1967: 153–64; Wheeler 1968: 126–33; Woolley 1954:35–36).

Notwithstanding the famous and indisputable case of Pompeii, recorded history offers even fewer verifiable cases of final destruction by nature than of final destruction by man. Destructions themselves are real enough and frequent enough, but as long as there are any survivors, they almost always rebuild. Constantinople (Istanbul) has been destroyed again and again, both by earthquakes and by fire, and has just as often been rebuilt, just as were San Francisco and other California communities after the memorable 1906 earthquake. Perhaps the most extreme example is provided by the town of St. Pierre on the island of Martinique, where in 1902 over 30,000 people died in a firestorm caused by the eruption of Mt. Pelée. Today St. Pierre is once again the second largest settlement on the island.

31

Why do people stubbornly rebuild their shattered homes in the wake of disasters that are as likely as not to be repeated? Clearly, lack of alternatives is not the answer. I can only suppose that there is a universal human impulse to outface adversity; to let the world—and the heavens—know that you are not licked. Even at Pompeii, we are told, the first thought of the survivors was to dig out and rebuild their city on a grander scale—a project that evidently foundered when the magnitude of the task was appreciated (Johnson 1954). This brings me to a point that I shall touch on later: that people's self-image is often closely bound up in the identity, and the fate, of their towns and cities.

In the face of the available evidence I think we have to conclude that neither natural nor manmade disaster offers a *sufficient* explanation for site abandonment. What calls for explanation is not the fact of destruction, which is all too commonplace, but the failure to rebuild, which is evidently much less common. It would seem that there has to be a specific reason for not rebuilding, and that reason is rarely the fear of a second destruction.

Disease, though not one of the more popular theories, has been suggested as a cause of site abandonment in the prehistoric Southwest (Titiev 1944:97–98), in highland Mexico (Wolf 1959:104), in Yucatán (R. E. W. Adams 1973:23), and in the late Roman Empire (Cottrell 1960:174; Schefold 1968:281; Settis 1972:30). (For a general consideration of the influence of disease on history see also Zinsser 1945: esp. 150–65.) Here again recorded history provides little corroborative evidence. Although the Black Death is estimated to have carried off one-third of Europe's population (Langer 1964; Ziegler 1976:94–95), and although the wholesale depopulation of rural districts is said to have resulted (Langer 1964), it is difficult to identify any single parish in Europe that never recovered from the plague. In the Southwest, Titiev (1944:97–98) has pointed out that no pueblo in historic times has been finally abandoned as a result of disease, notwithstanding the drastic depopulations wrought by epidemics in the eighteenth and nineteenth centuries. Disease seems to be another form of environmental insult (or divine insult, as earlier peoples would have had it) that communities are determined to overcome.

Demographic factors—i.e., declining fertility—have been invoked even less frequently than disease as an explanation for community decline. We do, however, find them at least hinted at in the case of Teotihuacán (Millon 1967), and quite explicitly suggested for the lowland Maya (Cowgill and Hutchinson 1963). These theories have not been widely accepted by anthropologists (see R. E. W. Adams 1973:29); indeed, most modern anthropologists, as good Malthusians, would probably insist that declining fertility is an effect of ecological or economic factors and not a cause in itself. Not all demographers agree (Langer 1964:111; Russell 1958:138), and at least one has marshalled some impressive statistics from late medieval parish registers to show that population fluctuations cannot always be correlated with external factors (Wrigley 1969:76–106). In general, however, neither archaeology nor history yields enough quantitative evidence on population to debate the question of declining fertility as an influence on community decline.

Environmental deterioration is, as we have seen, the theory most favored by anthropologists as an explanation for site abandonment. Included under this heading are such natural phenomena as desiccation and drought, erosion, flooding and silting, salinization of agricultural land, fluctuating lake and sea levels, and the disappearance of forests, pastures, and game and fish resources. One or other of these causes has been invoked to explain the abandonment of nearly every urban settlement in the New World not occupied at the time of the European conquest (see Table 2.1), as well as of settlements in the Nile (B. Bell 1971), Tigris-Euphrates (R. McC. Adams 1965:62–63; Jakobson and Adams 1958; Woolley 1954:245–48), and Indus (Lambrick 1967; Singh 1971; Wheeler 1968:126–33) valleys, the Aegean (Carpenter 1968:67), and Roman North Africa (Huntington 1945:544–46). (For general theories of the influence of changing climate on human settlement, see B. Bell 1971; Butzer 1964: esp. 416–71; Carpenter 1968; Huntington 1924: esp. 315–65; Raikes 1967: esp. 87–193.)

Documented cases of community death resulting purely from environmental causes are not so very common. The Dust Bowl towns of Oklahoma and Kansas, of course, spring to mind. Medieval Bruges declined to insignificance because its channel to the sea became choked with silt (McMullen 1969:89–90), and the growth of coral even more drastically affected the fortunes of the Red Sea port of Suakin (Wingate 1955:154). A number of Roman or pre-Roman seaports of the Mediterranean lost their utility because of a rising sea level, while Rye on the south coast of England, a thriving seaport as late as the fifteenth century, is now a quiet tourist village eight miles inland. In general, however, environmental change takes place so gradually that communities are able to adapt themselves to their altering circumstances—by developing new livelihoods or by removing physically to a new and more favored locality. It is only when all local possibilities of survival are destroyed that we can legitimately speak of environmental deterioration as the basic or final cause of community death.

Herein lies the fundamental weakness of the macrosystematic theories so dear to anthropologists. We are seemingly confronted with the simultaneous abandonment of *all* sites over very large areas (the Colorado Plateau, Yucatán, the Aegean Basin, and so forth), yet no one has suggested a drought, erosion, salinization, or cold so severe as to render these regions completely uninhabitable. If half the inhabitants had died out or left, there would presumably have been ample resources to support the other half. As Steen (1966:53) has suggested in the case of Canyon de Chelly sites, the last inhabitants must have left simply because they saw their fellows going. But if this is so, then migration per se rather than environmental change becomes the ultimate cause of site abandonment.

One of the few fairly convincing studies linking population shifts to environmental change is that of Robert McC. Adams in the Diyala Plains east of Baghdad (1965). Rather than offering a sweeping macrosystemic theory, Adams presents a closely reasoned analysis linking the conditions of abandonment in individual settlements to archaeologically verifiable, or historically documented, cases of silting, salinization, and failure to maintain irrigation works.

Exhaustion of natural resources may be regarded as the local and manmade aspect of environmental deterioration. It has been much less often cited as an explanation for site abandonment than has wholesale ecological change, although soil exhaustion has been suggested for the lowland Maya (R. E. W. Adams 1973:23–24) and for the Indus Valley site of Mohenjo-Daro (Wheeler 1968:126–33). Documented cases of community decline or even site abandonment as a result of resource depletion, on the other hand, are legion; we usually find, however, that it is export commodities rather than agrarian resources whose exhaustion leads to the demise of communities. Nevada and many adjoining states are dotted over with abandoned mining towns, and the successive depletions of coal, oil, and timber have had a severe effect on many Kentucky communities (see Cain 1972). Such one-industry towns are by no means unique to the industrial age: there were mining and lumbering towns in remote antiquity. Even in the late Stone Age, more than seven thousand years ago, the Anatolian settlement of Catal Hüyük is believed to have prospered from the mining and export of obsidian (Mellart 1965:84; see also Dixon, Cann, and Renfrew 1968). In my own excavations on the banks of the Nile I have encountered more than one pottery-making settlement whose abandonment was brought about, I believe, by the exhaustion of local fuel resources needed to fire the very large kilns (see W. Adams 1961 and 1962). I therefore suggest that exhaustion of local resources may be a more probable explanation for site abandonment than archaeologists have generally supposed.

To suggest that *migration* is a cause of site abandonment would probably be regarded by most anthropologists as tautological, and certainly as nonexplanatory. The current fashion is to work with rigidly determinist ecological models that have a built-in assumption of "least moves"—that is, that people stay in one place as long as they can and move no farther than they have to. It is somewhat ironic that these theories are especially developed with reference to the aboriginal Southwest (see Zubrow 1972), for here if anywhere we have evidence to suggest a restless, peripatetic people, seldom content to stay very long in one place even when there were no compelling reasons to move. Dean (1970:170–71) has shown that Tsegi Canyon sites of Betatakin and Kiet Siel—the major "urban" centers of the Kayenta people— were occupied for no more than 33 and 50 years respectively. With reference to the ethnographic evidence, both Titiev (1944:98–99) and Fox (1967) have suggested that the restlessness of the Puebloans is best understood in the light of internal, structural features of their society and not of external causes.

I have to reassert at this point that we are here talking specifically about migration and not about community death. Given the peripatetic habits of southwestern peoples, it follows that not many abandoned sites in this area can be legitimately equated with dead communities.

Maladaptation is a theory of community decline that has become popular with the return to favor of evolutionary theory in anthropology. What is meant is that urban centers, in particular, become overdeveloped in nonproductive areas, and place a greater strain on their resource base than it is able to sustain. This has been suggested for the lowland Maya cities (R.E.W. Adams 1973:27–28; Webb 1973:367–404), for the great midwestern ceremonial and trade center of Cahokia (Pfeiffer 1974:62), and even for a small Basketmaker village site in Arizona (Plog 1974:158).

The argument of the evolutionists, as I understand it, is that the Maya tried to achieve "too much, too soon." It is not argued that Yucatán today is incapable of supporting large urban centers with nonproductive elites, but only that the Classic Maya had not reached the evolutionary level where they were ready for such luxuries. A weakness in this argument lies in the fact that the Maya did somehow manage to support their temple centers and priesthoods for at least three centuries before giving them up. If the temple centers were genuinely maladaptive they ought to have become increasingly so with the passage of time, and we should observe a continual process of decay from the time they were first established. Instead we see progressive growth and enrichment until, we are asked to believe, the system broke quite suddenly under the strain.

A more fundamental weakness of maladaptation theories is that they are really descriptive and not explanatory. All human communities that do not produce their own food and other commodities needed for survival run a certain risk, and the greater their dependence on others, the greater the risk. They are, in other words, potentially maladaptive. Risk is minimized, but never fully eliminated, by establishing political, military, or economic control over the hinterland from which needed food and raw materials are obtained. When, for any of a variety of reasons, those controls fail, the town or city stands nakedly revealed as maladaptive.

The difficulty is that there is no very reliable way of predicting how much hinterland can be controlled, or for how long. The Romans, with a fairly primitive material technology but with advanced political and military ones, effectively controlled a hinterland so vast that the city could depend for its very survival on weekly shiploads of grain from across the Mediterranean (see Swanson 1975:585). Something comparable was achieved by the even more technologically backward Inca Empire in South America. On the other hand, cities with a much more advanced technical infrastructure than either Rome or Cuzco have failed entirely to secure effective control of resource areas, and their growth has been limited in consequence.

In the end, it seems to me, all that maladaptation theory really says is that anything that keeps growing will ultimately get too big. But how big is too big is a question that is subject to all kinds of situational variables, not all of which are explainable in evolutionary terms.

Economic change is frequently suggested by historians, but rarely by anthropologists, as an explanation for site abandonment. There appear to be two reasons for this, one essentially empirical and the other ideological. It must first be acknowledged that anthropologist-archaeologists have given the bulk of their attention over the years to the remains of relatively simple, food-producing societies, in which trade and economic specialization were not highly developed. Historians and historian-archaeologists, on the other hand, have always been primarily concerned with urban centers. This in itself reflects an important ideological difference: anthropology has a strongly proletarian bias (the legacy, presumably, of its intellectual origins in the Enlightenment), while historians, even if they would prefer otherwise, are confined by the elitism that is so evident in most of their source material. There are, obviously, weaknesses in both positions. Historians are unacquainted with the common man, and especially with primitive man, except as refracted through the eyes of upper-class observers. Anthropologists, on the other hand, are uncomfortable in dealing with complex societies in which man is not closely attuned to nature—which is probably why they always prefer ecological explanations to economic ones.

Economic change leading to community decay can be of several kinds. Probably the most common, and the most often suggested by historians, is the shifting of trade routes, resulting from changing political circumstances or changing transport technology. Speaking of America in the 1920s, Frederick Lewis Allen (1946:126–27) observed how "villages which had once prospered because they were 'on the railroad' languished with economic anemia; villages on Route 61 bloomed with garages, filling stations, hotdog stands, chicken-dinner restaurants, tearooms, tourists' rests, camp sites, and affluence. The interurban trolley perished, or survived only as a pathetic anachronism. Railroad after railroad gave up its branch lines. . . ." All these phenomena had their counterparts in the ancient world.

The region between the eastern Mediterranean shore and the Persian Gulf, familiarly known as the Near East, offers a particularly good opportunity to study the effects of shifting trade, for this was the pivotal zone and entrepôt in the great East-West trade, which for centuries was the world's richest commerce. Cities and even empires contended endlessly for the coveted position of middleman in the East-West traffic; deserted seaports on the South Arabian coast, and inland caravanserais like Petra and Palmyra, are monuments to the losers in this struggle.

Technological as well as political factors played their part in the shifting fortunes of towns and cities. The development of organized camel transport, in the last centuries B.C., gave a great impetus to overland trade, and to the flowering of such caravan centers as Mecca and Damascus (Nutting 1964:16–18). A few centuries later the introduction of lateen rigging, which greatly increased the ability of ships to sail close to the wind, tipped the balance back in favor of maritime trade (Parry 1963:72–74), and brought a corresponding decline in the overland routes and caravan centers. This, however, could be offset by political factors in individual cases. Aidhab, on the southeast coast of Egypt, was until the late Middle Ages one of the principal ports on the Red Sea and the main eastern departure point for pilgrims to Mecca. Its decline was precipitous after A.D. 1250, when the Mameluke overlords of Egypt and Palestine extended their dominion over the Hejaz, and thereafter promoted the overland pilgrimage route to Mecca in preference to the Red Sea route (Hasan 1967:78–82). So thoroughly was Aidhad ruined that today its remains are hard to find.

Another kind of economic change that we can observe in the ancient as well as in the modern world is the effect of declining markets on one-industry towns. One of my favorite examples is Aphrodisias, in the hills of Asia Minor, which prospered from the manufacture of Hellenistic marble statuary for a large part of the eastern Roman world. When Christian iconoclasm destroyed the market for ornamental statuary, Aphrodisias suffered a decline from which it never recovered, even though its supplies of marble were far from exhausted (Erim 1967 and 1972). Even more extraordinary was the history of the Sabaen cities of Yemen (South Arabia), whose prosperity derived from a worldwide monopoly of the export of frankincense and myrrh—two of the most precious commodities in the ancient world. The chief foreign consumers of frankincense were the Romans, who used it extensively in funeral pyres. When Christianity brought with it a change from cremation to interment as the normal burial practice, the Roman frankincense market collapsed (Van Beek 1969). Within two centuries the Sabaen cities and civilization were no more.

A final kind of economic change that merits discussion here is the overall decline of trade over large areas and for long periods of time. The more developed parts of the world have for millennia been subject to what are, in effect, macrobusiness cycles: periods of affluence and expansion followed by periods of impoverishment and contraction brought on by overproduction of nonessential goods and the saturation of consumer markets. My own feeling is that this was a major cause of the contraction so conspicuous all over Mexico at the end of the Classic period, as it assuredly was in Western Europe after the fall of the Roman Empire. The decline and outright abandonment of towns and cities at that time is much too well documented to require further elaboration here (see Hammond 1972:331–39; Pirenne 1956:15–37).

The economic benefits of the *Pax Romana*, even at the rural level, are well attested in the archaeological remains from Nubia, where I have been working in recent years. During the first three centuries when Egypt was under Roman rule (30 B.C.–A.D. 270), Nubia, the region immediately to the south of Egypt, achieved a level of prosperity never equalled before or since, down to the beginning of the twentieth century. Though not itself under Roman rule, and though extremely poor in agrarian resources, Nubia profited through its unique ability to supply three commodities that the wealthy Romans coveted: gold, ivory, and dark-skinned slaves. The prosperity engendered by this traffic can be measured in terms of the number and size of towns, the spaciousness of individual houses, and above all by the wealth of imported luxuries buried with the dead, not only in the major urban centers but in towns and even peasant villages all up and down the Nile.

Far in the interior of Africa, a thousand miles from the Mediterranean and 600 miles from the Roman frontier, the city of Meroë arose as a marshalling depot in the Nile trade. To the Greek and Roman geographers who heard of it but never saw it, Meroë was a fabled place (see Shinnie 1967:13–23), but the archaeological realities are impressive enough. Here, where no urban center has flourished before or since, were at least six temples (one of them over 500 feet long), several palaces, extensive iron smelters, and a full-scale Roman bathing establishment (for detailed description see Shinnie 1967:62–98). But after the time of Diocletian (A.D. 284–304) the prosperity of Egypt declined rapidly, and the fortunes of Meroë plummeted likewise. The Nile trade dwindled to a trickle, and within a century Meroë was given over to wild tribesmen from across the Nile (Shinnie 1967:56). At the same time rural villages all along the Nile declined in size, many were abandoned altogether, and the volume of material wealth buried with the dead markedly decreased.

Political change, except in its purely military dimension, has seldom been directly blamed for the death of communities, though Tula in Mexico is said to have been abandoned after the Toltec ruling dynasty transferred its residence to Chapultepec (Coe 1962:138), and internal factionalism is blamed for the collapse of the late Maya city of Mayapán (Proskouriakoff 1955). There are, however, a number of theories in which environmental changes leading to site abandonment are linked to political changes. Neely (1974:38–41), in Persia, and R. McC. Adams (1965:97–111), in Mesopotamia, have suggested that the weakness of central government under the Abbasid caliphs led to a wholesale abandonment of irrigation systems, resulting in desiccation and depopulation of large areas. On the other hand, Gibson (1974), while accepting the correlation between large-scale irrigation and strong central government, offers the intriguing countersuggestion that it was precisely the overextension of irrigation and the overexploitation of agriculture, in defiance of natural fallowing requirements, that led to so much salinizaton and soil exhaustion in Mesopotamia. Thus, we have strong government, rather than weak government, identified as the ultimate cause of depopulation.

Apart from instances in which political variables stand as intermediaries between man and nature, history gives us plenty of examples in which the death of communities can be linked directly to changed political circumstances. Ours is not the first civilization in which government is in and of itself an enormous industry; some of the ancient bureaucracies were vast in their own right (see especially Eisenstadt 1963). The cities of ancient China and of ancient Egypt were first and foremost court cities, often with little or no productive or commercial life, and the courts themselves were notoriously migratory. Thus, the annals of traditional Chinese history preserve the names of a dozen former capitals that soon crumbled (and many of which can no longer be located archaeologically) once the court had moved away. An extreme example of this that can be identified archaeologically is Tell el-Amarna in Egypt, founded by the "heretic-Pharaoh" Akhenaton as his new capital, and abandoned utterly after his death (Posener 1959:7–8). Throughout the ancient world many a provincial capital suffered a comparable fate, when for reasons of state or of strategy or of economy its administrative functions were transferred elsewhere. Just recently I was reminded, in watching a television program, of how the fortunes of Williamsburg suffered when the Virginia capital was moved to Richmond.

40

We should probably give some consideration to another kind of political change: the overgrowth and petrifaction of bureaucracy, which, according to Karl Deutsch (1969:28–30), leads to political bankruptcy, and which is now being blamed by Jimmy Carter and Ronald Reagan for many of the nation's ills. Something of the same kind is believed to have contributed to the decay and depopulation of cities in the late Roman Empire (Hammond 1972: 297–301).

Military change in the broadest sense, including enemy activity and enemy pressure, has been invoked more often than any other factor as an explanation for site abandonment. On the other hand, military change, in the more narrowly specific sense of changing technology or tactics, has rarely been considered by archaeologists. Here again, however, recorded history abounds with examples. The hilltop castle towns of Europe stand today as half-deserted reminders of an age when protection was a negotiable commodity, the chief concern of Europe's populace and the cornerstone of its political system (see Rudofsky 1971). Most of these towns were founded on previously uninhabited hills or mountaintops, while other, less defensible localities were abandoned. For example, we are told that Roman Conimbriga (in Portugal) was deserted because it possessed no defensible water supply that could be enclosed within the town walls (Alarcao 1970:47). The castle town was a product not so much of a new siege technology (most of the medieval siege engines were invented by the Romans) as of a new siege mentality. Yet the castle towns themselves fell into decay when protection ceased to be the prime requisite for survival—and when, in any case, they were rendered irrelevant by the development of heavy artillery.

Changing military requirements can affect the life of communities in another way. We have all heard the howls of protest from modern American towns when a nearby army base was threatened with closing; indeed, within recent years my hometown of Lexington, Kentucky, waged an all-out court battle to prevent the closing of an ordnance depot that had been militarily irrelevant for years. Again, this is nothing new: the western frontier of China is lined with the remains of abandoned garrison towns that did not long outlive the withdrawal of the troops (Stein 1964:esp. 155–68). According to the excavator, the same thing happened to the Anatolian town of Altintepe 2,500 years ago (Özgüc 1967:57).

Religious change in anthropological formulations always comes near

41

the end. For most of us religion is, I fear, no more than the "residual category of the non-rational"; we invoke it as an explanation only when all other explanations fail. (It is a standing joke in field archaeology that any unrecognizable thingamabob is catalogued as a "ceremonial object.") Thus, religious change has almost never been considered by anthropologists as a reason for site abandonment. The one case I have come across in the literature is that of Siemreap in Cambodia (the site of Angkor Wat); its decline is attributed by one authority to the otherworldly influence of Theravada Buddhism (Pym 1963:132–38). Needless to say, the author of this theory is not an anthropologist; the orthodox anthropological view is that Siemreap declined because of ecological factors (Shimkin 1973:291–95).

As a conventionally educated anthropologist, it has taken me years to appreciate fully the part that religion has played in human history, including in the life and death of communities. I have had to learn that religion is something more than a cognitive and behavioral system; it is also, and for millennia has been, a highly lucrative industry. As such it has spawned more than its share of one-industry towns, which, like other one-industry towns, have been vulnerable to the vicissitudes of market demand. Delphi and Olympia are prime examples for the ancient world. Both were flourishing international centers for the better part of a thousand years; both fell into utter ruin with the coming of Christianity (Encyclopaedia Britannica 1929b:175; 1929c: 779). Even Athens, though of course it did not altogether disappear, sank from a major city to a local market town after the closing of the philosophical schools that were its chief industry in A.D. 529 (L. Cottrell 1960:106). For modern communities that are vulnerable to a similar fate we need look no further than Lourdes and Mecca.

Religious change may of course be only a guise of political change, as in the dissolution of the English abbey communities by Henry VIII in 1536. Woodward (1972:2) has written that "In April 1536 . . . there were, scattered throughout England and Wales, more than eight hundred religious houses, monasteries, nunneries and friaries, and in them there lived close to 10,000 monks, canons, nuns and friars. Four years later, in April 1540, there were none." In this case a stroke of the king's pen accomplished what the Black Death (to an anthropologist, a more "natural" and probable cause of abandonment) could not achieve two hundred years earlier. We should not forget, however, that there are deserted monasteries all over Europe, in Catholic countries as well as in Protestant ones. Their abandonment is testimony to a more sweeping and fundamental religious change than the mere nationalization of the English church: a spirit of secularism that has rendered the monastic life and the monastic community irrelevant even in the eyes of devout Catholics.

Recreational change has never been suggested by archaeologists and is not well documented historically as a factor contributing to community decline, but it should probably not be altogether ignored. The case of Olympia, already discussed in connection with religious change, might be offered as one example. The famous games were, of course, an important industry in their own right, and they might have survived the coming of Christianity had not the Greeks simultaneously eschewed the cult of athleticism. More recently, the uneven fortunes of ski resorts, bathing spas, and gambling meccas all attest the influence of changing recreational patterns. In particular the decay of the once-elegant resorts so nostalgically celebrated by Cleveland Amory (1952) in *The Last Resorts* is a tribute to the impact of the automobile in America's recreational habits.

Archaeology and the Small Community

The archaeological and historical examples I have thus far cited are nearly all major urban centers, for the simple and sufficient reason that there is very little literature on the death of small communities. Their passing, it seems, has gone largely unrecorded by historians and largely unexplained by archaeologists. This is perhaps expectable in view of the elitist bias of historians, but the silence of archaeologists is less readily understandable. It is not that we fail to investigate small communities; there are far more archaeological reports on small sites than there are on large ones. Nevertheless, a more or less random perusal of one hundred reports on small sites, ranging in time from Neolithic to medieval,[4] has yielded only nineteen instances in which the author volunteered any explanation for the final abandonment of the site or sites. It would almost seem that we look upon abandonment as the natural and inevitable fate of small communities, something calling for no special explanation. Indeed, in the case of small sites it is often long persistence rather than abandonment that the archaeologist feels bound to explain.

To what extent is this view justified by the historical evidence? First

43

of all we can note that the majority of small archaeological sites do indeed give evidence of a fairly brief period of occupation—on the average, somewhere between a generation and two centuries. This is in part because many of our smallest sites were the residences of quite primitive and imperfectly sedentary peoples: practitioners of shifting agriculture, or farmers who continued to rely heavily on wild foods during the off season. Although there are many exceptions, there is nevertheless a very strong correlation between size of sites and length of occupation.

Another factor contributing to the transitoriness of occupation in small sites is the relative ease with which small groups can relocate en bloc, without permanent disruption of their social fabric (see Schwartz 1970). Thus, in the prehistoric Southwest, even when there were no very compelling reasons to migrate, people seem to have moved around a good deal simply because there was nothing to prevent them. This is of course possible only where no population pressure exists. The Near East, where there has been population pressure for a very long time, is also one of the few areas in the world where we regularly find quite small sites with a long occupation history.

Because of the migration factor it is very unsafe, in the case of small sites, to equate abandoned dwellings with dead communities, as we regularly (and I think legitimately) do in the case of large sites. I suspect, in fact, that the main reason why archaeologists have so seldom offered an explanation for the abandonment of small sites is their implicit assumption that the inhabitants had simply removed to some nearby location, though this has not often been explicitly suggested. Thus, it is only when a whole region is abandoned simultaneously that we envision the actual death of small communities.

We can further observe that throughout the world most of the inhabitants of small communities are food producers, while most of the inhabitants of urban centers are not. This fundamental division of society, we believe, goes back to the dawn of civilization. It follows inevitably that the circumstances of life and death are somewhat different in the two cases. Small communities are, we assume, more immediately vulnerable to environmental vicissitudes than are urban centers, while being proportionately less affected by failure or change in the economic, political, or religious spheres. Given the interdependence of city and village, however, it ultimately becomes true that what is bad for the one is bad for the other.

The Dead Community: Perspectives from the Past

Finally, we have to recognize that every city becomes, at least for some of its residents, a symbol of collective self-awareness in a way that primitive and peasant villages seldom are. As Frankfort (1956:52) has written in describing early Sumerian cities, "The city sets its citizens apart from the other inhabitants of the land. It determines their relations with the outside world. It produces intensified self-consciousness in its burghers, to whom the collective achievements are a source of pride." Once a city has acquired an identity and a history, then, the mere fact of its existence is sufficient reason to keep it going, and to rebuild it in the wake of disaster, even when the original reasons for its founding have long been forgotten. In short, the city exemplifies what John Bennett (1976:848) has so aptly termed the "time-binding" aspect of culture. The same appears to be much less true in the case of village dwellers, whose totemic allegiances are less explicitly bound up with their places of residence.

Making allowance for all of the above considerations, both archaeology and history nevertheless suggest that small communities may die in all the same ways and for the same reasons as large ones. To begin with, they are of course much more vulnerable to violent and total destruction, both by man and by nature. Not only is physical destruction more easily accomplished, but there are not, for the reasons just discussed, the same symbolic incentives to rebuild on the same site as in the case of the city. From the prehistoric Southwest we have a fair number of seemingly incontrovertible examples of the violent and final destruction of small communities (Haury 1958; King 1949:140; McGregor 1965:384). And, of course, small communities can be totally wiped out by disease, as has been suggested (but not proven) for rural European villages at the time of the Black Death (Langer 1964).

Because there is so little literature on the subject, I shall have to turn primarily to the results (partly unpublished) of my own excavations in Nubia to exemplify some other causes of death in small communities. I have already alluded to the various pottery-making sites that I believe were abandoned when local fuel supplies were exhausted. (Another case of local resource depletion is provided by medieval villages on the island of Öland, which are believed to have been depopulated when the herring departed from the Baltic on one of their cyclic migrations; see Hagberg 1976:117.)

The village of Meinarti, situated just at the foot of the Second Cataract of the Nile, was occupied continuously for more than 1,200

45

years (for excavation reports see W. Adams 1964b, 1965, and 1968b). It had almost no agrarian resources, and owed its prosperity to its strategic position in the Nile trade. Here cargoes had to be offloaded from large to small boats, for passage through the cataract, and here in consequence the Nubian kings maintained a customs post or tollhouse, according to medieval Arab chroniclers (see Burckhardt 1819:494). When Ottoman economic policy destroyed the Nile trade at the end of the Middle Ages, Meinarti was abandoned and never reoccupied.

Another effect of changing economic conditions can be seen in the decline and impoverishment of many Nubian villages that accompanied the diminution of trade with Roman Egypt, as detailed in earlier pages. Effects of political change are apparent at the townsite of Qasr Ibrim, a regional administrative center off and on during its 3,000-year history. When, in the sixteenth century, the rapaciousness of the Ottoman garrison forced the local governing officials to remove themselves to the neighboring town of Derr, the newly established administrative center prospered while Qasr Ibrim became little more than a filthy and dilapidated barracks.

The effects of military change are particularly evident in the rugged Batn el-Hajjar region, extending upstream for about seventy miles from the Second Cataract of the Nile. This is the poorest and least productive reach of the entire Nile Valley, but because of its rocky, mountainous nature it also presents an unusual number of easily defensible sites. Between A.D. 1200 and 1800—Nubia's feudal age—the Batn el-Hajjar boasted a population considerably in excess of today's.[5] A great deal of it clustered in sites clinging dizzily to the tops and sides of rocky promontories, the Nubian equivalents of Europe's castle towns. Every one of these sites was abandoned by A.D. 1800.

Over the past 4,000 years Nubia has had three "established" religions: the Ancient Egyptian, the Christian, and the Islamic, and each has developed its local cult centers. The Egyptian colonial overlords of the second millennium B.C. established temples and temple-estates at many places, and most of these were kept up under the native empire of Kush, which arose in the aftermath of Egyptian rule. With the coming of Christianity in the sixth century, some of the old temple centers were quite promptly abandoned, while others became places of Christian worship, and at least six were adorned with cathedrals. The arrival of Islam a thousand years later rendered the cathedrals (as well as a great many local churches and monasteries) obsolete in their turn,

46

and towns like Faras and Qasr Ibrim, which had flourished as local pilgrimage centers for millennia, fell into decay.

Some Concluding Reflections

My own views on the subject of community decline and site abandonment should be sufficiently clear from the foregoing discussion. I am not much impressed either by the catastrophism of historians or by the unrelenting determinism of anthropologists; the theories that seem to me most believable fall somewhere between these extremes of particularism and generalism. Factors of an economic, political, military, and social nature have, I believe, been far more influential than disaster or environmental decay.

If there is a common theme running through the theories of community decline that I find most believable, it is the failure of systemic linkages—the ties that bind communities to the larger societies, economies, and polities of which they are a part. Very few communities are, and very few large communities ever have been, self-sufficient and self-contained; they exist and can survive only within a network of interdependent relationships with other communities. When for one reason or another those relationships are weakened, either because the community is no longer able to obtain from other communities the things that it needs or because it is no longer able to supply the things that others need, decay and death are the result. As I have already suggested, the commodities of which I am here speaking are not necessarily material ones; they may be political, social, religious, even artistic or recreational.

Most excursions through history's pages seem only to prove that there is nothing new under the sun, and it appears that this one has been no exception. I have not identified any causes of community death in the past that are not relevant to the present, or vice versa. On the contrary, as a convinced "uniformitarian," I am always suspicious of explanations offered for one time or place in history that are not applicable to other times or places (see W. Adams 1973:28).

There is consequently a lesson that is continually borne home to me by the contemplation of the historic past, and that is to be wary of excessively or exclusively materialist explanations for social phenomena. I think we have to remember in this connection that communities are often born, or suddenly blossom, for essentially irrational or even trivial reasons, and they are prone to die for the same reasons. The whim of a drunken Alexander creates a thriving provincial capital; the vision of an unlettered girl gives the world a great religious center; a backroom political tradeoff determines the siting of a military base, or even a state university.[6] The resulting communities have no obvious economic or geographical reason for existence, but they may endure for centuries. By the same token they are vulnerable to death or decay when their sometimes fragile links to the larger society are disturbed.

THE SYMPTOMS OF COMMUNITY DEATH

When we turn from the question of why communities die to the question of how they die the archaeologist finds himself on safer ground, for he is now in the realm of description and inference rather than of explanation. He also finds that the evidence of written history seldom contradicts his interpretations; the historian has had little enough to say about everyday life at the best of times, and still less about life in the dying days of towns and cities. On the other hand the better-preserved archaeological sites, particularly in the world's arid regions, often give a quite detailed and even poignant picture of the circumstances of life in a community's last days. Comparing this with our picture of life in earlier and more prosperous times, we can identify a number of specific, archaeologically verifiable conditions that appear to be symptomatic of the dying community.

Physical contraction may seem so obvious as hardly to require mention. Since most communities die because people leave them, it necessarily follows that they become gradually smaller until they reach the vanishing point. We are apt to think of this, however, in relatively short-range terms, perhaps extending over one or two generations. Archaeology, on the other hand, shows that community death may be the culmination of a very long contraction process. In deeply stratified sites like Teotihuacán (Millon 1967), Knossos (Hutchison 1962:300–303), Troy (Blegen 1963:171), Ur (Woolley 1954:245), and Mohenjo-Daro (Wheeler 1968:127), we consistently find that even before it began its final decline the city was not as big as it had been in earlier times.

Lack of new building is another condition that seems intuitively obvious, but is nevertheless worth mentioning as an archaeologically verifiable condition. It is specifically noted at Tikal (Culbert 1973a:2–4) and Mohenjo-Daro (Wheeler 1968:127), and in a number of stratified sites I have excavated in Nubia.

Since building activity of one sort or another is almost always going on in lively and flourishing communities, we find in most occupation horizons the remains of both old and new buildings. (Age is attested by the extent of dilapidation or the accumulation of indoor refuse, which in primitive and peasant dwellings sets in very rapidly after initial construction.) In the uppermost occupation levels, however, we are apt to find that there are only dilapidated buildings. We assume in these cases that the people with initiative enough to build new houses were also those with sufficient initiative to move away.

Dilapidation is, then, another conspicuous symptom of the dying community, specifically observed by the excavators at Dzibilchaltún (Andrews 1968:46), Mayapán (Proskouriakoff 1955), Minturnae (Johnson 1954), Mohenjo-Daro (Wheeler 1968:127), and several Nubian sites. Not only is there an absence of new houses, but the older ones—as well as public buildings—are allowed to deteriorate beyond the point at which, in earlier times, they would have been repaired or replaced. On the basis of observations in my own and other sites, I would conclude that the general standard of housing in a community's last days is apt to be lower than at any previous time in its history.

Neglect of public monuments is one of the most commonly noted and suggestive evidences of community decline. Neglect of the church in the last days of Christian occupation is notable at Qasr Ibrim and at least half a dozen other medieval Nubian communities with which I am familiar. A similar unconcern is reflected in the building of potter's workshops within formerly sacred precincts at Ur (Woolley 1954:247) and Mohenjo-Daro (Piggott 1952: 227–28); in the accumulation of rubbish within temples at Dzibilchaltún (Andrews 1968:46) and Kawa (Macadam 1955:27); by late-period rubbish in kivas at several southwestern pueblos (Hill 1970:90; Rohn 1971:27); by the dilapidation of royal pyramids at Meroë (Shinnie 1967:56); and by tomb-robbing at Tikal (Culbert 1973b:78) and in the sacred necropoli of Egyptian Thebes (Wilson 1951:283–88). In one way or another the decline of civic pride and/or loss of faith in the city's tutelary deities is probably reflected in each of these instances.

Disorderly town development, or, in other words, the gradual departure from an orderly arrangement of buildings toward a seemingly haphazard or opportunistic one, has been noted at Teotihuacán (Millon

1967) and Mohenjo-Daro (Wheeler 1968:127), as well as in my own excavations at Meinarti (W. Adams 1968b:191–95). It is presumed to be indicative of the decay both of central authority and of civic pride. (For a discussion of the relationship between centralized political authority and town planning see W. Adams 1968b:198–99).

Refuse accumulation is evidence that can cut in two directions. The gross volume of garbage generated by a community is of course a measure of its affluence and not of its poverty (for a lively and informative discussion on this see Rathje 1974). Garbage disposal is, however, another matter. In times when every house is occupied, and when the streets and plazas are busy places, people may be obliged to dump most of their rubbish at the edge of town even if they are not particularly civic-minded. With impoverishment and depopulation comes increasing litter within the town, as has been noted at Mug House (Rohn 1971:27) and Pueblo Bonito (Judd 1954:20) in the Southwest, at the Maya city of Dzibilchaltún (Andrews 1968:46), and certainly in many of my own excavations in Nubia. Slovenly living habits are not, however, an infallible sign of community decay; although we nearly always find them characteristic of the community's last days, we sometimes find them in prosperous times as well.

Declining standards of craftmanship are attested for the dying stages of many communities: inferior houses at Teotihuacán (Millon 1967) and Mohenjo-daro (Wheeler 1968:127), inferior temples at Mayapán (Proskouriakoff 1955), inferior pottery at Teotihuacán (Millon 1967) and in Nubia (W. Adams 1970:118).

Cultural and artistic diversity—another evidence of the decay of central authority—has been cited in the case of heterodox religious practices in the last days of Tikal (Culbert 1973b:74–80) and Mayapán (Proskouriakoff 1955), and in the local differentiation of pottery styles among the late Mayan (Culbert 1973b) and late Mycenaean (Samuel 1966:133–34) cities. Ceramic diversity has also been noted in the Andes in connection with the decay of the prehistoric cites of Tiahuanaco and Huari (Bennett and Bird 1964:148–49).

Neglect of the dead may be cited as a final symptom of community decay. It may take several forms: the dilapidation of funerary monuments at Meroë (Shinnie 1967:56), the diminishing wealth buried with the dead at Meroë (Shinnie 1967:56) or lavished on funerals at Minturnae (Johnson 1954), and, in several places, the unceremonious interment of corpses within the town precincts (Johnson 1954; Wheeler 1968:129–31).

One word of caution must be inserted here: none of the symptoms of decay that have been discussed in preceding pages are diagnostic and indisputable evidence that a community is dying. Periods of decline and decay, when many of these symptoms are manifest, occur from time to time in the history of many long-established communities. Indeed, stratified archaeological sites in the Near East seem to evidence an almost rhythmic cycle of growth and decay. Generations of neglect and dilapidation end in a sudden revitalization, when quite abruptly—perhaps within a matter of a few years—nearly every house in the village is rebuilt or repaired, the streets are cleared of rubbish, and the local temple or church is given new plaster and decorations. Then, it seems, the deterioration process begins anew.

Decay processes in and of themselves are just as normal as growth processes: both are going on simultaneously throughout most of the life of the community. When the rate of decay threatens to overwhelm the rate of growth, some revitalizing influence intervenes and sets the pendulum temporarily swinging in the opposite direction. This is conspicuously observable in the archaeological remains of the two Nubian sites of Meinarti and Qasr Ibrim, both of which showed all the symptoms of dying more than once before their times actually came.

What happens when communities finally die, evidently, is that normal or expectable revitalizing forces fail to materialize. It is that failure, rather than the normal and predictable fact of decay, that we are called upon to explain.

The Death of Communities and the Decay of Civilizations

Up to now I have avoided any mention of the sweeping "decline and fall" theories made popular by Spengler (1932), Toynbee (1962), Sorokin (1962), and others, but these too have sometimes been invoked in explaining the death of communities. (For general review of such theories see Sorokin 1963.) Like the macrosystemic theories of anthropologists, they link the decline of communities to larger systemic failures; unlike the theories of anthropologists, they look upon human history as a series of repeating cycles rather than as a generally upward course interrupted only temporarily by environmental reverses and imbalances. To the cyclic theorists decay and death are as inevitable in the human experience—both communal and individual—as birth and growth, and as such require no explanation in terms of external causes.

In speaking of prehistoric civilizations like those of the Indus Valley and the Aegean, the argument from decline of civilizations to death of cities is tautological. In these cases the civilization *was* the cities, in the sense that we have no other surviving evidence of it except the archaeological remains of its communities. Even in the historic period, however, when we can supposedly separate the ethos of a civilization from its physical embodiment in town and city, we often find an implicit or explicit assumption that the final death of a city is sufficiently explained by the decay of the civilization of which it was a part. (This seems to be particularly true as regards Roman cities; see Matthews 1957:46.)

Cyclic theories are easy to discount, and easy to refute, when pushed to the deterministic extremes represented by Spengler (1932), Toynbee (1962), and Sorokin (1962). When all that is said, and when every allowance is made for the possibility of circular reasoning, there remains nevertheless an uncomfortably real correlation between the decay of individual communities and the decay of larger sociocultural systems. Edward Stillman (1968) in a semifacetious article called "Before the Fall," lists the following as generally recognized symptoms of cultural decadence: mannish women, glorification of the flesh, violence and crime, faddist art, alien cults, alien garb, gleeful tastelessness, glorification of disorder, the cult of squalor, the decline of fellow feeling, tumorous government, and class war (the terms in each case are his). It is startling to notice that more than half of these conditions—and nearly all those that leave recognizable archaeological traces—have their localized counterparts in the symptoms of community decline that we have discussed in preceding pages.

NOTES

1. A number entry in any box in the table indicates that a particular explanation (vertical column) has been suggested for the abandonment of a particular site (horizontal row). The numbers themselves refer to relevant literature, listed immediately following the table. For full citations see the Reference list at the end of the volume. Asterisks (*) identify the theories advanced by anthropologist-archaeologists.

2. The dichotomy is not as dramatically illustrated as it might be in Table 2.1 because I have lumped together on a single line a large number of environmental explanations for the abandonment of individual sites in the Southwest, Yucatán, and Mesopotamia.

3. Richard E. W. Adams is one of the few and honorable exceptions to this generalization. He has suggested that we ought to seek different explanations for the abandonment of different Classic Maya cities (R. E. W. Adams 1973:33).

4. The primary criterion of selection was that all the reports were in my personal library, since I undertook this exercise on a day when the university library was closed. This means that there was a somewhat heavy weighting toward Southwestern and Nubian sites, but many other areas are also represented.

5. That is, in excess of the population in 1964, before its enforced removal occasioned by the Aswan High Dam.

6. This happened in my former hometown of Flagstaff, Arizona, which was awarded a teachers' college—now Northern Arizona University—as a kind of consolation prize when it was decided not to build the state insane asylum there.

3

The Dying Community: The Natural Resource Base

MARION CLAWSON

Resources for the Future
Washington, D.C.

The extent and the closeness of the linkage between the community and natural resources depends on the definitions of each.

To this economist, there are at least three senses in which the term *community* may be used: (1) as a collection of people in a more or less defined geographic area, such as a village, a town, or a ward of a city; (2) as economic, or as production and consumption of goods and services by the inhabitants of such an area, for their own use or for export and exchange with other areas; and (3) as a set of social relationships or of roles among the people who inhabit the area or who are close enough geographically to maintain such relationships.

My concern in this chapter is primarily with the first two of these concepts, while the other papers in this volume are concerned primarily with the third concept, as the introductory essay by Gallaher and Padfield makes clear. The three kinds of community are closely interrelated. Where my conclusions or statements might seem to have different applicability for one definition as compared with another, I shall try to make clear the differences.

If natural resources are broadly defined, then communities (in each sense) are closely and directly linked to them; if a more limited or more restrictive definition of resources is employed, the linkages are less direct and not as close. My definition of natural resources, evolved over many years of reading, thinking, and talking about the subject, includes four major elements: (1) Any quality of nature which (2) the culture knows how to use (3) economically (4) to an end which is sought.

The first part includes the physical-biological aspects of nature—soils, forests, waters, minerals, climate, and the like—that are often thought of as the whole of natural resources. They are indeed important, but their importance is not uniquely determined, because it depends upon the other parts of the definition. Moreover, the characteristics of nature that constitute natural resources at one period in history may not do so at another. Natural resources are a changing or dynamic concept, not a static one.

The second part of the definition includes the technological means by which man translates some quality of nature into some good or service for direct consumption and use. Unless such capacity exists, the quality of nature is not a resource. I have pointed out elsewhere that, to the Plains Indians of 200 years ago, the petroleum deposits so important to today's economy of Texas and Oklahoma did not exist—the Indians did not suspect the existence of the oil under the land over which they hunted, would have had no means of bringing it to the surface had they known it was there, and would have had no use for it if brought to the surface. Examples of this kind of technological change are numerous if not infinite in number. A chemist friend once remarked that, up until about World War II, uranium was a minor element, almost a chemical curiosity; but after the first atomic explosions, it became one of the most valuable natural resources in the world. This role of technology is sometimes summarized in the statement that natural resources do not exist—they become. Even mines are made, not found.

But it is not enough to know where some natural quality occurs and to know how to use it; the result must also be an economic one, in the sense that the labor, capital, and managerial talent required in the process are rewarded at least as well, and preferably better, than the use of the same human resources anywhere else. For example oil shale exists, the oil is in demand, the technology for its extraction exists, but so far the costs exceed the values so created. Or, the desalting of seawater is technically possible, the supply of seawater is virtually limitless, and the water could be used for irrigation to produce cereals and other staple crops for food badly needed by people in many countries. The catch is that the costs, for the present and the foreseeable future, are a whole order of magnitude greater than the values (Clawson, Landsberg, and Alexander 1969). The economics of a particular natural resource use depend not only upon the circumstances surrounding that particular resource, but also upon the availability and costs of alternative sources of the same commodity or of substitutes. The economic dimension of natural resources sometimes changes rapidly, and thus changes the content of the natural resource basket available to any community.

But the definition of natural resources is not complete without including the goals or the desires of the persons who may use the goods or services so produced. There are many circumstances in which it would be possible to produce something, which the society would reject. To take one grotesque example, we do not grow human beings to serve as food for other human beings or as food for our animals. Or, as another example at the other end of the scale of social attractiveness, the sunshine and climate of Florida were not much of an asset until we developed an economy and a culture with a large leisure (including retired) quota. As our contemporary culture changes, the importance of cultural attitudes toward natural resources seems to increase.

COMMUNITY GROWTH AND CHANGE

A community, in the economic sense, is never wholly self-sufficient or wholly self-contained. There is always some trade of goods, services, and ideas with the "outside." The community is always to some degree "open" in the sense that goods, services, and ideas flow in and out; indeed, a considerable part of the human energy of the community may be devoted to the management and servicing of such flows. The openness of economic communities is greater today and in the economically advanced countries than it once was or than it is today in the economically less advanced areas.

To a considerable extent, the foregoing statement applies to the social community as well as to the economic one. No community today is completely isolated from the rest of the world. Most American communities, however physically distant they may be, are linked by radio and television to the rest of the country.

Within the demographic community, the processes of birth, death, and migration are constantly changing the makeup of the mass of individuals who form the economic and the social communities. The number of people may change slowly or quickly, upward or downward, by a combination of these demographic processes. The rates of change differ greatly among different communities, from rapid inflow when a new gold strike is reported to an equally rapid outflow when it becomes apparent that the strike was small or nonexistent.

The economic community is likely to move rather closely in parallel with the demographic community. When a community is growing in population, it is likely to be at least moderately prosperous economically; it requires prosperity to attract or to hold people. A community declining in population is likely to be economically depressed; people move out slowly and in response both to pull from other areas and to push from their former location, and typically move only as adverse income or employment situations develop. There are, of course, numerous exceptions to the idea of closely synchronized population-income changes, and in a particular situation these divergences may dominate the picture.

But the social community changes over time also, especially as the demographic and economic communities change. Merely holding the population of a small town constant or slowly growing, and merely having a modestly prosperous local economy, does not necessarily prevent substantial social changes. For one thing, though numbers of people may stay the same, the individuals making up the total may change. For instance, in the past decade many rural communities in the United States have had relatively constant or slowly growing populations, but made up of declining numbers of older residents and increasing numbers of younger immigrants with greatly different life-styles.

Thus, though one can talk about *community* in any one of the three senses outlined, or about *resources* in any definition chosen, the relationship between community and resources is likely to be a changing one.

MAN-NATURE RELATIONSHIPS

Man and nature interact, and always have. Man adapts himself to nature, including the nature and the form of the resources that he is able to use. Great natural catastrophes, such as floods, droughts, hurricanes, and earthquakes, often reveal how limited is man's control over nature and how dependent man is upon nature. But nature is affected by man also. There exists no situation on the earth where man has not left his mark today. Possibly such a situation existed for a few millennia before the ancestors of the American Indians arrived from Asia, but it exists no longer.

White, black, red, and yellow men have greatly affected nature in the modern United States. Before the coming of white men, the red men had only fire as a major tool, but they used it to their own ends and with substantial effect in many areas. On the one hand, modern man has developed natural resources in the United States, by the application of technology, to such an extent that one can properly speak of creating resources. On the other hand, he has destroyed or altered many other resources. One can hardly imagine any process by which this part of the world's surface could go from a population of about 1 million with an Indian culture 500 years ago to a population of about 220 million with a highly advanced technological culture today, and at the same time leave nature undisturbed. One need not, of course, argue that all changes have been for the best or that all disturbances were unavoidable. But basic changes in nature were an inevitable result of population growth, and the clock cannot be turned backward.

In relatively recent times, the United States has seen the development of a mass environmental movement. We are no longer so complacent about the environmental results of our actions as we once were. Major efforts are now being made to reduce environmental impacts or to reverse past environmental damages. The resource-environmental situations are often complex, the relationships among factors are poorly known, the element of risk and chance is very great, and yet as a nation we are now determined to reduce the environmental damages. Resource use of all kinds in the future will increasingly feel the impact of these popular attitudes toward the environment.

With the increase in population, the development of new technology, and the increase in economic output, the United States has continually poured more labor, capital, and management into the productive processes based upon the natural resources. The input-output curve, or production function between resources and other productive inputs, has constantly shifted to the right and upward while at the same time shifts of inputs along the curve were occurring. Some of the shifts were irreversible, as when some species became extinct, but others were within the reversible range, as when soils were cultivated more or less intensively or when forests were cut and regrown.

In the man-nature relationships, it is a grave error to underestimate the resilience of natural ecosystems. Given any chance at all, a natural ecosystem will rebuild partially or fully. Land cleared for crops reverts to forest when no longer cultivated, though it may take several human lifetimes to restore the original kind of forest. After all, plants and animals have all had to cope with enemies and forces other than man throughout their long evolution, and if they had not had the capacity to recover, they would not have persisted. Existence today is ample proof of capacity to have met yesterday's challenges; it does not guarantee capacity to meet tomorrow's challenges, but it is surely suggestive of such power.

Part of my definition of natural resources is technology, the primary means whereby one form of natural resources replaces another. Coal replaced wood as a fuel, only in turn to be largely replaced by oil and gas, in each case as new technologies made previously unusable natural resources productive and valuable. The man-nature relationship is not a static one.

CHARACTERIZATION OF NATURAL RESOURCES

With this general background, some (most, but not all, perhaps) of the natural resources may be characterized as they affect the existence and the health of the economic community.

First, there are extractive resources of various kinds—the fossil fuels, the metals, the inherited virgin timber—all of which have been and most of which still are important in the economy and culture of the United States. They are not renewable; they exist. While the usable supply can often be augmented by increased recovery, there is a finiteness to these nonrenewable natural resources. These are often what is meant by *natural resources*, but, as indicated above, these are far from the totality of natural resources in this or in any other country. Popular language often refers to their being *mined out*, or exhausted. The deposit or the stand of timber may indeed be used fully, but often the process is rather different from the usual depiction. The initial mining may take the richest deposits, which are quickly used up, but further mining may be able to utilize thinner deposits. This is what has happened with most metals; progressively poorer ores are used, but technological changes in the past have held the real costs of metal nearly constant. At some point, however, the ore deposit is wholly gone in each local area.

In contrast to the extractive resources are the renewable resources, including sunlight and water circulated by the hydrologic cycle, and especially soil and the vegetation that can be grown thereon. The soil can indeed be washed or blown away, and to this extent is subject to extraction or depletion; but it can also be used continuously over long periods of time—thousands of years in the Nile Valley, for instance. New soil is formed continuously in most natural situations. The growing of crops is nearly the only practical means yet invented of using solar energy; although photosynthesis captures only about 3 percent of the energy in the sunlight that falls on a particular part of the earth, it is still the best means so far devised for economically capturing any of that energy. The amount of plant growth that is possible on earth is vastly greater than often realized; plants could produce annually a biomass containing several times as much energy as people everywhere consume annually in all forms, including fossil fuels. The United States has emerged in recent years as the chief producer of food crops for export, with somewhere around three-fourths of the world's capacity of food export. We can also grow wood in large volume and at reasonable cost, and as the inherited stocks of largely nonreplaceable timber are used up, the growing of timber is becoming more important in our national economy. The growing of crops and timber typically result in a population that is spread thinly over the land, but their service communities form population concentrations generally not large but still significant.

Locational resources are often important in community existence and function. Transportation nodes, particularly water-land junctions such as seaports, have been the reason underlying economic communities from the beginning of time. Such locational matters as a ford across a river, or the emergence of the mountain pass to the plain, and others have long been factors underlying the local economy. The importance of a node depends very much upon the technology of the transport, of course. A site that may be ideal for a great international airport may have had little significance for oxcart travel, or the easy ford across the river may long since have been outmoded by bridges on shorter routes. While the specifics of transportation nodes may change, this type of natural resource is likely to remain important almost forever.

Climatic resources have always been factors in population locations, but the importance of attractive climate has risen in the world in recent years. An attractive climate draws people for recreation, providing employment and livelihood to those who serve them. But an attractive climate may draw people as permanent residents, who constitute a labor force, which employers and jobs then follow. The population growth areas of the United States during the past quarter century have been dominantly those where climate was the major natural resource—the Sun Belt. One might hazard the generalization that the importance of climate rises as the average per capita income rises; when a person, or a group, or a nation is poor, then living where an income can be secured may be imperative. When incomes reach or exceed some minimum, and when factors other than the basics in life loom large, then one may choose to live where he or she thinks life is pleasant, and to seek to find ways to earn a living there. This relationship may well become a major factor in community structure in the next generation.

Some economic and social communities have been and are located because of some cultural resource—a religious center, an educational institution, a seat of government, and the like. The culture made the place into a resource and now the place has resource characteristics. I am much impressed by this because I live in the largest such community in the United States. As people say in Washington, we are a company town, the company being the federal government. Direct employment and direct income from the federal government has increasingly been matched or exceeded by indirect effects—the drawing together of large numbers of people who have business with the government, or who serve government people and clientele. This particular economic community has its special social community or communities. But ancient religious shrines, or ancient seats of learning, have always provided a base for support of economic and social communities.

Finally, some groupings of population are where they are today because an economic and/or social community has been there for decades or generations. That is, every human community is to some degree its own resource; its very existence today is reason for its continued existence. There exists a great momentum in both economic and social communities, in the sense that what is, tends to continue. This does not in the least deny the importance of growth and decline, the latter of which is the subject of this symposium. But many a settlement will continue and function when it would not be reestablished were the slate to be wiped wholly clean. The many bonds—economic, technological, commercial, social, political, and others—in any modern community, especially one of fair size, are powerful factors for the continuation of the community. If part or much of it is destroyed, by flood or tornado, it is likely to rebuild even when its economic base is shaky, simply because of these numerous inherited intracommunity forces and ties. Some illustrations of community change in the United States are provided later in this article.

NATURAL RESOURCES AND COMMUNITY LOCATION

Where natural resources, in the foregoing definition of the term, exist, economic communities will almost surely arise and persist, and associated with them will be social communities. Part of the economic community will be resource-dominated, the people engaging directly in resource extraction, management, processing, transport, and the like. To these people engaged directly in resource use will be added many in service occupations or roles—provision of essential services to the resource enterprises, or in essential services to the persons engaged in resource work directly. Every oil field provides employment for servicing and repair of well-drilling and other machinery, for instance, as well as in the transport and handling of essentials for the resource extraction or use process. Agricultural towns typically have farm machinery dealers as one of their major commercial enterprises. But the people who work in resource use must also be serviced (by grocery stores, other stores, beauty parlors and barbershops, bakeries, printing establishments, and scores of others), and these service people in turn must be serviced. The direct employment has sometimes been described as community-forming, because its volume and type often set the limits for the economic community; the service employment has, in the same terminology, been called community-serving. The line is not quite as clear as these terms suggest. The quality of the service in a retirement or recreation community may do much to form its economy, including the numbers of people attracted to it.

Although these factors may be responsible for the general location of groups of people, other factors are likely to be responsible for their precise location within a general area. Initial extraction and processing must take place where extractable resources occur, of course, but subsequent processing may be there or at any location up to the point of final consumption. Availability of fuels, water, and other supplies; economies of scale in processing, which may dictate larger but more distant plants; and weight-losing or value-accruing characteristics of the materials may all play a major role in decisions about the location of processing plants and communities to serve them. Even the location of villages to serve a farm population depends upon scale economies in provision of services—economies that may take the form of quality and variety of services as much as or more than monetary economics of price or cost. The locations of such villages may often reflect an older transportation network—the intersection of wagon roads that followed the easiest topographical routes.

The geographers have a large body of literature on this matter of community location, size, and function. It is not my intention to review, much less to appraise, this literature. I only call it to the attention of those interested in the sociological aspects of the community.

RESOURCE BASE AND COMMUNITY SIZE

If the foregoing inclusive definition of natural resources is accepted, then the number of people in the human community or communities will be related to, though not precisely determined by, the size of the natural resource base. If the resource base expands by discovery of a new ore deposit, or by a previously known deposit becoming profitable to exploit, for instance, then the economy based on such resources will almost surely grow. The technology of resource transformation may greatly influence the amount of labor input, hence the size of the direct employment, and hence, probably, the amount of indirect employment, and thus the size of the population. But these relationships are not invariable; more or fewer persons can be sustained on a given resource basis, and at different levels of personal income. In these modern days of rapid personal transport, the place of living and the place of working may be separated by many miles; the labor supply for a new enterprise may be recruited from a not-too-distant town without necessarily producing any settlement near the actual place of employment. An expanding economy is likely to be a place of high personal incomes, in perhaps both real and apparent terms, for it often takes the inducement of higher incomes to draw people to a new area. The actuality of incomes may be different from the expectations; most great gold rushes of the West seem to have drawn many people who never realized their income expectation.

When the natural resource base (as defined above) shrinks, the population is likely to decline also. The shrinkage of the economy may be in numbers of people or in per capita income, or both. With exceptions, the path of shrinkage is not likely to be the same as the path of expansion. That is, as the natural resource base shrinks, people will be loath to leave, hoping that some alternative base will develop, or not knowing where to go, or counting the costs of moving, or all of these. If an inducement was necessary to draw people to an area, because of both economic and social costs of moving, those same costs serve as a barrier against outward movement. Typically, a declining community takes a long time dying, if it ever dies completely. There are likely to be many persons hanging on who would not move to the community for the living conditions that they now find there. There are exceptions, of course; many a boom mining town has collapsed as quickly as it rose, but this has as often been due to the attraction of another boom town as to the decline of the first.

Many of the ancient civilizations of the world have experienced major population declines, some to the point of extinction, as the chapter by Adams in this volume documents fully. The Mediterranean and Middle East regions of the world have some of the best known such examples, but other continents had their examples as archaeological research reveals. Great empires flourished and thousands of people lived in places where today and for centuries there have been few or no persons. The Mesopotamian Plain once was the home of a large population, including many cities. Various factors have been responsible for declines of ancient civilizations; it is beyond the scope of this chapter (and the competence of the author) to engage in a comprehensive review of such population declines. One can only say, as one surveys long periods of history worldwide, that impermanence of settlements is more striking than permanence. In our preoccupation with the present, we unconsciously assume that what we know, or some reasonable evolution of it, will continue, perhaps indefinitely. Maybe so, but the statistical experience is against any such easy assumption.

CHANGES BY TYPES OF TOWNS IN THE UNITED STATES

The mining towns of the western United States are classic examples of fast growth and fast decline. Many a mining town sprang up in a matter of months, if not weeks, with thousands of miners and would-be miners, many hangers-on, some business service people, and almost always a printing press as an early establishment. Plans would be developed for vast cities, land subdivided, lots sold and resold rapidly and speculatively, and everything under high pressure with extravagant claims and anticipation for the future. Many of these towns declined as rapidly as they rose. There are sites scattered over the West today where settlements of a few thousand people at the peak were established, rose, and fell to zero, all within two or three years. These were the sudden-death mining towns. But there have been others where nearly everyone left, but a few persons lingered on, eking out an existence in some way. And some of these old mining towns have recruited new residents—and I do not mean the rejuvenated ones, such as Aspen. Some mining towns may die, some may be dying but not yet dead, and others may be only lingering. The social structure of these ephemeral towns was often curious and, in any case, ephemeral also.

There are substantial numbers of fossil fuel and metal-mining towns and regions in the world where the present resource base will someday be gone. This is true for all of the great Middle Eastern oil sources of today. By and large, the leaders of these people realize that their present prosperity rests on a declining and ultimately vanishing natural resource, and this is what worries them greatly. There are metal-min-

66

ing complexes in various locations around the world where ultimate exhaustion of economically minable ore is also a certainty, although the timing may be uncertain. Many of these areas try to ignore their basic problem in the same sense that the average Californian ignores his earthquake hazard. My main point is that population declines are not all in the past; not only will there be some in the future, but today we can identify some likely candidates.

The lumber camps of the United States of seventy-five or more years ago were a very special kind of economic and social community. Mostly they were inhabited only by men, often men in young-mature ages, often only seasonal in occupation, often with different individuals in each season, and presumably with all the sociological problems such communities generally face. Many of them were moved from time to time, as timber supply in the immediate vicinity was harvested. Although some of the lumber towns were more permanent and have even endured to this day, hundreds of old lumber towns in the Pacific Northwest disappeared with scarcely a discernible trace (Erickson 1965). Many of these were flimsily built with the expectation of an early demise, so that investment was held to a minimum. Since these lumber camps and towns were mostly harvesting an inherited timber stand, which bore many resemblances to a metal or fuel deposit, their history naturally bears some resemblance to that of the mining towns, except that the extreme speculation of the latter was generally absent.

Agricultural service towns and villages are by far the most numerous case of declining settlements in the United States, for the past century or so and for the present. Although sometimes this decline was caused by the loss of a resource base, as in some farming support towns of the Northeast and South, where agriculture gradually lost the economic ability to compete with better-endowed farming areas to the West, on the whole the decline of the agricultural service town has been due to changes in the utilization of resources. American agriculture has undergone a virtual revolution in the past two generations; from the same area of cropland, or less, the output of agricultural commodities has more than doubled, while the labor input on the farms was declining by much more than half. The explanation is technological changes, such as the development of improved varieties that will yield more under identical conditions, but it is also the greater use of especially fertilizers and other chemicals, and more machinery.

To a very large degree, the technological revolution in agriculture has been due to the increased specialization of agriculture. Two generations ago, the typical farmer grew his own seeds, produced his own fertilizer (animal manures), was likely to make his own containers in which to sell his produce, and was likely to do a good deal of its marketing as well. He was often his own blacksmith, shoeing his horses and repairing his farm machines. Today, all this is done by nonfarm specialists; and many farmers today buy many of their inputs from other farmers, as the cattle feeder may buy both cattle and feed. In the earlier days, the cost of purchased inputs into agriculture were roughly half of the value of farm output—the value added by the farmers was half or more of their gross output; today, production expenses are nearly three-fourths of gross output, and value added is not much over a fourth of gross value.

This specialization has shifted the employment in the total agricultural process away from the farms, mostly toward fairly large cities. But within the generally agricultural areas there have been important shifts away from the former agricultural service towns, due in part to changing transportation methods and in part to changing demands of the former for farm services and of the farm family for consumption and social services. With the modern auto or pick-up truck, today's farmer can go ten times as far in an hour as his grandfather could go with horse and buggy. The farmer would rather go to a somewhat more distant but larger farm town, where the machinery dealer is more likely to have the part he needs for his farm machine, than he is to stop at the very small town where his grandfather would have patronized the blacksmith. But the farm homemaker is no longer satisfied with the small country grocery store; she wants the variety and the freshness of foods from the larger supermarket, just as much as does her town-sister. This desire for the better services that only somewhat larger towns can provide extends to educational, religious, and other cultural services, as well as to the provision of essential commodities for living and for production.

As a result of these changes in agricultural production methods, thousands of agricultural service towns throughout all parts of the United States have fewer people today than they had at their peak, as we shall discuss in more detail in the ensuing section. Some former towns may indeed have died, and disappeared, but more have simply declined, and are unlikely to wholly disappear, at least for a long time.

They may or may not be dying; they are not dead. Their economic function has often become one of supplying the "convenience goods," such as gasoline, the simpler and less perishable groceries, the more common drugs, and so on. In this respect, they are similar to the neighborhood store, which can no longer compete with the large supermarket on a full range of goods and services, but manages to hang on, and sometimes do very well, on a smaller range of goods, on more convenient hours, or on closer location, or some combination thereof.

POPULATION DECLINES IN THE UNITED STATES

The frequency—indeed, the ubiquity—of population declines in the United States is not well appreciated, even by demographers, geographers, economists, and other students of population change, land occupancy, and resource use. In our obsession with growth, we have ignored or underestimated the declines. In my judgment, no really comprehensive and adequate analysis of population decline in the United States has yet been made. Though I have made some studies of this matter, most of which are unpublished, I feel that I have only scratched the surface of a very big subject.

The units of time and of area used in an analysis of population change, and more particularly of population decline, will dominate the findings. The most common source of population data is the decennial census, but over a ten-year period many population changes average out; annual data, or even seasonal data (like that for summer recreation areas), would show a greatly different picture than the ten-year enumerations. National data will reveal one picture, state data another, county data still another, and finer-grained geographic analysis will show still another picture of population change. The population of the United States has risen from one census to another, and there has never been a year in which the population of the whole country did not increase; nearly all states show population increases from census to census, though there have been exceptions, especially in recent decades; but accurate annual population data by states, for a long period of time would almost surely show rather dramatic changes, including decreases, for some states in some years. A brief overview of population changes by counties is presented below; but at this point it may simply be said that many counties show population declines over ten-year intervals between censuses and one suspects that even more would show declines for shorter periods if accurate data were available annually for long periods of time. But population changes take place within counties; some parts, notably the larger towns, may be gaining while the whole county is steady or losing, thus clearly showing that the other parts of the county were losing more heavily.

An analysis of population change is also bedevilled by the matter of the degree of change; at least the following situations may logically be differentiated: (1) population increases greater than the excess of births over deaths within the area for the time period, made possible only by a net immigration; (2) population increase, but less than the excess of births over deaths, thus showing some net out-migration, but at a comparatively modest level; (3) absolute or near absolute population constancy; believe it or not, there are a few counties with exactly the same number of persons in two successive censuses; (4) small population decline of less than the deficit of births over deaths, where deficits exist, showing modest net immigration; and (5) large population declines of a scale that necessarily involves net out-migration.

For all of these, except the third, different degrees of change could also be shown—changes less than the national average, changes greater than the national average, or changes either less than 10 percent and over 10 percent, and so on.

The combination of different time periods, different geographical areas, and different degrees of change clearly lead to a very large—an impossibly large—number of permutations and combinations for analysis. Sheer unavailability of data will rule out some theoretically possible combinations—one could not, even if one wished, make extended analyses of annual changes in county population, for accurate annual data over a considerable period of time do not exist. Partly on logical grounds and partly as a realistic compromise between the desire for both temporal and geographic detail and the practicalities of analysis, I have confined my studies of population decline to county data and to decennial census periods, and I have limited my analysis to a simple separation of counties into two groups: those that gained and those that lost population over the decade. This analysis obviously cannot reveal many of the details of population change over time and area, but even it produces a volume of data not easy to digest and hold in mind.

The number of counties losing population rose in each decade, from 1900 to 1970, with the exception of the 1930s, from about 400 to about 1,000 (Fig. 3.1). Until 1920, the increase in proportion of total

Number of counties

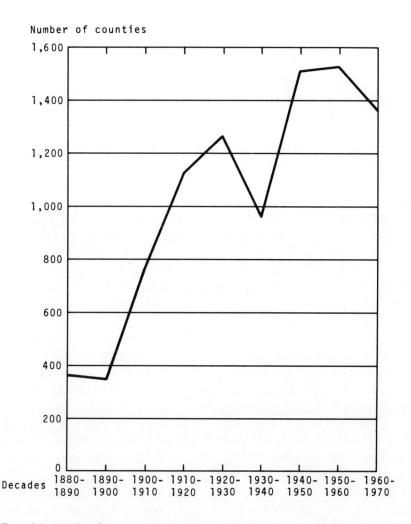

Figure 3.1. Number of counties in the United States losing population by decades, 1880–1970.

number of counties losing population was somewhat less than this figure would suggest, since the number of counties was also increasing. But since about 1910 or 1920, the number of counties in the United States has been nearly constant, at about 3,000. Thus, since about the time of World War I, close to half the counties have lost population each decade. The conspicuous exception in the trend up to 1970 was the experience of the 1930s, when fewer counties lost population than for several decades earlier and later, but this was more a sign of weakness than of strength. In the extreme depression of the 1930s, with its massive unemployment, life often seemed better on the farm or in the rural town than in the larger city, and so some of what would otherwise have been normal migration backed up. The number of counties losing population in the 1960s also declined, modestly. With so many counties losing population in each of five decades, obviously a large proportion of them lost in more than one decade. There is both a persistence and an ubiquity to population decline.

This matter of population decline can be approached in another way. The Bureau of the Census has prepared and published a map showing the census date when each county reached its maximum population. A substantial number of counties had their maximum population in 1900 or earlier; some of these are western counties, whose earlier mining booms had peaked and receded, but the largest number are rural, essentially farming, counties scattered across Ohio, Indiana, and Illinois, with a particularly large number in Iowa, Missouri, and eastern Kansas, and eastern Nebraska. Other large numbers of counties peaked by 1920.

Among the many patterns of change, I have identified those counties I call *steady losers*—those that declined in population in each of the three decades of the 1940s, 1950s, and 1960s, and (except for the newer West) in two earlier decades as well (Fig. 3.2). The western Corn Belt and eastern Great Plains show up strongly here, as do some southern, essentially Piedmont, counties. One can find some fascinating examples among these steady loser counties—counties that have lost population in every decade since 1880. Essex County, Vermont; Bracken County, Kentucky; Talbot County, Georgia; and Noble County, Ohio, lost some population in every decade from 1880 to 1970. Madison County, Virginia, lost in every decade from 1880 to 1960, but in the 1960s posted a small gain. Bourbon and Washington counties in Kansas; and Bates, Knox, Monroe, Montgomery, and Schuyler counties,

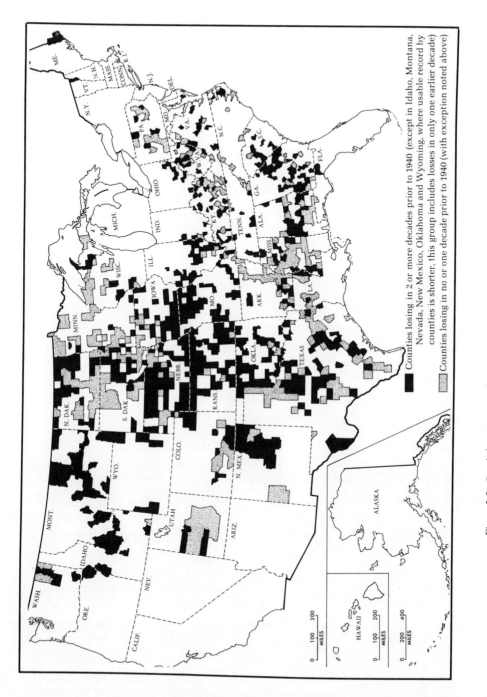

Figure 3.2. Steady loser counties (lost population in the 1940s, 1950s, and 1960s).

Counties losing in 2 or more decades prior to 1940 (except in Idaho, Montana, Nevada, New Mexico, Oklahoma and Wyoming, where usable record by counties is shorter, this group includes losses in only one earlier decade)

Counties losing in no or one decade prior to 1940 (with exception noted above)

Missouri each posted population losses in every decade from 1890 to 1970. While some of these decade losses were only a few persons— some of these counties never had many people—the persistence of the loss is impressive. It is noteworthy that no western state makes this list, but that may be because the West is so much more recent in settlement. Most western states and counties had very few people by 1880 or 1890.

There are a considerable number of counties that have lost population in several decades, sometimes continuously, sometimes with decades of loss interspersed by decades of gain, but they do not make my steady loser list. I shall not try, in this paper, to show some of those other, and generally more complicated, patterns of county population loss. In a large number of cases, these other counties with population losses in several decades, but not as persistently as my steady loser group, lie interspersed in the "holes" of the steady loser chart or on the fringes of the groups of those counties.

If one equates population size with natural resources, as my earlier discussion does to a large extent, then these population changes reflect declining natural resource bases. The significance and the meaning for social policy of these population trends is that they reflect the judgments of the local people, who choose to stay or to leave; they do not depend on some outsider's judgments on economic prospects. As we have noted for agricultural villages, the resource base may stay the same, or even increase by some measures, and yet the number of residents may decrease, as more of the activity associated with the natural resources shifts elsewhere, so that the equivalence of population and resources is not exact.

The record would not be complete without taking notice of the fact that the population has increased in recent years in many nonmetropolitan areas, many of which are rural, and by amounts that indicate net immigration. These increases are measured by relatively new data on annual population by counties; they are not yet decade data, since the period of increase began not much before 1970, and one cannot know how well the recent trends hold up for the whole decade of the 1970s. One can be even less sure whether these recent increases mark the beginning of a new and long trend of population decentralization or whether they represent a relatively modest aberration on the earlier trends. One can find many examples in the historical-geographical record of counties losing population for several decades,

74

either after a period of gains or before one. That is, reversals of population losses by counties have occurred in the past and may well occur again.

These population changes by counties do not directly show intracounty changes, but one can reasonably conclude that such intracounty changes were considerable. In some cases, even a casual inspection of the available data and/or personal knowledge will indicate that the county seat or other larger town (even though small, by national standards) was gaining while the county as a whole was losing, indicating that the rest of the county was losing population at a more rapid rate. Various studies have indicated that the smallest towns and villages tend to lose population while the larger ones tend to gain— "smaller" and "larger" being relative to the size of towns in that particular part of each state. The correlation is far from high, and other factors also enter.

None of these data on population change gets directly at the matter of the community, in the sociological sense of the term, but the data may be suggestive. Migration is always a selective factor: the younger, the abler, the better educated, and the more venturesome move in proportionately larger numbers. Continued out-migration produces sociological effects: I paired up steady loser and steady gainer counties in Illinois and Iowa (omitting metropolitan counties from each group) and found that people were older, more poorly educated, with lower incomes and poorer housing in the steady loser group than in the steady gainer group (Clawson 1975). Many studies by sociologists have explored these relationships in far more detail than I could. But population gains after a period of population loss may not restore the older sociological community—they may not even restore the older economic community, including its labor market and its retail trade. We can generally expect that population losses and population gains had sociological effects, even if we cannot be sure what those effects are without more study.

STUDIES AND MODELS OF GROWTH AND DECLINE

Scores, if not hundreds, of studies have been made of economic growth—theoretical models, predictive models, balanced growth, unbalanced growth, growth of the less developed countries, growth of the advanced industrial countries, Marxian models, pure competition models, international trade models, and many others. Economists, planners, econometricians, geographers, futurists, and many others have constructed models or have made empirical studies or both. There is an immense professional literature of economic growth. When growth is clearly under way, the processes by which it continues are fairly well understood. While population is treated variously in such models, from an exogenous variable, to neglect, to a central position, all implicitly or explicitly involve population growth to match in some degree the economic growth. Most do not consider the geographical pattern of population distribution, nor do they usually deal with the community in the sociological sense, but most have implications for that community.

In the dramatic and sharp contrast, there is much less professional literature dealing with the process of economic decline. Some studies have been made of historical situations, such as the long-continued population decline in Ireland, or the decline of certain towns or areas of industries in the United States. But there is virtually no theorizing about economic decline. I exclude the Club of Rome in its first version, partly because the same group has since been recanted, but partly because their shotgun approach could as easily yield anything from rapid growth to catastrophic decline. One can only conclude that serious professional students simply assumed that extensive and persistent economic decline would not occur or would be too rare or too unimportant to warrant their attention. There is, of course, an extensive economic literature on the business cycle, showing how depressions begin and feed upon themselves until some sort of corrective forces come into play, but this either explicitly or tacitly assumes that economic growth will resume when the depression is over.

This relative neglect of economic decline is the more surprising both in view of the frequency of population and economic decline, as outlined previously, and because the processes of decline are as fascinating, theoretically and in human terms, as are the processes of growth. It would be most interesting to have some of our growth specialists turn their attentions and abilities to economic decline—what starts it, by what processes it spreads within the local economy, how or when or why it flattens out or growth resumes, and the social strategies for coping with it. It would be interesting also if more specific studies were made, to see to what extent generalizations about economic decline could be made.

There are, in the United States, and in some other countries, groups with no growth as their economic objective, as there are zero-population growth groups. These no-economic-growth groups start with an assumption that economic growth is socially bad; they attribute all the ills they see in modern society to the economic growth that has occurred in the past, and they assume that if the growth could be stopped, the ills would diminish or vanish. These groups are better known for the fervor of their views than for the rigor of their logic. They do not, in any case with which I am familiar, face the fact that no-growth might itself create problems—problems greater than those created by growth. The sociological consequences of a stationary economy and a constant income per capita, especially if compounded by a stationary population, would be substantial. Such a society would have relatively many old people, economic advancement for the individual would be slow, the younger persons would move up the economic and social ladder only as the old ones died or retired, living conditions would be static, and all the sociological and psychological characteristics of a chronically depressed area would be present.

This is not the place, and I am not the person, to propose a new theoretical structure to deal with population and economic decline in all their ramifications, economic, demographic, sociological, and geographical; but I would like to see at least a few of our growth modelers turn their attention to decline as a process.

COMMUNITY DECLINE, DEATH, REJUVENATION, AND TURNING POINTS

Some economic and/or social communities die, as the chapter by Adams makes clear for many ancient communities and as earlier parts of this paper have suggested for American communities. All of the communities that died went through a period, long or short, of decline; and in addition, many other communities have declined but not died—at least, not yet. Decline may be a way station on the road to death, but not invariably so, since rejuvenation can and does occur.

The growth-decline-death sequences and processes for economic and social communities do not exactly parallel similar processes and sequences in biological organisms, including man. There are many similarities, it is true, but there are also important differences. One major difference is that the timing of the process and of the end result is far less predictable for a community—granting that the timing is unpredictable for a biological organism, also. But the greater difference is that the end result is not as inevitable for the community as for the biological organism. The possibility of rejuvenation is vastly greater for the community. Man has dreamt of personal rejuvenation since the beginning of time, but results have been negligible to date.

Important as the processes of growth and decline for a community are, once these processes are clearly and firmly under way, the turning points from growth to stagnation and to decline, or the reverse, are more significant. Processes of growth and of decline for U.S. local areas, measured by the available population data, have shown numerous reversals in the past. That is, counties losing population for several decades have later entered onto periods of population growth; or, conversely, extended periods of population growth have been succeeded by long periods of population decline. Readily available data do not permit easy measurement of such economic factors as personal income or of such social factors as community organization associated with these population trends, but one can rather confidently predict that economic and social relationships did change as population changed. These changes in population trends have been quite numerous in the United States over the past hundred years or more. My rather limited knowledge of economic history in the rest of the world suggests that reversals in population trends have been common everywhere.

Why do reversals in population trend occur? How far in advance are reversals in population trend foreseeable? What are some of the advanced indicators? Are the forces leading to reversals of population trends indigenous to the local area or exogenous to it? How far are reversals of the local economy or changes in the local social structure causes of reversals in population trends and how far are they consequences of it? Are there discernible persons who are prime movers and, if so, where did they come from, and why did they direct their attention to this local area? Or, how far did the new population trend seem to arise from some rather general, perhaps somewhat indefinable, economic or social forces, without any evident prime mover?

78

ALTERNATIVE STRATEGIES FOR A DYING COMMUNITY

What alternatives are available for an economic or social community experiencing population and/or per capita income decline and perhaps death?

The very phrasing of this question presupposes two matters of fact: (1) that some form of community, in the sociological sense, exists; and (2) that it chooses to do something about its decline and possible death. Unless the individuals of the village, city, region, or other geographical unit have common aspirations, goals, standards of life, and other human attitudes, it is most unlikely that they can agree on any effective line of action. Even when the individuals do have such common attitudes, they must have institutions capable of bringing these attitudes to a focus, into some form of a program that they will support with a real commitment of themselves, their time, and their assets. They must also have some political organization, such as a unit of local government, or a powerful voluntary association, through which they can work to their common ends. Needless to say, many collections of individuals lack one or more of these common goals, means of crystallizing their desires, and means of effective action, in which case the people of the area let nature take its course as far as their future is concerned.

Even when there exists a common desire, known and expressed, and a social-political mechanism that might enable the people to take effective action, they may prefer not to do so. This may be for one of several reasons: lethargy or unwillingness to exert effort and make sacrifices, satisfaction with life as it is and an unwillingness to disturb it, or a rejection of any form of life and action that might reverse their downward trend. Many people who would not consciously formulate their choice in these terms might nevertheless in fact choose a policy of nonaction, simply by procrastination and unwillingness to face up to unpleasant facts.

But supposing that there exists a community in the sociological and political senses, and that it does choose to do as much as is within its power to arrest its economic and demographic decline and to prevent its probable death: what alternative lines of action are open to it, and where do natural resources fit into this strategy?

The most realistic alternative often is: nothing. If a community based on resource extraction is gradually exhausting the deposits that made the community possible, or if a community based on a transportation node is faced with a complete obsolescence of that node, or if an ancient shrine no longer commands respect and admiration of visitors, or if, in any one of the other resource-based communities described previously, the old resource has lost its economic relevance, there may be very little the community can do about it. Like old persons approaching the end of life, such communities may best simply enjoy such life as they have, relaxing in the pleasure of their existence while it lasts, and accepting the future as inevitable. In my view, a frank recognition of this situation and a deliberate choice for it is a rather different course of action than the drift that arises from sheer inability to choose. Both individual and community can find many ways to enrich life under these circumstances. It is here that some good theory about the processes of decline would be so helpful; for what parts of the community economic and social structure should the most effort be exerted to retain, what parts can most readily be sacrificed and in what order, at what point does the community cease to try to manage its own affairs? All of these community choices are paralleled by the choices the aging individual must make.

Sometimes the community may find new ways to use the old resources that have been its mainstay for many years. The dwindling timber supply may be manufactured into more highly finished products—doors, windows, and their frames, instead of unfinished lumber, for instance. Or some of the metal processing may be shifted to the community, based on ore extraction. Or the recreation community may find new activities for visitors, or even manufacture artifact souvenirs to sell, instead of importing them. Other examples could be given. The idea may sound appealing, but the execution will not be simple. If such community support has never been sought or never been effective in the past, what reason is there to think it can be made effective now that the community has begun to decline? Nevertheless, the first place any community should look, as it seeks to improve its economic and social future, is to the factors on which it has traditionally rested. How can the old resources be used better, before any effort is made to invent or develop new resources?

Sometimes the community can find some new resources on which to base its economic and social future. In this western region of the

United States, but elsewhere in the world also, old towns originally founded for one purpose have acquired wholly new directions and new leases on life by using old resources in wholly new ways, so that they are really new resources. Aspen, Colorado, is surely one of the best known and most sensationally successful such towns. Aspen today bears very little resemblance to the Aspen of bygone days. Recreation has frequently been the basis of old town revival. The old mining towns, old lumber towns, old fishing villages, and other old towns may possess a character appealing to enough people to take on a wholly new life as a recreation town. Typically, these towns lose much of their original flavor in the process. It might be argued that this process is one of new town birth, not of old town revival; but at least some of the latter is always involved. This process of making a town into a recreation attraction usually requires outside capital, outside managerial capacity, and, often, outside leadership and inspiration. Moreover, it is not foolproof; not every old town has a future as a new recreation center even under the most skillful management, and merely having something old is not a guarantee of success.

As the number of persons on retirement or other income transfer as a source of livelihood rises, the opportunities for older economic communities to continue to exist and even to prosper is much increased. If people do not need employment for income, and can live as well one place as another, then the settlement that has pleasant climate, or attractive community ambience, or that somehow appeals to some group of such transfer-supported persons may be able to play a useful role in the whole economy and society, as well as improve its economic prospects in the process. Again, not every decadent or declining or old small town has the capacity to attract such people. While the attraction of retired and other income-transfer people probably requires less promotion, less skill in getting them to the community, and less skill in caring for them after they arrive, than does the specialized recreation settlement, still these things often do not come "naturally." If a small town seeks retired and other income-transfer people, it may have to take active steps to attract and to hold them.

A town or small city might, of course, seek some new kind of economic activity, especially of the "footloose" kind, which can about as well be located one place as another. A labor force, a water supply, a sewage system with capacity, a pleasant climate, or good

81

transportation and communications connections to larger cities might serve to attract small manufacturing plants or small data-processing plants to a small town that had previously lacked any such employment. In effect, some of the town's old resources take on new meaning, becoming really new resources. While this sort of small town stimulation or rejuvenation has taken place in a number of cases, the initiative of the local community seems to have comparatively little to do with it. A manufacturer or processor wants a new location outside a major city or metropolitan area and he casts about. There have been instances when the first the local people knew about such enterprises was the public announcement by some firm that it was planning to build a new plant in their town.

While any social community faces up to the fact that its economy is sliding downhill, or to the fact that such declines are highly probable in the foreseeable future, with all their economic, social, and political consequences, the first question that an outsider may ask is: what have you done with the income you earned and the capital you accumulated in the past, when you were prosperous? Or, as the old hoboes used to say, what have you done with your summer's wages? How far has the community income gone into the development of education, research, cultural, and service facilities, or how far has it gone into current consumption or been exported from the community? For the community already well on the downward path, such questions are important even if the course of history cannot be reversed, for they will tell much about the prospects for doing something about the decline. For the community still booming, but based on an exhaustible resource, such questions are extremely important, for something can be done about them. Such questions are critical to the current oil-rich countries, for instance.

In my judgment, it is far from certain that any economy based on exhaustible natural resources can accumulate capital and use it so wisely that, when the exhaustible resource is gone, the community can continue and prosper. At best, it is a difficult process; more likely, the present flow of income will support a level of current consumption that cannot be maintained later. The oil-rich countries are building universities and research institutions, as well as social infrastructure, but they are also spending substantial parts of their oil revenue for armaments that have dubious value today and will be impossible for them to maintain when their incomes drop. Few nations, communities, or individuals are able to face the fact that their current prosperity is temporary and that they should put a lot of their current income aside for the inevitable rainy day. Honesty compels me to admit that often, if they did put present income aside for future consumption, it would be lost or decimated by some process over which they had little control.

Economic and social communities are born, grow, and sometimes prosper; many also decline, and some actually die. Is community death as inevitable as individual death, and as unpredictable?

4

Dependence on External Authority and the Decline of Community

ART GALLAHER, JR.

Department of Anthropology
University of Kentucky

Except for Arensberg and Kimball (1965), Redfield (1960), and Steward (1950), anthropologists seldom have been interested in either the empirical or theoretical question of what community is. Most of us have been content to do "community studies"—where we analyze problems and social processes in the context of community—but not to get involved with the larger issues of community theory. Despite this lack of explicit concern, a number of tacit premises emerge from these and other studies, and, taken together, reveal to us how anthropologists view the nature of community. I should like to review briefly some of these premises to set the perspective against which my concerns for external authority and threat to community become relevant.

Maurice Stein, in his very fine *The Eclipse of Community* (1960:chpt. 10), notes what probably is the major premise held by anthropologists on the human community. Citing particularly early works by Sapir (esp. 1924:401–29), Benedict (1938:161–67), and Radin (1953), he notes in their thinking the pervasive view that a society ought to provide its members with the full opportunity to grow socially and to gain individual satisfaction. This widely accepted view relates to the added notion that it is in the community that the individual confronts the larger society and culture. Consistent with these observations, Stein concludes, and I think rightly so, that:

> It almost seems as if community in the anthropological sense is necessary before human maturity or individuation can be achieved, while this same maturity is, in turn, a prerequisite for community. (Stein 1960:248)

It follows from the above that anthropologists have always accepted the universality of the little community, and in its complete form have viewed it as the smallest unit to encompass the range of institutions necessary for a human group to ensure its sociocultural future. This view, incidentally, is compatible with the largely functional bias that has guided anthropological research in communities, where the effort typically is to view all forms of behavior as interdependent parts in the context of the whole (Steward 1950:21). We thus have addressed the community as a laboratory, as a unit representing a total pattern of living, which can and ought to be studied in its totality. Our interest has been less in communities as representative phenomena in a given society, rather more in the social processes representative of a given society that can be examined in the community context—the kind of study that Conrad Arensberg (1954:109–27) labels *in vivo*.

The thrust just indicated has been misinterpreted, I think, by some as too parochial—as conceptually modeling community after our notions of tribal societies. While some anthropologists have fostered this limited view of what we have been about, many others have held out the notion that one community is, in fact, always impacted by other communities. To cite only two of the better known theorists: Redfield (1960:chpt. 8) suggests that one of our models of the little community be that of a community within a community; and Steward (1951) addresses in a comprehensive way the matter of determining levels of sociocultural integration. More pragmatically, studies by anthropologists in little communities throughout the world have established that increasingly they are being pulled into the social and cultural mainstreams of the larger wholes with which they are identified. There is occurring, it seems, a leveling of culture patterns in little communities.

The process by which this leveling occurs is diffusion, viewed graphically as being either of a market or administered variety (Warren

1963:21). In the first case we are talking of changes relatively unplanned, a process that accounts for the wide distribution of many material and nonmaterial culture traits in our own and other societies. Crucial variables in explaining this type of change are the social and physical isolation of the community. If either or both of these are diminished, it follows that we can expect an acceleration in market diffusion. All of the studies done in little communities indicate that this is, in fact, happening in all regions of the modern world.

Administered diffusion, or directed change, on the other hand, is the deliberate introduction of innovations into the little community. The source directing the change may be in the community, as for example, a public school, a denominational church, or the local branch of a national firm; it may be from outside the community. The increased interest of central government in social planning, the increased bureaucratization of all segments of our society, and the refinement of mass media techniques, all combine to intensify this kind of change. Significantly, directed change—especially that which originates in the political and economic processes of the society—has a more explicit content and direction than does nondirected change, and has the effect therefore of accelerating the tempo of change at the community level. Furthermore, diffusion administered through the bureaucracy often is accompanied by built-in rewards and/or sanctions, either of which customarily is designed to facilitate the level and rate of acceptance of innovations.

One final point influencing my perspective: in all communities in this country, and indeed this seems to be a pattern emerging elsewhere in the world, there are local units that belong to both the community and to extracommunity systems. Every community thus is subject to controls from within and without, with neither type of control ever operating completely independently of the other. The local branch of the bureaucracy, the school, voluntary associations, the branch firm, are at one and the same time local and extralocal, we-oriented and they-oriented. Depending on the situation, however, in any given instance one set of controls usually carries more weight than another.

Without belaboring the point further, one of the major premises held by anthropologists about community—especially germane to the concerns of this chapter—is that one community exists in relation to other communities. It follows, then, that part of the dynamic of a community typically occurs around this relationship. I should like, therefore, to address the notion of *dependence upon authority* as one of the principal elements in the interaction that develops between one community and its other communal frames of reference.

DEPENDENCE ON AUTHORITY

As I am employing it, *dependence upon authority* does not address dependency as a psychological phenomenon; that is, it is not my intention to explore why some persons are voluntarily more dependent than others. My intention, rather, is to follow the usage of Homer Barnett (1953:65–72) and to seek those conditions that encourage the shared attitudes and predispositions that lead the members of a group to depend consciously on those who command some kind of authority and who, because of it, influence critical life-chance decisions. Authority in this context may rest on power, on prestige, on influence, or, as is so often the case, on the control of knowledge. Dependency so viewed is a normal consequence of communal life and, indeed, is a characteristic of many elements in a community's customary division of labor. The issue thus is not its presence or its absence, but rather has to do with (1) the qualitative basis on which such authority rests; (2) whether the authority attaches to positions internal or external to a community's social system; and (3) the nature of the sanctions that may be tied to such authority. It is, in short, an important aspect of the social organization of a group. It is not, however, a principle to be invoked in every examination of alternatives, and it does not therefore explain all of the change taking place in the culture of a given community.

Though the construct *dependence on authority* incorporates within it what many writers label *bureaucratization*, I want to make clear that bureaucratization is not a necessary condition for such dependency to exist. In a society as complicated as ours—where a highly developed division of labor results in extreme specialization—we are accustomed, for example, to relying on the knowledge of nonbureaucratized specialists to see us through the normal routine of daily life. This is nothing new to us, or in lesser degree to societies everywhere, though we have assumed that the number and kinds of dependency are qualitatively different in the little community from dependency in the city

(Durkheim 1933; Toennies 1955; Becker 1950; Redfield 1947:292– 308; 1953).

As little communities everywhere confront the alternatives of the greater traditions with which they perforce identify, and as the greater expectation of change that results takes hold, there is a concomitant expansion in the number and kind of authorities on whom people in the little community must depend. This is inevitable as they partici- pate in the more elaborate and specialized systems of the greater cul- ture. Involved in this whole process, and of special significance to this essay, is the critical view that develops in the little community as its adequacy to satisfy expanding needs is assessed. In a small village in this society, for example, not only can the consequence of accepting a new standard of living cause a population to lose confidence in many of its local institutions, but for some segments, such as the merchants who have geared their investment to traditional consumer behavior, the results can be disastrous. Such situations as that described are common and inevitably they threaten solidarity in the little communi- ty (Gallaher 1961:234).

As indicated above, then, our concern is not with whether depend- ence on authority can be established for a given community. Our premise rather— based on the evidence—is that such dependency is a normal part of the social system of any community and as viewed here relates to matters both internal and external to it. Viewed at one level, modernization seems always to require that the little community sur- render certain of its decision-making prerogatives in order to survive. Economic reforms, for example, especially in such fields as agricul- ture, welfare, civil rights, education, and health innovations, all in- volve issues so complicated that the little community has no choice but to relinquish many decisions to bureaucratic levels, which have their locus elsewhere. Typically this process also involves the defini- tion of those in helping roles as authorities in matters of change. Survival thus is assured, the community maintains enough of its sense of integrity, although changed somewhat in its sociocultural configura- tion, and the role of external authority initially is judged supportive.

Viewed at another level, however—and this is the concern of this volume—there are situations in which the intrusion of external au- thority threatens the very basis for community identification. Based partly on a review of the literature, and partly on my own research in

Europe and this country, three patterns of external dominance, each of which weakens the solidarity of a community, emerge. Operating singly or in combination, these represent activities in the surrounding political order that lead to (1) sociocultural suppression, either intentional or unintentional; (2) expansion or contraction of the social structure; and/or (3) cultural cooptation.

SOCIOCULTURAL SUPPRESSION

The pathways of westward expansion are littered with evidence of communities, and indeed of whole societies, that have disappeared. In addition, as Professor Adams notes, there is evidence from prehistory to indicate that community and societal dissolution are not confined merely to the historic periods. Unfortunately, whether dealing with history or prehistory, the specific circumstances and the actual processes of decline are seldom known in detail.

My concern here is not for those situations in which the demise of community—on whatever scale one chooses to conceptualize it—is the result of genocide. That extreme case, it seems to me, speaks for itself—if all the people in a community are killed, then no community is possible. My concern rather is for those situations in which an external authority, with dependency relationships already established with a community, sets out intentionally to destroy the basis for that community's solidarity.

The classic and clear case is that of the greater society employing political and other measures to *force* the structural and cultural assimilation of those communities with ethnic or subcultural features deemed too much at odds with the dominant norms. A case in point—one of many we could cite from various nation-states around the world—occurred on a massive scale in this society during the 1880s. After earlier having segregated American Indian tribes on reservations, thus assuring rigid boundary definition and constraints on their cultural systems, U.S. policy shifted to effect their ethnic assimiliation into the national culture. The assimilative strategy was simple—to detribalize Indians by the General Allotment Act of Congress, passed in 1887. This act recognized that communal ownership of land provided a major boundary-maintenance function for Indian culture; it sought, therefore, to dismantle many of the reservations by assigning shares of the communal land base to individuals. The Secretary of the Interior at the time noted the act's assimilative intent when he observed, "The enjoyment and pride of the individual ownership of property is one of the most effective civilizing agencies."

Combined with the steps just indicated, political authority also moved to appropriate the major socialization functions of the Indian community by removing many children to boarding schools. Indian languages and other traditional elements, which contribute significantly to community boundary maintenance, thus were discouraged.

The strategy just described failed miserably. Not only did it fail to deliver the assimilative results desired, but had the effect of encouraging even further the social disorganization of a great many Indian populations. The process of change attempted by the government in this case was to direct a massive replacement of cultural elements in Indian social organization. The integrity of Indian communities was threatened in all cases, and in many was destroyed. The community into which it was assumed the Indian would assimilate his newfound culture, however—that of the dominant anglo society—did not emerge as the viable replacement intended.

The example just cited illustrates that the *minority* community seems destined always never to have its cake and be able to eat it too. Seldom, for example, is there a pluralistic tolerance adequate to meet its needs, though a few instances appear in the early social science literature of adjacent ethnic groups showing little interest in either borrowing or exercising an active dominance one over another (Handman 1934: 86–111; Tax 1941:27–42; Mandelbaum 1941:19–26). The case for a ubiquitous intolerance is even more apparent when we examine communities where the lines drawn are more subcultural than distinctively ethnic. It is a fact, for example, that in most societies the dissident and disaffected frequently innovate as a way to insulate their belief and sentiment systems. The Dukhobors of Georgian Russia, Father Divine "kingdoms" in American cities, and "hippie" back-to-nature family-communes in several states during the late sixties and early seventies, are wide-ranging examples that come to mind easily from among literally hundreds that we could cite. In all cases, however, the extent to which the dissident community can survive depends as much, or more, on the external authority on whom it must depend for its protection. That same authority, it is to be remembered, is subject also to pressures to raise questions, to take actions, to break through and render ineffective the boundaries of such communities, thus forcing assimilation. Viewed in this way, the consignment of communities to death in the modern nation-states of the world is a frequent phenomenon.

Of a different order and becoming increasingly common, but still involving the intentional demise of community, is the *expulsion* of populations from specific territories. Forced removal of this order is not, of course, something new. A number of conditions, however, are focusing new attention on this phenomenon. At issue particularly, both in this country and abroad, is the resettlement of communities to facilitate public works projects. The magnitude of this problem, for example, can be deduced from the African situation, where four major dams already have dislocated a quarter of a million people, and where one estimate places the number to be affected on completion of some thirty more dams at more than one percent of the continent's total population (Brokensha and Hodge 1969:9).

Displacing populations to facilitate public works projects sometimes involves efforts to relocate whole communities intact (Drucker, Smith, and Reeves 1947). The success with which this is managed, that is, the extent to which a sense of community can be sustained during the relocation effort, is a function of adequate lead time and proper preparation (Brokensha and Scudder 1968). Total community displacement in time and space, however, even under the most ideal of conditions, can never replicate the sense of community in a new setting that existed in the old. This is especially true of agricultural villages. Again, drawing upon the experience gained in Africa, we can generalize that resettlement is apt to involve a complex of situational adjustments, which, taken together, typically generate considerable change. These are adaptations to the new geographic setting, adjustments to the indigenous groups in the resettlement area, acquisitions of new agricultural and other economic skills, accommodations to new settlement patterns, housing styles, readjustments of kinship and neighborhood relations, some traditional religious and political officials' loss of authority, new forms of political and economic organization, changes in world view, and the increased use of ideology to "make sense of" the experiences of the relocated populations.

To note these problems is not to bemoan the fact that resettled communities are unable to replicate their prior communal experience. It is rather to make the point that the human cost of such resettlement would be less if a positive sense of community can be sustained in the transition. There is some evidence, in fact, that receptivity to innovation is heightened during resettlement activity, and, with proper planning, this disposition might be turned to improvements in community life, including the acceleration of favorable economic development schemes (Brokensha and Hodge 1969:9).

Of greater concern ought to be those public works projects that destroy a community and leave to the affected individuals all of the problems of integrating into new communities. This is a common pattern in this country, one that produces anxiety for all concerned. The threatened loss of familiar institutional moorings—commonly labeled community—frequently produces what Anthony Wallace calls the "dilemma of immobility." He says that "rather than face the anxiety of cultural abandonment, individuals will cling for years to a disordered sociocultural system, in which events do not follow reliably upon their supposed antecedents." (Wallace 1970:204)

This syndrome is reported by Philip Drucker and a team of Kentucky students who for several years have studied a community threatened by a Corps of Engineers dam project. They note, for example, that many people scheduled for relocation refused to believe this would happen to them until the day the government property sales negotiator arrived. They managed thus for several years to fool themselves about their fate (Drucker, Smith, and Reeves 1974).

I want to shift the focus now to those situations in which an external authority makes decisions that have the potential effect of destroying a community, though not intentionally. The classic case, which occurs frequently, is the single-industry-based community, in its extreme form a company-owned town. This is the type of community associated particularly with mining, lumbering, and, in some parts of the world, plantation agriculture (Steward 1956; Hutchinson 1957; Norbeck 1959), all enterprises typically located in remote regions.

It is true that a company that dominates the economy of a local community may know that its decision to halt production or otherwise modify its activity may lead to the demise of that community. The basis for such decisions, however, is not the desire to destroy a community, as discussed in the first case above, but rather relates more to company production, profits, or to changes in technology. Thus, decisions made in distant boardrooms, involving variables not addressing human needs per se, have the incidental effect of destroying a human community.

An excellent case in point is the famous study by W. F. Cottrell (1951:358–65) of Caliente, a railroad community whose future was threatened by a changeover from steam to diesel-engine power. This case is interesting for our purposes because Caliente, though not a company-owned town, owed its existence primarily to jobs provided by the railroad company. In this sense it more nearly approximates current conditions here and abroad where those who plan for small communities frequently gamble their futures on the attraction of single industries.

The community of Caliente took shape in a remote desert region in the West because there was a need for people to be in that place. "So long as the steam locomotive was in use, Caliente was a necessity. With the adoption of the diesel it became obsolescent" (Cottrell 1951: 358). Their own obsolescence, however, was not projected by those who made of Caliente a community. In this regard, they did not differ from people elsewhere who are enmeshed in the rhythms of a technology too complicated to comprehend and who must, therefore, depend on the authority of those who do understand such matters.

> Based upon the "certainty" of the railroad's need for Caliente, men built their homes there, frequently of concrete and brick, at the cost, in many cases, of their life savings. The water system was laid in cast iron which will last for centuries. Businessmen erected substantial buildings which could be paid for only by profits gained through many years of business. Four churches evidence the faith of Caliente people in the future of their community. A 27-bed hospital serves the town. Those who built it thought that their investment was as well warranted as the fact of birth, sickness, accident, and death. They believed in education. Their school buildings represent the investment of savings guaranteed by bonds and future taxes. There is a combined park and play field which, together with a recently modernized theatre, has been serving recreational needs. All these physical structures are material evidence of the expectations, morally and legally sanctioned and financially funded, of the people of Caliente. This is a normal and rational aspect of the culture of all "solid" and "sound" communities.

94

Similarly normal are the social organizations. These include Rotary, Chamber of Commerce, Masons, Odd Fellows, American Legion, and the Veterans of Foreign Wars. There are the usual unions, churches, and myriad little clubs to which the women belong. In short, here is the average American community with normal social life, subscribing to normal American codes. Nothing its members had been taught would indicate that the whole pattern of this normal existence depended completely upon a few elements of technology which were themselves in flux. For them the continued use of the steam engine was as "natural" a phenomenon as any other element in their physical environment. Yet suddenly their life pattern was destroyed by the announcement that the railroad was moving its division point, and with it destroying the economic basis of Caliente's existence. (Cottrell 1951:358–59).

The people of Caliente thus made their commitment to a technology complicated beyond their ken—as people seem to do everywhere—and in the process committed themselves to make of Caliente an ideal community. Unfortunately, as Cottrell (1951:365) observes, those whose behavior most nearly approximated the ideal were those to suffer the greatest cost when faced with the dissolution of their community. I believe this point to be the most critical in our thinking about those decisions by external authority that have the potential to destroy a community—the residents who are asked to make the greatest investment, emotionally and otherwise, typically are those who then sustain the greatest loss. This pattern has been repeated with monotonous regularity in frontier, new town, and other forms of developing communities throughout the world. The cost, and here I am referring less to economic and more to psychological, has seldom been accounted in the type of situation cited.

EXPANDING AND CONTRACTING THE SOCIAL STRUCTURE

In considering the expansion and contraction of social structure there are two points to keep in mind. First, the basic units of social structure are statuses, that is, the positions people occupy in social life. Statuses aggregate into groups, and the systems of interrelated groups, which serve the basic ends of social life, we label institutions. These

95

are our referents, then, for discussing the role of external authority as either adding to or taking from a community's social structure. Second, to reaffirm a point made earlier, following Redfield our perspective is that the little community is to be viewed always as a whole within a whole. Operationally this means that national institutions serve as bridging mechanisms between a community and the greater society, existing alongside those that exhibit local autonomy. Viewed from within the community, then, the extent to which external authorities operating through these bridging institutions determine goals, policies, and operations at the local level, assumes considerable importance. By its actions, for example, the surrounding political order may impose new directions through new institutions, or it may treat established institutions in ways so as to reduce their communal properties. Significantly, in the modern world either tack more often than not follows on efforts intended to lend assistance to a community. This will become more apparent in some of the examples to follow.

It is important to keep in mind, however, that whether a social structure is expanding or contracting, *the real issue is how this impacts a community's decision-making autonomy.* Our premise is that this critical dimension of autonomy is threatened whenever external authorities either (1) dilute the communal properties of institutions by appropriating critical statuses and/or groups; or (2) overload a community with statuses and/or groups that owe their identity, scope, and function to sources outside the community. As is frequently the case, both of these actions occur simultaneously.

When I speak of external authority acting to *reduce* statuses at the community level, I do not wish to imply necessarily the element of deliberateness. Such actions may be deliberate, as in Egypt when, following the Revolution, the traditional office of the village headman (omda) was abolished. The omda traditionally maintained order at the local level, and represented local interests in all matters with central government. The revolution, however, created administrative districts. This caused villagers henceforth to work through several bureaucratic agencies to secure functions formerly aggregated in the omda role (Fakhouri 1972:120–21). Examples similar to this one abound in the ethnographic literature.

The more common pattern, however, is that the reduction of statuses locally occurs as an incidental or latent function of other activities directed by external authority. In the United States, for example, any community as old as fifty years will show a decline in the occupations and service agencies that formerly were autonomous to the community setting.

For example, I grew up in a small frontier community in western Oklahoma, and though in my youth in the 1930s the community was only a few years old, people already were reflecting on the shrinking occupational base. Popular sentiment held that the community's days were numbered, that it would fall a casualty to progress. I do not recall that anyone felt this a problem, or that it was a process to be countered. Quite the contrary, decisions made at the state level to consolidate schools and to improve transportation facilities, and the struggles of saddlemaker, bootmaker, broom manufacturer, baker, and independent grocer, against the mass production and merchandising techniques of outside economic interests, elicited little concern locally. The same was true of the tinsmith and the newspaperman, both of whom gave way to encroachments on their traditional territory by the more modern and less costly products of outside chains. And the moves by agricultural extension and soil conservation agencies to innovate practices, which could lead only to consolidation of holdings and fewer ranches, hence fewer needs to be met by local tradesmen, simply were not questioned. All of these changes initiated by external authority were rationalized locally as in the nature of progress. In fact, the local sentiment of those affected was that if one did not like it here there was always relief in flight to another frontier—to the West, to the outside—to become a part of the very success syndrome that seemed inevitably to be causing the community's demise. Parents talked of the out-migration of their children with some pride and always in the context of "out," "upward," and "onward."

Several years later, now as anthropologist, I spent a year in Plainville, a community in the northern Ozarks experiencing interference by government and private interests very similar to that which I had known in my hometown (Gallaher 1961). Plainville is a much older community than the one I knew as a youngster, with a very different settlement pattern. The town was settled early in the nineteenth century by migrants from the hill country of Appalachia. Its people in 1955 felt the community to be in decline. Dire predictions of its demise were common. When asked for their evidence of this, people talked of the decline of occupational statuses and, concomitantly, their feeling of impotence that anything could be done to revitalize the social struc-

97

ture. They talked despairingly of the long history of out-migration, always in the context that their young "had to leave," and they noted with great concern the growth of elderly age-grades in the community. In short, the indicators for community decline that they discussed among themselves, and that they verbalized to me, were drawn from the social structure and functions deriving therefrom. Unlike the people in my hometown, however, where the frontier ethos prescribed that one move on, Plainvillers struggled with how to hang in there and maintain a viable community. Thus, while experiencing substantial transformation in their community culture, which increasingly made them dependent on the greater society around them, Plainvillers continued nevertheless to define themselves in Jeffersonian terms—as self-made independents who stood before the world as "free" men and women. It was almost as though Plainvillers felt they could become part of the mainstream of urban, U.S. mass culture—indeed, expected bureaucratic change agents to bring such culture to them—but have their community remain the same. Their dilemma came in the realization that contractions in communally based elements of their social structure could not yield the same quality interpersonal relations as those which they nostalgically remembered from former years.

Before leaving the issue of status reduction in community, I should like to note a special case that is increasing steadily in incidence. I refer to those situations involving a *temporary* reduction of statuses. At one extreme, for example, a political decision may be made to conscript elements of a population for labor or military service. Less extreme but no less significant are those random decisions to site industrial plants in locations that draw workers from several surrounding communities. This can sometimes cause a disequilibrium in the normative role patterns, which, over a prolonged period, threatens community identity and proves stressful for individuals. Sue Abbott (1974), for example, tells of a Kikuyu village north of Nairobi, Kenya, which, during the week, loses most of its males to jobs in Nairobi. Since social relationships in the traditional Kikuyu household are dominated by males, Abbott reports that their absence forces women into unfamiliar roles determining household policy. Strains between these new obligations and those that are more traditional produces for them increased emotional stress. Again, the ethnographic literature is filled with similar examples. In this country, it is not uncommon for established communities to lose their vitality when they develop into bedroom communities, with the work force leaving each morning for jobs elsewhere. This situation frequently develops when decisions are made to consolidate or to mechanize industries, thus reducing the range of status options in a community so suddenly as to have a traumatic impact on those who live there. In this instance we refer not to the situation of total dependence on a single industry, as in the railroad town cited earlier, but to the more pervasive one of primary dependence. So often in this case, a major enterprise departing a community will set in motion a ripple effect that will be felt in many areas of the community. Institutional supports, such as banking and credit, may start defining such areas as high risk, and a reduced tax base may precipitate a reduction in social and community services. In this type of situation failure becomes its own cause—it begets more failure. Levin makes this point elsewhere in this volume in her discussion of institutional and group responses to dying communities.

It is appropriate to observe that a recurrent theme in the examples of community demise caused by status reduction is that decisions so frequently disruptive of community social organization and culture are those premised on a profit motive. It may well be the time now for technologically based societies, such as the United States, to rethink the man-machine relationship. Rather than operating from the premise that the thrust of productive technology should always be in the direction of labor efficiency and greater profits, we should think more in terms of *appropriate technology*. By *appropriate* in this instance I mean those technical innovations that improve quality and quantity of product but not at the expense of worker jobs. The primary concern thus shifts to quality of life.

I should like to move now to a discussion of external authority impacting the local community *through* expansion of the social structure. This is, of course, a primary strategy in community development and frequently represents the turn-around of a community in decline. Success in this case typically follows the ability of the local population to occupy the new statuses added to its community. Not infrequently, however, the new statuses demand behavior based on skills, attitudes, or knowledge not available locally and for which no preparatory program has been provided. Extensions of the central bureaucracy—usually in the form of helping agencies—commonly are of this order. Not only do outsiders follow the bureaucratic bridges into the community, but their roles often are those of change agents who link the bureaucracy systemically to local targets (Loomis 1959:383–90). As change agents they are thus arrayed in opposition to traditional norms; as representatives of the bureaucracy they frequently manage rewards and sanctions, which impose new authority and prestige patterns in the community. In addition, and one sees this most clearly in developing areas, representatives of the bureaucracy become generalized gatekeepers for many of the processes and procedures that originate with external authority. All of these activities thus intensify the dependency of locals and erode the traditional roles through which they link to the "outside."

I have witnessed the process just described in two quite different communities; Plainville, already referred to, and a peasant farm community in the west of Ireland. Though both demonstrate a shift away from dependence on those who command traditional modes of adapting, to those who represent external authority as channeled through helping agencies, the Irish case is more typical of that found in developing areas. It might be helpful, therefore, to take a brief look at the Irish example.

Without going deeply into the ethnographic base established for my research, we can note that dependence upon authority was very much a part of the Irish peasant farmer's social system as that culture was described by Arensberg and Kimball for 1932 (1940). The primary thrust of this dependency, however, was *internal*: that is, upon the older gatekeepers of tradition, who, because of their status, served as regulators in the social structure of contact (Spicer 1958:433–40) with the outside world. There was in that contact situation some dependence upon external authority, as represented mainly in the priest, teacher, government agent, and big-farmer cattleman roles, but it was of secondary importance in the decisions peasant farmers were required to make in their management of everyday affairs. The elements of status, prestige, influence, and, as I am using the construct here, authority, thus were all vested in age and tradition. Furthermore, the shared attitudes and predispositions that settled such authority on the old, ramified throughout the entire social fabric, supported by sanctions such as gossip, verbal censure, and ridicule of those who dared to deviate too far from the norms. Tradition thus equated with success and, as such, carried value.

My inventory of the social welfare, health, housing, education, land, and agriculture schemes avilable to Irish peasants in 1971 came to well over a hundred. Considering that many of the schemes subdivided into particularistic programs, an obvious conclusion was that the peasants in the community under study literally were being assaulted by efforts to direct changes in their culture. A number of generalizations can be made about these schemes. For example, most of them appeared well after the 1932 baseline established for my work. Further, participation in the schemes typically involved some contact, usually direct, with agents of the central or local government, said agents required customarily to visit peasant homesteads. These agents came mostly from outside the community with, in some cases, noncommunity affiliation being a requisite for the job. Also, practically all schemes were sanctioned by monetary inducement, either as reward for cooperating, as a share of program cost, or as outright subsidy. Without belaboring the point further, we can conclude, then, that among these peasant farmers the central government had established high visibility as the primary advocate of sociocultural change.

In examining the above details with respondents, there was agreement among them on two points: (1) they were aware that over the years they had become increasingly dependent upon the central government; and (2) they believed that social life had become too complicated to solve through traditional means, and it was right and appropriate therefore that the government assume for all people its heavy involvement in innovation. Further, their concern for innovation divided into two elements: (1) the direction that change ought to take; and (2) determining the innovations and means for implementation.

These peasant farmers thus verbalized the dependence of their kind upon government as a source of change, aware that this dependency had been growing steadily each year. In recognizing the role of government, most agreed simply that it could deal with their problems better than could those who advocated traditional norms. They noted, for example, the complexity of health, education, income, land acquisition and development, changing life-styles, and production and marketing problems. They coupled this understanding to the feeling that solutions lay mainly in the technology of science. This did not mean that as a class they were ready to throw over all tradition-based solutions. It did mean for most, though, a belief that survival is based in an *expectation of change* that will address the complexities of production and marketing in ways beyond their ken. Not to make this accommodation is to go the way of many who have disappeared before them—to make the accommodation may well mean survival in a community context other than that now present.

Their dependence on central government for direction, and for the innovative means to problem solution, received added impetus from a related source that should be noted here. Irish peasants—in common with marginal agriculturalists everywhere—face perennially the problems of scarce capital reserves and limited capability for capital formation, either through savings or credit. Thus, for many, the acceptance of innovations is based less on their technical worth than on the desire to acquire the cash incentives that accompany them. Whether this strategy has the effect ultimately of producing genuine change is not my concern here. I do note, however, that it does intensify dependence on the source of innovation by making of it a capitalizing agent. In a milieu of scarce risk capital, even a meager economic inducement in an innovative process can become an end rather than the means. Over a period of time this kind of capital dependency can become structured, thus lending immense power to those who link the community to the "outside."

The above process is occurring among the peasantry of western Ireland. In the community being studied, however, the impact of this type of power is not so negative as one might assume. Because of the development of small regional industrial schemes, statuses which require skills that can be met by the local population are being added to the social structure; hence the power of some change agents is reduced. There is, however, one interesting result worth noting. Detected among the more progressive farmers is some hostility toward neighbors who place economic inducement above the value of the innovations they presume to accept. This hostility, verbalized on rare occasions even in public meetings, derives from the progressive farmer's fear that the motives of his conservative fellows will not generate the intended changes in behavior, and the planners and policy makers, therefore, will discredit the capacity of those like themselves to benefit from government assistance. The potential for the kind of factionalism mentioned here, as concomitants to externally generated impacts on a community, thus weakening the sense of community that previously existed, is a common theme in the anthropological literature. The evidence seems clear, however, that typically this potential is of little concern to external agencies.

The expansion of social structure that accompanies extensions of the bureaucracy into the little tradition constitutes a kind of structural assimilation of the community into the greater tradition. The Irish parish just referred to, as it receives more and more statuses that link it to the larger, surrounding community, is undergoing just this kind of structural assimilation. The process, albeit subtle, nevertheless is real. A more explicit form of the same process occurs, however, when interest groups vertically intrude into a community. I am referring here to units such as political parties, religious or other sodalities, economic cooperatives, labor unions, or other types of voluntary associations. Since such interest groups are national or even international in scope, they provide the important function of relating the individual to the political, economic, and social processes of the greater society (for example, Gallaher 1961; Geertz 1968; Nash 1974; Smith and Reyes 1957:973–1002). The more complex a society becomes, the greater the reliance on associations to mediate the "inside-outside" interface in the local community. This is a common process noted by observers of the United States (for example, Warner 1953), and one being noted increasingly in the social science literature accumulating on other societies. The Andersons, for example, in their interesting analysis of *The Vanishing Village*, note particularly the role of voluntary associations in the rapid incorporation of a community into the greater tradition, in this case urban Denmark (Anderson and Anderson 1964).

I should like to note one final impact on local community through expansion of the social structure. I refer to the common decision of planners to develop a community merely by swelling its numbers. The notion that numbers sharing a given territory automatically come to share a sense of community is patent fallacy. Those who stand for the historical continuity of a community customarily find that a rapid infusion into the population frequently atomizes them to the point where they cannot effectively sustain communal properties in their institutional behavior.

CULTURAL COOPTATION

The cooptation of culture—by which I mean the loss of community identity as a function of complete acculturation into the larger society—follows when the boundary-maintenance devices by which a community sustains its social identity are relaxed. We have, in fact, already broached a major dimension of this process in our discussion of structural extensions, either through statuses or groups, by the greater society into a local community. The point is obvious that such structural linkages as are created do not exist in a vacuous situation; rather they function as conduits for the transmission of attitudes, values, sentiments, ideologies, and the appropriate symbolic systems for transmitting these social meanings.

In addition, we should keep in mind the extent to which a community is influenced by nondirected diffusion. I refer particularly to media influences, such as movies, television, radio, newspapers, and magazines. These, when coupled to improved transportation and other devices, force a continual confrontation with alternative life-styles. It should, therefore, come as no surprise to those of us exposed to popular advertising to know that as potential accepters we are subject to the influence of authority figures no less than those who experience directed change situations.

Influences of the kind mentioned here are ubiquitous. Frequently aggregated under the label *urbanization*—referring to their locus in the mass culture of the greater society—they exert a constant pressure to change on all social units. This pressure, especially as it develops in the greater society, has been noted as a threat to the little community by observers reporting from a wide variety of social contexts. James West, for example, who studied Plainville fifteen years before I did, spoke of that community and others like it:

> For better or for worse, they are doomed as "traditional" communities. As their ancient value'system crumbles under the blows of a new "tradition" imposed from outside, their problem is to learn to participate more fully in the cultural rewards of the greater society. (West 1945:225)

My analysis in 1954–55 revealed that the people of Plainville, indeed, had begun to participate more fully in the greater society:

> A major result of the Plainviller's increased contact with American mass culture is new expectations of what constitutes the desirable in various areas of his life. Among other things, he has developed new standards of adequacy based on models drawn from urban America, that is, cities and more urbanized farm communities. These are mirrored in the dominant pattern of change—a newly defined standard of living involving expecta-

tions of material and nonmaterial comfort and efficiency. This pattern, axial in a complex of economic changes, permeates and, in large measure, integrates most of the changes which have occurred in Plainville since 1939– 40. (Gallaher 1961:228)

A similar point is made by Morton Rubin in his study of a community in the plantation South:

> The effect of the mass culture in promoting cultural and social change in the plantation areas has been to create forces which are causing the new patterns to be dysfunctional and inconsistent with the old ones. . . . Old ways are being redefined, but compromise is slow. The young people of the plantation area will have to examine the old ways and the new ways with clear and analytic minds in order to discover that goal of a good life they want and deserve. (Rubin 1951:204– 5)

And writing of still another type of contact situation, Julian Steward suggests the growing dependence of small, homogeneous communities upon external sources for necessary innovations to be a critical element in the process of modernization:

> Trait transmission from state-level societies to simpler societies may operate as between tribal societies. In one respect, however, it may be so different that it is quite inadequately conceptualized as "diffusion" in the traditional sense. Whereas diffusion between tribal societies ordinarily implies that the borrowing society incorporates the trait as part of its largely self-sufficient system, borrowing by a simple society from a complex state often involves adoption of traits upon which it comes to depend but which it cannot reproduce itself. The simple society, therefore, becomes institutionally dependent upon the state, for example, through trade. (Steward 1967:5)

Steward is telling us that the fate of virtually all tribal and peasant communities is to acculturate to the framework of state political, economic, and ideological systems, to the point of losing their identity. A similar point of view is made by Redfield, who says, "In our days many peasants are changing very rapidly. For the future it may be said that peasantry are ceasing to be." (Redfield 1956:137)

Cultural cooptation is accelerated when those who plan and advocate innovations establish in potential accepters a dependence upon them as authority in matters of change. Through the manipulation of rewards, especially economic, and sanctions, frequently rationalized through the political process, genuine control is exerted over the direction and rate of change in a culture. Critical in this situation, it seems to me, are the strategies that those in authority control, because it is in them that a community comes to assess its future cultural viability.

My own experience has been mainly in economically marginal and politically vulnerable communities, the kind noted for high out-migration of the educated, with residual populations of high economic dependency (for example, Ford 1973). The strategies employed by change agents to motivate such communities to change frequently are based on relative deprivation premises; that is, to keep before the population models of "the good life," easily reducible to material referents, which they should come to feel it is their right to share. This model for growth is purely economic, though during the brief O.E.O. effort in this country there were attempts to include improved power and decision-making capability as part of the model for change.

In all cases, those in the business of helping, those on whom the communities depended for assistance, defined problems, goals, and solutions at a level of complexity that could only reinforce the dependency of those who needed help. Perhaps the contemporary world is this complex, and helping agencies have no alternative but to structure development models in the way they do. If that is the case, then local conceptions of viability under these conditions can only register on the negative side, and communities must take whatever measures possible to rationalize subordination to the greater society. Some will cling to the little community ideology, as in the case noted by Vidich and Bensman in their *Small Town in Mass Society* (1958). They tell us that the people in this upstate New York community still cling to the traditional image of their life as eminently more desirable than the life of the city. Still the urban culture is much more a part of Small Town than the people who live there will permit themselves to believe. This condition exists because they have accommodated successfully to their situation by developing two systems of social control. One supports the Small Town ideology and the other, through a well-integrated leadership group, insures that local affairs will be adapted to the pressures of the greater urban society.

Suffice it to say that not all communities manage an identity crisis as well as do the people of Small Town. Many, as do Plainvillers, engage the popular U.S. rhetoric about small town life but in their behavior passively acculturate to the mass culture. And the literature abounds with examples of others plunged into conflict between old and new,

106

factionalism, or other activities that demonstrate social disorganization. Occasionally, when its problems seem about to get out of hand, a community may turn in on its own cultural tradition, glorying in its values and exclusiveness, what Linton (1943:230–40) labeled *nativism*. Or, it may self-consciously attempt to construct a more satisfying cultural system through rapid change intended to achieve "revitalization" (Wallace 1970:188–99).

In summary, then, I suggest that in both directed and nondirected diffusion there are sources external to the little community that are likely to be vested with authority in matters of change. Further, a likely source is the central government bureaucracy. The responsibility for innovative solutions to problems, and for the direction change will take, thus rest with agents and the bureaucratic agencies they represent. Typically, the locus of ideas, values, attitudes, and other dimensions of culture, are in the mass culture of the greater society; hence, change is cast in that direction. As a consequence of their activities, change agents thus frequently generate expectations of change on the part of those who have problems. A common strategy that they follow is to employ economic models of the good life, which, since they are not now available, should cause the potential accepter to feel a sense of relative deprivation. Such intrusions into the culture of a community, either because of success, or lack of it, may evoke a number of responses, one of which ultimately is to surrender the sense of local community to a larger communal frame of reference. It is all very natural, all done in the interest of helping others to solve their problems. It is a process striking in its subtlety.

EPILOG

In the comments that have gone before I have attempted to explore how the activities of external authority can impact on the little community so as to cause it to experience decline and, perhaps, ultimately cease to be. My basic premise has been that such activities can impact on both the social and cultural dimensions of community, and that in either case there are occasions in which complete sociocultural suppression is possible. In exploring the problems set for myself, I have not intended to attach value to whether a community survives or dies. This has not been easy for me, and I may not have been successful at it, because I share with my anthropology colleagues the notion that a community ought to provide its members with the full opportunity to grow socially and to gain individual satisfaction. Thus, if pressed, my position is that if a community is losing that capability, or if there are forces impacting a community so as to prohibit its meeting its obligations to its members, then that community or the external intrusion has to be assessed negatively.

I adhere to the view, however, that deteriorations and decline also are natural processes for a community to experience. The issue thus is not whether these processes are known to occur, but rather whether rational interventions ought not to be attempted. I adhere to the notion that rational intervention should be attempted, and the added notion that such intervention not be biased toward either saving or terminating the little community. Rather, those who plan should operate from the premise that the primary objective always is to secure the best quality of social, political, and economic life possible in a specific communal context. It may well be that we should begin to rethink radically the forms of social organization through which this objective can be achieved.

5

Revolutions in Community Structure

ARTHUR J. VIDICH

Department of Sociology
New School of Social Research

IMAGES OF COMMUNITY IN SOCIAL THEORY

In western thought, at least since the decline of feudalism, social and historical thinkers (including Marx, Weber, Durkheim, Toennies, and Maine) have tended to conceive of contrasting types of communities. [1] These included community-society, folk-urban, Gemeinschaft-Gesellschaft, organic-mechanical, sacred-secular, traditional-rational-legal, feudal-capitalistic. In setting up contrasting types of communities, these thinkers used an image of the preindustrial world as a basis for highlighting the emergent institutions of the industrial, capitalistic, liberal societies that they studied.

Our conceptions of community structures within industrial society continue to be shaped by the contrasting image of folk and urban society. According to this imagery, the historic-folk communities developed their central characteristics because they were spatially isolated from other societies and because they were small. Their separation from other societies and the resultant density of interpersonal relations allowed them to develop distinctive cultures that supported and reinforced the individual even as he was submerged in and by this community culture. The community was characterized by a deep sense of

person-to-person emotional commitment, a strong sense of community identity, and a stability of tradition from one generation to the next.[2]

In theory, it was the spatial isolation of the community that allowed
for the development of distinctive cultural, organizational, ceremonial, and ritual forms. Spatial isolation reinforced tradition, which framed
and limited the behavior of community members. The frames and the
limits provided the cultural bases for the activities of the members of
the community and supplied them with the motivational structures
required for participation in the community. Individuals were not
plagued by the problems of choice because few alternatives were available. The conflicts in value that did exist were limited because the
isolated community tended to have an overarching hierarchy of values
that served as a basis for its institutional integration. The community's
values were expressed in all institutional areas. Political, economic,
religious, and family activities were all part of a single fabric and
institutional specialization and differentation as we know it did not
exist.

Anthropologists in their studies of preindustrial communities have
underscored the absence of institutional specialization by their stress
on kinship institutions as the coordinating nexus of all relationships. In
communities where descent and kinship provide a foundation for economic, political, and religious relationships, the person is surrounded
by an integrated pattern of values even if these values included such
phenomena as political domination, sex domination, or caste and
status inequalities. The result of such integration of values was to
present the person few choices and thus to severely limit his opportunities for individual expression. He could not experience himself as
having a strong sense of his own individuality and subjectivity, and so
could not threaten the institutional integration of the community. In
sum, anthropologists have described communities whose institutions
have remained unspecialized and have been identified with slow rates
of change and a strong orientation to tradition. In this respect the
theoretical orientations of anthropology have been guided by images
similar to those used by Marx, Weber, Durkheim, and Toennies in
their discussions of feudal society.

Of course, while it is understood that this image reflects an underlying reality for the preindustrial world, Europe, even under feudalism,
was not wholly isolated or separated from other equally powerful traditions of community in which individuals' community relationships

110

were not based on space or kinship. The idea of the civic community, whose origins go back to the demos, has always been central to the idea of the political community. The demos is linked to the idea of citizenship, which in the West has been associated with urban life since its beginnings. Again in the West, as Max Weber has stressed, there was a relatively early and definitive separation of communities of religious faith from communities based on kinship or blood ties. Weber, in his work on ancient Judaism, notes the Judaic step from tribal gods to the only god and, subsequently, the rejection of all tribal limitations in Pauline Christianity. The latter step created the basis for giving religious sanction to communities that transcended all ties of blood or kinship. In this tradition we find the seeds for the growth of an active sense of the community into larger units, continuing thus far up to the idea of the nation-state, to whose commitment communities based on clans, tribes, castes, or hereditary sects are of secondary importance.

Such traditions suggest that within the history of western civilization there have been from very early times specialization and differentiation of community structures. For the most part, however, the conceptions of community utilized by modern writers have not stressed these alternative principles as foundations for community structures because their attention was focused on the forms of relationships that were under assault by the emergent institutions of capitalism. Thus, our present conceptions of community derive from an intellectual tradition that was itself part of the process of the transition from a politically decentralized, agriculturally-based, nonurban, feudal system to an industrially-based, centralized, urban civilization. The thinkers upon whose ideas we rely saw the concrete consequences of the effects of modern industrial capitalism on European civilization. In their view the factory, the market system, the specialization and division of labor, the internationalization of labor markets, and the breakdown of the ancient culture were the concomitants of emergent commercial and, later, of industrial capitalism. Viewed in economic terms feudal civilization, and the classes it supported, were based upon land wealth. Industrial civilization and its classes were based on urban-centered wealth ultimately derived from an exploitation of nonagricultural resources.

To the extent that industrialization has become a worldwide phenomenon, the revolutions that those thinkers experienced and tried to comprehend in the nineteenth century have continued to manifest

111

themselves in all areas of the world where industrial capital has become dominant and/or more intensively utilized. After the demise of feudalism and with the beginnings of industrial civilization, the all-pervasive spirit of industry has transformed the spatial isolation and the primitive simplicity of the preindustrial community. Large-scale urbanism, industrialization, mass institutions, and centralized bureaucracies have everywhere engulfed ancient traditions and the institutions of traditional communities. The shift from community to society, from folk to urban, and from mechanical to organic reflects a shift in the center of wealth and civilization from agricultural to industrial and urban.

It is understood by historians of civilizations that the social forms and culture associated with preindustrial society both in the West and in the formerly primitive societies do not simply disappear with a change in the economic basis of society. Older cultural traditions and institutions may continue to persist even as newer institutions and cultures arise and take their place beside them. Thus, for example, the ancient institutions and cultures of Christianity, Judaism, or Mohammedanism continue to persist in areas of intensely developed urbanization and industrialization. Communities based on religious belief have been known to be relatively impervious to changes in economic forms. Another example of such imperviousness may be found in communities based on ties stemming from ethnic descent. Groups such as the Jews, Poles, Armenians, or Chinese may continue to form spatially bounded or unbounded communities within the framework of advanced capitalist or communist nations. Because the cultures and traditions of the past may continue into the present, an archaeological perspective is essential to an understanding of the growth, decline, and persistence of community institutions and traditions over periods of time that may even embrace revolutions in political, social, and economic institutions.

Archaeologists have registered the growth, decline, and death of great civilizations and of small isolated communities. Because of the nature of their speculations, however, it has been difficult for them to examine the living social fabric of the communities that were located at the sites they study. Their data are the complex of artifacts associated with a region, place, or site. They speak of such complexes as traditions rather than communities. They have had the advantages, however, of being able to view the growth and decline of community and civilizational traditions over long periods of time.

112

The cultural traditions of world history stand in complex relations with each other. A. Kroeber in his book *Configurations of Cultural Growth* (1944) and R. Linton in *The Tree of Culture* (1956) described the history and process of cultural continuities and discontinuities over vast periods of time. These authors noted that new styles of living may emerge and merge with previously existing cultural traditions. Older styles may decay or become mummified and be resuscitated at a later time in a different place. Older styles and traditions may survive even when their economic basis changes, or they may continue and become associated with new social and psychological attitudes on the part of those who have been the bearers of the traditions. Most likely, however, the history of tradition and civilization is one in which new styles do not completely replace old ones, but simply become accretions to them. Innovations in styles of life thus increase the complexity of traditional modes of behavior because older styles can coexist and merge with new ones. In light of this, combinations and even recombinations of closely related traditions are a continuous possibility and one of the common historical processes accounting for the continuity of and change in tradition.

Archaeology as a field itself has been a major factor in the revival and perpetuation of cultural traditions. From the point of view of modern civilization, it has salvaged and brought back to our attention traditions long since erased from human memory. For example, the ancient traditions of Egypt, Greece, Persepolis in the Old World, and the Aztecan, Mayan, and Incan civilizations in the New World have been retrieved by archaeological investigators only within the past hundred years. Once these sites were rediscovered and exhumed, they could supply the raw materials for the absorption of some of their elements into modern culture. Certainly Aztecan design and architecture have been incorporated into modern Mexican culture, and their use has deepened that culture, even though the selective utilization of the past is not intrinsically related to the present. Archaeology by its own example teaches us that cultural traditions do not easily disappear and that they may be re-created by archaeological craftsmen who redefine the artifacts and symbols of the past for modern consumers. By utilizing the rational procedures of investigation available to modern science, archaeology contributes to the rational production of Old World cultures, and the culture that is produced often enters the worldwide marketplace without regard to intrinsic spatial or historical

113

limitations. In this sense, cultural and social forms may have lives of their own, independent of their origins or original use.

But, as we have already suggested, the sources from which traditions are drawn, the traditions themselves, and the continuity of tradition are not uniquely interrelated with the existence of the community. A community involves not only the traditions and life-styles on which it is based, but also the interaction of its members with outsiders and their culture.

Almost all observers of communities have noted a difference in the types of community interaction found in towns or villages and cities. The distinction between rural and urban has been central to almost all social theory about communities. Professor William Adams in his essay (p. 44 above) makes this same distinction between small communities and urban centers and stresses that the interdependence between them has been the critical fact in the history of civilization. He says:

> We can . . . observe that throughout the world most of the in-habitants of small communities are food producers, while most of the inhabitants of urban centers are not. This fundamental division of society, we believe, goes back to the dawn of civilization. It follows inevitably that the circumstances of life and death are somewhat different in the two cases. Small communities are, we assume, more immediately vulnerable to environmental vicissitudes than are urban centers, while being proportionately less affected by failure or change in the economic, political, or religious spheres. Given the interdependence of city and village, however, it ultimately becomes true that what is bad for the one is bad for the other.

From ancient civilization onward, the city has been the site of diverse ethnic populations who converged on the city from surrounding agricultural regions. Where crossroads of trade and travel became the sites of cities, urban populations have been drawn from far distant ethnically, linguistically, racially, and religiously heterogeneous immigrants. Usually such immigrant populations created distinct communities, each based on ethnic, linguistic, racial, and religious differences. Frequently such urban ethnic settlements, at least during the life span of the first generation of immigrants, retain many of the features of rural and agricultural social organization characteristic of the immigrants' community of origin. These same rural institutions are transformed, adopted, and distorted to the requirements of urban life and are diffused throughout the city, adding to the content of city culture. The ghetto in the city is sometimes no more than a transplanted rural community.

The history of cities has also shown that ghettoes may survive long after the expiration of the immigrant generation. Second, third, and fourth generations retain distinctive ethnic, racial, religious, or linguistic habits. Over time, ghetto boundaries may become more clearly defined and sometimes legally reinforced. Ethnic leaders may emerge who claim to lead on the strength of maintaining the integrity of the groups' identities, which, in turn, rest in part on territorial and institutional claims. The modern ghetto is clearly a form of urban community that may trace its roots to rural society, but is an urban community form in its own right.

Because of the ethnic and racial composition of urban populations, cities have been distinguished by the great variety of cultures that they absorb and contain. In some cases these cultures have remained separate and isolated from their milieu, like the populations that have been their carriers, but more frequently they have diffused and have interpenetrated other cultural groups giving the city a plurality of cultural styles. Some groups, such as the Jews, have had long-standing identification with the city and have accepted urban values while retaining religious separateness. But the same heterogeneity of the city and its receptiveness to a wide variety of beliefs, values, religions, and lifestyles has made it an object of hostility to those who are threatened by the existence of other than dominant traditional ways of life. Thus the city has always had an uneasy relationship with the surrounding countryside.

Part of the complexity of urban community structures is related to the complexity of urban class systems. Except for the period of European feudalism, the city historically has been the place of residence of upper classes, whether their wealth has been based on land, tribute, office-holding, or administration. Even under modern industrialism, the newly emergent upper classes have maintained urban residences, while also maintaining secondary rural estates and tertiary residences in the world's elite recreational areas. The other conspicuous class that developed in the cities is the urban poor. They became an underclass and a "proletariat" if they could not return to the countryside and a burden to the rural dwellers if they did. The middle classes have created new cultural styles and have left their stamp on the ways of urban life. Urban classes may thus represent a complex form of social organization, which includes new life-styles and institutions that do not conform to our conventional images of the community, and which are far removed from the "rural" communities of urban immigrants.

The record from archaeology encourages us to pay attention not only to rural and small-scale communities but also to community forms and structures that have been characteristic of cities. The interpenetration of cities and surrounding countryside has always been a decisive factor affecting the fate of not only towns and cities, but of whole civilizations. Nonetheless, the dominant tradition in the study of communities by sociologists and anthropologists has not reflected this idea of interpenetration, in our epoch a global phenomenon.

The Penetration of Industrial Civilization

The original thinkers who set up the image of the isolated spatially distinct community based their observations on an abstract conceptualization of feudal society (Marx, Weber) and primitive communities (Durkheim) against which they could contrast emergent industrial society as they saw it in the nineteenth and twentieth centuries. Industrial society, they observed, resulted in:

1. an enormous growth of industrial and trade-centered cities and vast dislocations of rural populations from the countryside to industrial centers.
2. the development of machine technology and the factory as crucial to the redefinition of class structure, wealth distribution, the division of labor, and the separation of economic activity from family relationships.
3. the growth of centralized government, and the development of the corporation as the legal instrument for organizing large-scale economic projects.
4. the development of bureaucracy as the key form of social organization in industrial society and the use of bureaucracy as the major tool of societal administration.
5. the development of mass communications, universal literacy, and the breakdown of the psychological isolation of the world's communities by the penetration of the new means of communication. It was, after all, Marx, who, when he used the slogan "Workers of the World, Unite," understood as early as anyone

116

the power of mass communications in gaining the attention of mass audiences over unrestricted territorial spaces.

6. the worldwide penetration of the institutions of industrial civilization based on both an inexorable search for the raw materials needed to supply industry and the long-term tendency toward a worldwide division of labor. Over the long run, the processes of rationalization inherent in the modern industrial system have led to the calculation and inventorying of raw materials, labor, marketing, distribution, and consumption worldwide.

Of course, industrial civilization and its institutions have penetrated different parts of the world at different times, rates, and intensities over the past 300 years. Examples of such penetration and its consequences can be found throughout the anthropological literature dealing with the acculturation of primitive peoples. Everywhere primitive communities have become dependent on commercial markets and wage labor and are subjected to the vagaries of sudden and abrupt changes in the structures of those markets. From the point of view of the traditional preindustrial and relatively isolated communities of the world, the consequences of this penetration have varied from place to place depending on the intensity of the penetration and the capacity of local populations to absorb or deflect it:

1. In parts of the world where indigenous communities were small and stood in the way of the goals of their western conquerers, such as in Tasmania and many parts of the Western Hemisphere, indigenous populations were dispersed or obliterated. Violent conquest has been one of the major mechanisms used by industrial civilization for destroying the preindustrial communities of the world.

2. In other parts of the world, such as Africa, Asia, or the Pacific region, where populations were too large to displace or destroy or where the labor of the population was indispensable to the conquerer, the indigenous population was preserved while it was simultaneously integrated into the institutions of industrial civilization under various forms of colonial rule.

3. The deepest penetration of industrial institutions has occurred within the most advanced industrial countries. In these areas of the world, industrialization in the tradition of liberal, large-scale, corporate capitalism continues to sustain its dynamism based on growth in scale of enterprise and continuous displacement of

older forms of wealth and their replacement by newly created sources of wealth. This has meant vast movements of ethnic and racial populations from rural towns and villages to transoceanic urban centers where industrial frontiers attracted migrants and persons already displaced by the industrial penetration.

The above forms of penetration, which we may label for purposes of convenience genocide, colonialism, and metropolitanization, have resulted in the death and transformation of communities and in the creation of new community forms. So long as modern industrialization continues its inexorable growth and spread over the face of the globe, these processes will continue unabated until such time as the isolated, primitive, rural community will have no existence in reality even in the remote areas of the world. Let us attempt to delineate the processes by which community structures have changed as a result of the penetration of industrial society and to describe some of the forms of community that have replaced those destroyed by these processes.

Genocide and the Preservation of Primitive Communities

Less than a hundred years ago, the small, primitive community was almost completely vulnerable to conquest or genocide by those who would choose to invade it. Where such communities were small and isolated, they were unable to resist the overwhelming power with which they were confronted and were without recourse against their conquerors. The defeat of such communities has continued to the present wherever the preindustrial world confronts for the first time the full force of capital-intensive development. One contemporary example of this process was the encounter between the opposing forces and the primitive hill tribes of Vietnam during the twenty years of war in Vietnam. The primitives were uprooted and displaced, and their social units frequently were separated from each other. Another example is the displacement of Amazonian primitives by the construction of the Trans-Amazon highway into the Peruvian headwaters of that river. Many other examples could be cited. At this time there are only a few places in the world where remote groups have somehow escaped the full force of these processes.

Yet while the most primitive and most remote of such groups have historically been least able to defend themselves, groups like these have now found that they have self-proclaimed protectors within the centers of advanced industrial civilization. Anthropologists, missionaries, and other professional groups, whose occupational concerns traditionally have been either the study or the salvation of primitives, have been more aware than other groups of threats to the existence of primitive populations. From its beginnings, anthropology has sponsored an ideology that has favored the preservation of the primitive because the latter were "original men," "children of mankind," and the "living museum" of early man. Missionaries have wished to save primitives not only from their own paganism but also from the vice, corruption, and degeneracy of western civilization. In the course of their jobs, these field workers have seen at first hand the tragic defenselessness of small-scale communities. Moreover, as part of their occupational ideology, they have tended to identify with the primitives' plight on the grounds of the inhumanity and immorality of the civilization of which they themselves are a part. Thus, it has been relatively easy for these occupational groups to take the step from simply identifying with the plight of the primitives to becoming their active defenders in the court of world opinion.

Organizations such as the American Anthropological Association, the United Nations, and Cultural Survival, Inc., have begun to act as spokesmen to world public opinion for these endangered primitive groups. Excessively rapid detribalization, and wholesale transplantation or slaughter of tribes tends to evoke the sympathies of sectors of world opinion. An apt example is the community of "stone-age" men "discovered" in the Philippines by Charles Lindbergh. As a result of his discovery, a vast public relations campaign has protected them while projecting them on television. Where campaigns to protect primitives are successful, they may act as a restraint against the forces that would destroy those of the world's remaining primitive communities. Mass communications and the electronic media have given the primitives a form of defense that they did not have earlier. As civilization has advanced, it has produced the means by which defenseless communities may be defended.[3]

It is possible that some communities that might otherwise have been destroyed will be saved. If they are saved it will be as a result not of their own efforts but of the efforts of individuals and groups who have chosen to save them. Insofar as the initiative to preserve these communities is external to the community itself, the terms under which they will survive are contingent upon the same civilization that would destroy them.

Heretofore, anthropologists have preserved in the world's museums the material cultural artifacts of tribal communities. As industrial civilization has penetrated more deeply, more and more of the preindustrial cultural traditions of the world may be found in such museums. The preservation of these traditions in museums is paralleled by the preservation of extinct and disappearing species in the world's zoos. Industrial civilization has been impartial in its exploitation and conquest of the living species of the world.

Colonialism and the Transformation of Primitive Communities

Colonialism, only recently abandoned as a policy by the industrial West, had the effect of preserving selected indigenous institutions while freeing the energies of parts of the population to serve the interests of the metropolis. Its larger interest was the exploitation of the labor of indigenous populations for the purpose of profits, capital accumulation, and military bases. Colonies offered a ready-made, low-cost labor force whose consumption requirements were met by the indigenous economy, while their labor produced for the international economy, thus further adding to the process of accumulation. Paralleling the history of western colonialism has been the internal colonialism of countries such as Russia and Japan where industrialism was imposed by an elite on feudal indigenous populations within an emerging, industrializing nation-state. In these latter cases a dominant region or class has managed the imposition of industrialization over the traditional agricultural and/or nomadic populations. In the case of Japan, Japanese "internal colonialism" created a surplus population of erstwhile peasants who could not be absorbed by Japan's cities. They were therefore exported to become the colonial vanguard in other states, such as Korea and the Philippines. Internal and external colonialisms have been a central mechanism for transforming the social, psychological, and institutional bases of preindustrial communities. Though colonialism as a historic process has been characteristic of early stages of industrialization, its impact on preindustrial communities has had long-term consequences, which remain its legacy to the present.

The outside colonial administration enters a community that is already structured in terms of social values as well as political, economic, and other differentials. Administration brings with it new skills,

120

new techniques, and patterns of administration and organization that create new positions in the society, new sources of income, and new values. From the point of view of the members of the indigenous community, the outside administration, its jobs, and its values represent so many new forms of opportunity.

If these opportunities—for education, clerkships, policy duty, factory work—are seized by already privileged groups within the community, such groups have behind them not only the power, privilege, and prestige connected to traditional institutions, but they have the authority and prestige of the outside power to bolster their position with the indigenous community. This was especially the case in India where the British supported the rule of the traditional Raj, who then would claim authority both in traditional and British terms. Where such groups have been successful, they have succeeded in destroying the traditional internal checks to their status claims and to their own power, traditional in their society. When the sources of power, privilege, and prestige of both the traditional systems and colonial society are combined within one group, the traditional community has been revolutionized and its indigenous traditions can no longer be said to exist in their previous form.

If, on the other hand, groups who are marginal in traditional society respond to the new opportunities, they then possess a basis for making claims for prestige, status, and power on the strength of the new values and resources. These emergent groups tend to develop influence, power, income, and prestige with reference to colonial administration and industrial civilization, but are outside the pale with reference to traditional values. They then become a threat to the older traditional leadership and privileged groups who regard them as parvenus and carpetbaggers in their own society. For them the conflict between informal power and income position and their unrecognized prestige position results in their attempt to legitimatize themselves within the indigenous structure. They do so by attempting to buy into the traditional status symbols and titles of native society, and/or they attempt to change the social values of the society so that their new positions can have the prestige formerly attached to the older positions. The Shah of Iran and Kwame Nkrumah of Ghana were examples of this. In such cases there is usually a struggle between groups who make their political and status claims on traditional values and those who transform tradition in order to bolster new claims. All of this also

121

involves the revolutionizing of the society and its values, and it means degrading traditional values and institutions.

In both cases, colonial administration has fundamentally altered the structure of the traditional community, has contributed to the transformation of traditional institutions and has linked the previously isolated community to the institutions of industrial civilization. Once this process began it was irreversible and the future of communities in colonialized societies became linked to the same social and economic processes as rural communities in the industrialized nations of the West. Wherever a community cannot adjust to the social and economic impact of world political and market forces, its chances for survival are reduced.

These same processes of colonialism occurred during the industrialization of Japan and of Russia, to which we have referred as cases of internal colonialism. In these countries, under the administration of organizations such as the Communist Party or the Zaibatsu, the traditional institutions of preindustrial communities were either utilized in the service of industrialization or, when they obstructed it, eliminated. Stalin's thesis on the nationality problem in the Soviet Union was a policy guide to the administration of community institutions; all political or organizational forms that were thought to stand in opposition to centralized administration or industrialization were assaulted frontally. On the other hand, cultural institutions such as language, dress, ceremony, and dance were not attacked, but were used to supply the basis for ethnic and cultural nationalism for the first generations of those ethnic and cultural minorities who experienced the full impact of the industrialization process. Thus the partial preservation of traditional community institutions facilitates the transition to industrial society by temporarily preserving what must ultimately wither when industrialization reaches the level where it can produce its own cultural forms.

Where industrial civilization has been introduced under the management of a centralized leadership class or planning bureaucracy, rationally calculated decisions have been the basis of the survival or elimination of communities and their institutions. But even in the United States and other parts of the Western Hemisphere where central planning was not utilized during early stages of industrialization, a similar process occurred. In these countries, the forces of "pluralism" tended to be sustained by the immigrant's dress, language, ceremony,

122

and food while absorbing his strength and talent in the industrial system. Blacks presented a special problem, especially in the United States, because they were brought in to serve a large-scale but technically backward agrarian, plantation society and were isolated from the industrial system.

Community Structures in Metropolitan Society

The processes of industrialization, urbanization, and bureaucratization continue to penetrate ever more deeply into the social fabric of the advanced industrial societies. In the United States the Civil War decided the preeminence of industrial as opposed to agricultural capital and the twentieth century has seen the industrialization of agricultural capital. In Europe, the historic resistance to industrialization and capitalism by the rural, middle, or gentry classes has all but disappeared. The purpose for the creation of the European Common Market as far as agriculture and rural society is concerned has been to rationalize its labor and productive power on a transnational basis. While France and Germany have regulated and controlled the reduction in the rural labor force by supporting the prices of agricultural commodities, the long-term trend has been a reduction in both the rural labor force and the size of distinctly rural segments of the population. The small European towns and villages become increasingly suburbanized as European industrial capitalization penetrates the hinterlands. Where traditional European towns and villages retain some of their ancient charm, this is the result of the work of travel and tourist agencies and local real estate interests, which have a keen eye for the foreign tourist, especially the American, whose nostalgia for the preindustrial past is so powerful that it enables him to accept the illusion of the quaintness and charm of the facade erected by the promoters of tourism. Industrial society includes among its capacities the ability to preserve and to reproduce the appearances of ancient culture.

Since the beginnings of industrialization in both the United States and Europe, the small town and the rural community have been characterized by instability in both their economic basis and their population composition. Since its beginnings the American small town and the village community have continuously been penetrated by the current forces of business and industrial civilization. Each economic period in American history has left behind its dying and dead communities upon which, however, in archaeological-like fashion, new economic and social forms have been superimposed. The following illustrations briefly suggest this process of death and rebirth.

1. The original New England farming communities have long since disappeared only to be replaced by mill towns, which have also disappeared. Many an older New England farm village and mill town are archaeological sites. These sites have since been reoccupied by the recreational industry and by the growth in ownership by the middle classes of the weekend second home, essentially a process of suburbanization.

2. Many copper, ore, gold, and lumber towns of the late nineteenth and early twentieth centuries died with the exhaustion of the resource on which they were based. This is also true of railway round house, shop, and junction towns, which have withered along with the industry on which they were based. Many of these ghost towns from the earlier period have been remodeled as tourist attractions. In some cases they have been retrieved from their ultimate fate by new homesteaders, who attempt to build new rural life-styles on the salvaged foundations of what would otherwise have become archaeological sites.

3. Older towns and villages located in relation to the logics of older systems of transportation (such as the railroad) have been bypassed by the new interstate highway and airplane systems, which in the past twenty years have connected all parts of the country into a single interconnected road and air network. The growth of automobile, truck, and air transport has resulted in airport towns, truck transportation centers, motel culture, and C.B. radio communities defined and located within the framework of electronically based verbal communication between people moving from one place to another.

From the point of view of the traditional community, this has meant that wherever communities have been based on less capital-intensive methods of production, they have been unable to survive in their original form whenever newer more intensive capitalization of agriculture has occurred. Such communities have survived only when they were able to transfer their economic base from the older to the newer

124

forms of capital investment, and as sites where the affluent benefactors of urban business and industry can enjoy rural, environmental consumerism. The history of traditional small towns and village communities in the advanced industrial societies is a history of progressively deeper penetration of societal institutions, paralleled by a continuous weakening or transformation of preindustrial cultural forms, even as these forms are celebrated and refashioned to maintain ideal images of the past.

So far in the history of industrial capitalism, the death and decay of older small towns and rural communities have always been paralleled by the growth of new settlements and communities linked to newly emergent forms of capitalization. Each successive stage of more intensified capitalization, however, represents another nail in the coffin of preindustrial culture.

In a place like the United States, depending on how one wishes to count generations, we are now at the stage (since 1945) where the life experience of at least two generations has been totally embraced by modern culture. As the industrially advanced metropolitan societies approach the end of the twentieth century, we enter a stage where almost all living generations will have had their total life experience within an immediately present industrial civilization.

With reference to the sociology of the community and the sociology of community culture, this means the creation of greater and greater psychological distance from the traditional primitive, tribal, ethnic, and national cultures of the past. Thus the long-term drift of modern industrial civilization mocks all those who would attempt to construct a theory of community structures based on images of preindustrial society, whether feudal, ancient, or primitive. The utopian hopes for industrial civilization of some earlier thinkers like St. Simon, Comte, and Marx have not been realized. Primitive culture or national cultural forms of the past are the cosmetics for a new, more urban industrial capitalism. The fulfillment of industrial society and capitalism has pointed in the direction of vast bureaucratic organizations, huge state administrative organizations and the rational calculation of investment, production, and, to some extent, distribution on a worldwide scale. The question must be asked: what have been the consequences of these trends for the community structures of both the former colonialized societies and the advanced metropolitanized societies?

SOCIAL AND PSYCHOLOGICAL CONSEQUENCES
OF PENETRATION

The rate and density of penetration of the institutions of industrial society throughout the world has transformed the institutional and psychological matrix of small communities everywhere. The net result at an institutional level is that in almost all areas of the world the internal life of the community, including politics, and class and status arrangements, is based on new skills that have their value vis-à-vis the larger world. The penetration of primitive and rural society has tended to destroy all older forms of identification, ritual, loyalty, and ceremony traditionally associated with small-scale preindustrial communities. Thus, the self-confidence of indigenous populations in their own traditional institutions is attacked because of the dominance and superiority of industrial society and its technology. Indigenous values and religious beliefs are destroyed by the overwhelming superiority of industrial civilization. Frequently, however, these values have been destroyed before they have been replaced by other values that would substitute for those that have been destroyed. When clan, tribe, caste, sect, and village ties have been surrendered, they have not automatically or concomitantly been replaced by urban communities, civic communities, universal religious communities, or loyalties to a nation-state.

Paralleling this breakdown in self-confidence in indigenous institutions is an admiration and envy of the techniques and institutions of industrial society. Consumption standards associated with advanced industrial society have been used everywhere as a model of comparison for indigenous standards. Historically such admiration and envy has resulted in programs and plans to transform society for the purpose of achieving higher consumption levels. This has been done without regard for the consequences of such transformation on indigenous institutions. Modernization has almost always gained over traditionalism and reactionary resistance; i.e., in no area of the world does the attempt to restore the status quo ante appear to be a dominant movement.

Instead, an attack is made not on the technology but on the foreign control of technology. The ambivalent attitudes toward indigenous tradition and industrial civilization separates the instrument from the wielders of the instruments. By this mechanism the resentment against the dominant institutions and their wielders can be expressed directly either against the hated foreigners who live within the community or

126

against the seats of central government and multinational corporations within the metropolitan society itself.

The hatred of outsiders, foreigners, and the centers of foreign power allows for re-creation of a sense of community identification based on a nationalism whose claim to loyalty and commitment rests on hostility and resentment. Nationalism replaces localism and traditionalism as a basis for the psychological cohesion of the community. The central characteristic of the emergent community identity is thus a negative one because it is shaped by a hostility to the same institutions that they hope would replace their own traditional institutions. But since even nationalism has not yet become firmly embedded as a source of commitment and loyalty and newer universal values have not been absorbed and integrated as a basis for new community formations, the psychological source of community integration comes to rest in xenophobia.

Paralleling the breakdown of tradition and the development of xenophobia is an attempt to re-create images of past traditions that will be consistent with the new hopes and aspirations to achieve the benefits of industrialization. Efforts are made to locate symbols of the past, including the archaeological past as in Mexico, Egypt, Persia, and China, which will serve to reinforce the negative identity based on hostility to industrialized areas. The cultural items that are selected as symbols are almost irrelevant except that they are consistent with industrialization and that some form of identity can be formed around them. Thus the forms of community identification and loyalty upon which psychological integration rests are themselves part of the larger historic processes of industrialization and rationalization. At the level of individual psychology, this represents the disenchantment of preindustrial populations on a worldwide scale. In this fundamental sense one can speak of the death of the spatially isolated community and its distinctive cultural, organizational, ritual, and ceremonial forms.

The disenchantment of preindustrial populations with their own traditions and institutions, however, has been replaced by a hope for a share in the material benefits to be derived from industrialization. Leaders of all but a few countries have committed themselves to the industrialization of their economies. It is expected that successful industrialization will make it possible for these countries eventually to emulate the life- and consumption-styles of countries whose industrialization is already advanced. Thus, hope for the future combines with xenophobia and together they act as substitutes for the older traditions and community structures of preindustrial society.

Hope for the future is based on an image of life in advanced industrial countries, particularly the United States (less so in Russia), which serves the world as a model of the good life. Seen from a distance, however, this image excludes the negative features of industrial civilization that are now becoming apparent to those groups and classes within the metropolis who are the beneficiaries of some of the successes of industrialization, i.e., the middle and the upper middle classes, privileged youth, grandchildren of immigrants and slaves, some academic intellectuals and free intelligentsia. Environmental pollution, chemical threats to life-support systems, gargantuan bureaucratization, mass culture, and relentlessly progressive specialization of labor have violated for them the utopian expectations originally inherent in industrialization. Visions of the classless society, of equality, and of fulfillment of the individual's inherent creativity have been delayed indefinitely at best and sidetracked permanently at worst. Disenchantment with industrial civilization by some groups is similar to the disenchantment of primitives with their traditional values and institutions. Thus the admiration of industrialization by those who pin their hope for salvation upon it is paralleled by a disenchantment with industrialization by some of those who have already received its benefits.

Some of those who are already disillusioned with industrial civilization have begun to place their hope on a return to simpler forms of industry and community life in the form of subsistence agriculture, hand-crafted production, communal living, other-worldly asceticism, and a rejection of that preeminent symbol of industrial civilization, the city. They admire those same life-styles and forms of organization that the preindustrial world is abandoning as part of an effort to achieve industrialization. It is too early to say how deep the reaction against industrial civilization will penetrate the industrialized metropolis, but even at its present rate such a reaction is sustained by a utopian image of preindustrial life. It is one of the ironies of the times that the industrializing world sustains itself partially by its own myth of a utopic industrial future while the metropolis sustains itself partially by the myth of a return to a preindustrial past. Thus, the two worlds are psychologically integrated by idealizing the myth that the other is superior. In this sense one may speak of a dialectical worldwide community whose central characteristic is that all its members are joined to each other by their reaction either positive or negative to deepening penetration of industrial civilization.

It is apparent that as industrial civilization penetrates more deeply within the highly industrialized countries of the world, the older rural-urban, sacred-secular, traditional-rational-legal images lose their capacity to reflect reality. It is also apparent, however, that industrial civilization continues to live off older cultural forms and institutional traditions no matter how much these forms and traditions have been modified to meet the exigencies and requirements of modern industrial civilization. One result of this latter process is that the older theories of community continue to be used as a model, even though they fail to embrace such dominant tendencies as the deeper intensification of computerization, bureaucratization, capitalization, and internationalization of the world's labor force. Another result is that the theory itself takes on the quality of an ideology that is used to reject in whole or in part the industrial civilization that it was originally designed to comprehend. Hence, ideologies built on primitivism, ruralism, small townism, peasant culture, and preindustrial or nonwestern life-styles become romantic and (where such ideologies are practiced) heroic defenses against the drift of world civilization. The professors of such faiths based on a commitment to ancient culture join those who continue to embrace the structures of belief of the world's classical and not so classical religions. Industrial civilization appears to be able to absorb and tolerate all such ideologies and faiths not only because they constitute no threat to it, but, equally important, because they supply a basis for community identifications and loyalties that industrial civilization fails to supply. Thus the attackers, rejectors, critics, and defenders of industrial civilization supply for their own group the ideologies and belief systems that act as a substitute for a lost past. In this sense, the primitive and preindustrial community structure characterized by lack of individuality and an integrated pattern of values is re-created in the midst of modern industrial civilization.

This "solution" to the problem of community in advanced industrial civilization, however, is not available to everyone. To the extent that the individual is unable to identify with such ideologies, recourse may be had to identifications with an organization, bureau, occupational group, professional association, residential community, or "big brother." Failing the possibility of such identifications the individual may seek other forms of "community" affiliation. At this point recourse may be had to categories of association, which, though first examined by an earlier generation of anthropologists who still had the opportunity to study primitive society at first hand, now begin to appear to be applicable to the study of community formations in industrial society. Our reference here is to the increasing categorization of individuals into age grades (infants, adolescents, youth, middle-aged, aged, octogenarian, etc.), sex groups (male, female, lesbian, homosexual, heterosexual, transsexual), or by employment status (student, graduate student, unemployed, employed, recipient of unemployment compensation, retired), warrior status (recruit, draft-dodger, conscientious objector, veteran, disabled veteran, dishonored veteran), health status (paraplegic, disabled, hemophiliac, arthritic, cardiac, diabetic, epileptic, mentally ill), descent status (Jewishness, blackness, Italianness, Polishness, Irishness, Indianness), and so forth. As bureaucratic organization becomes larger and grander in scope, its capacity to organize entire populations rationally by specific functions and age, sex, or other status categories results in the uniform treatment of the individuals who fall in the defined category. The prior existence of the category may then become a basis for the formation of a community based on the social characterisitic so defined. Modern bureaucracy has the capacity to organize such populations on a national scale and thus displaces by its methods of categorizations the older traditional forms of community organization based on place of residence or locality.[4]

Spatiality and isolation, the hallmarks of traditional communities and cultures, have been overcome as limiting conditions for the formation of communities. Industrial civilization has made possible the concentration of vast numbers of people in metropolitan, urban, and suburban regions. Moreover, these populations are relatively unrestricted in opportunities for movement from place to place and, hence, escape the necessity of forming their associations and communities from among those who are their immediate neighbors. Density of population and spatial mobility supply the opportunity for the individual to select and choose from a vast number of possibilities those others one wishes to make part of one's community or communities. By the choices, commitments, interests, preferences, and tastes that are expressed, the individual creates his or her own communities. Thus, one may participate in communities based on special interests in religion, sports, games, hobbies, travel, music, physical fitness, or antique collecting.

Other communities may be based on occupational or professional activities, which, because they are common to all those in a given occupation or profession, supply the common denominator requisite for the formation of a community. Sociologists like Erving Goffman have noted the existence of total institutional communities (prisons, mental institutions, hospitals, or schools) that bring together under administrative management all those who have been similarly categorized in relation to a specific social or cultural condition.

At another level, transitory or even permanent communities may be formed on the basis of a common interest in opposing the very trends and tendencies of industrial civilization that are destroying older traditional community structures. Such communities may be formed on the basis of opposition to the development of nuclear power plants, urban renewal projects, public works projects like dams or highways, and utilization of animals for medical experimentation. Over time, these newer forms of community may develop social, ritual, and ceremonial forms that supply for participating members the same social and psychological functions that were supplied by the spatially isolated traditional community.

It is one of the ironies of advanced industrial civilization that ethnic communities have begun to be revived in many metropolitan societies where descendants of these earlier ethnic communities may be three or more generations removed from the original community. However, this rediscovery of ethnicity is now associated with populations that no longer live within spatially bounded areas. Like the Jews, these ethnic communities can be transnational in the spread of those who identify as members, thus creating at a new and higher level forms of community heretofore more closely associated with primitive and preindustrial forms.

It is not yet apparent to what extent the community structures emerging in industrial civilization can be described by the social categories developed by anthropologists to describe primitive society. It is clear, however, that the similarities in the usefulness of the descriptive categories to describe both primitive society and the community structures of industrial civilization will not be paralleled by a similarity in the psychological sense of community experienced by the respective participants of these societies.

In recent years some anthropologists have revived an interest in studying the applicability of Marx and Marxism to an understanding of a primitive society. Perhaps we may account for this revival by noting the characteristics of Marxism and how these characteristics contain within them an inherent appeal to modern anthropology. Marx and Marxism face in the direction of both the future and the past. On the one hand, the works of Marx speak to a Rousseauean view of the world, which is both precapitalist and even pre-Occidental in its image of the possibilities for a utopic world. At the same time, Marx's critique of capitalism and its civilization has supplied the critical perspective and framework for those who reject the civilization of which they are a part. Marxism, itself, thus is a dissident product of capitalism's own development and allows anthropology to speak in a language and vocabulary that is comprehensible to those who both reject and accept but do not choose to understand the civilization of which they are a part.

NOTES

1. I wish to thank Stanford Lyman, Mike Hughey, Art Gallaher and Harland Padfield for their helpful comments on earlier drafts of this paper and Joseph Bensman, with whom I have worked on other projects that helped to shape the ideas presented in this paper.

2. See Bensman and Vidich (1975) for a further discussion of this theme.

3. Another group that has had to rely in part on the protection of civilizations that would destroy them are the Jews. Perhaps, their long history of near genocide and survival, ghettoization and new statehood (Israel) among enemies provides a strategic research project. Anthropologists have not studied very much the survival capacities of the Jews. Perhaps this is because the Jews have historically been a predominantly urban population and anthropologists have heretofore largely relied on a conception of community that largely excludes urban groups from investigation.

4. For a further discussion and analysis of both the problem of community structure in industrial society and emergent forms of communities in this society, see Vidich and Bensman (1968, 1975).

6

Social and Demographic Processes of Declining Nonmetropolitan Communities in the Middle West

WAYNE ROHRER

Department of Sociology, Anthropology, and Social Work
Kansas State University

DIANE QUANTIC

Department of English
Wichita State University

In their efforts to discover why communities change, social scientists have identified population composition, private and public investment, transportation, war, and natural resources as important forces. Identification of several reasons for social change contrasts with sociological research on communities, which has concentrated on studying growth. Studies of organization in growing and declining communities are used in this paper to make available maximum information to those people who want to deal with decline where they live.

This chapter is based on the novelistic and sociological literature on middlewestern communities.[1] Two general processes are revealed in these bodies of literature: millions of people moved in or out of midwestern communities during the nineteenth and twentieth centuries, and interests or purposes of some residents conflicted with those of

133

fellow residents. On the other hand, each body of literature included contradictions: farming was done in a slough of despond or in a fertile garden; towns were socially stifling occupational traps or were places where contented people prospered; cities offered dehumanizing environments or unbridled opportunities. Fiction and sociology are similar in these aspects.

The processes of population movement and conflict influence today's communities but in different ways from the past. Migrants moved to the region during one century, but moving from the region has become popular in the last twenty years. In fact, declining communities are often described in terms of the number of people who have moved away. Furthermore, one reason given for community development is to provide jobs to keep youths at home. Much of yesterday's conflict concerned nationality differences. That cleavage has been replaced by one between races in practically every place with a population of more than five thousand in the United States. The processes of migration and conflict result in change, influence the ways residents organize their communities, and provide reasons for community development and organization.

DEMOGRAPHIC AND SOCIAL ASPECTS OF CHANGING NONMETROPOLITAN COMMUNITIES

Intercensal population changes for three types of midwestern communities included in Table 6.1 indicate that the rural areas absorbed most of the increases of population until 1880, that the 41 larger cities increased most rapidly in the next half century, and that the suburban or nonmetropolitan cities have grown most since 1930. These data suggest a succession of general reasons for population migration: first, to acquire land; second, to obtain urban jobs; and, finally, to find suitable residences. In the last instance, a social instead of economic reason for moving is observed. Since 1900, the region's rural population actually decreased in half of the periods. Declining farm neighborhoods and villages have been part of the midland scene for several decades.

Other demographic trends indicate massive population changes in the twentieth century: more than 60 percent of the population was rural in 1900, more than 70 percent was urban in 1970; 26 million

TABLE 6.1
INTERCENSAL CHANGES OF POPULATION FOR TYPES OF
MIDDLE WESTERN COMMUNITIES FROM 1800 TO 1970
(numbers rounded to closest thousand; 000 omitted)

Intercensal Period	Middle West Total	Larger Cities: 100,000 or more residents in 1970		Other Cities: suburbs, nonmetropolitan urban places		Rural Population: small towns, villages, farm population	
1960–70	4953	141 or	2.8%	4859 or	98.1%	−47 or	−0.9%
1950–60	7158	625	8.7	6365	88.9	168	2.3
1940–50	4318	1358	31.4	3696	85.6	−736	−17.0
1930–40	1549	213	13.8	873	56.4	463	29.9
1920–30	4574	2639	57.7	1936	42.3	−1	−0.0
1910–20	4131	2598	62.9	1691	40.9	−157	−3.8
1900–10	3556	1922	54.0	1399	39.3	233	6.6
1890–1900	3923	1446	36.9	1302	33.2	1176	30.0
1880–90	5046	1879	37.2	1341	26.6	1826	36.2
1870–80	4383	716	16.3	780	17.8	2887	65.9
1860–70	3884	727	18.7	712	18.3	2446	63.0
1850–60	3693	400	10.8	364	9.9	2929	79.3
1840–50	2052	243	11.8	126	6.1	1683	82.0
1830–40	1742	62	3.6	26	1.4	1654	95.0
1820–30	751	27	3.6	2	0.3	722	96.1
1810–20	567	10	1.8	0	0.0	557	98.2
1800–10	241	3	1.2	0	0.0	238	98.8

Source: Table 3 of each state's 1960 census of population report, entitled *Number of Inhabitants*, was the source of data for 1900–1960. Data for earlier and later censuses were obtained from counterpart tables in published U.S. censuses.

persons lived in the Midwest in 1900, nearly 57 million in 1970; the Midwest's population slightly more than doubled, while the population of the remaining states of the nation nearly trebled during this century; finally, the region that received millions of migrants during the nineteenth and early twentieth centuries has been more recently typified by an out-migrant or stable population. Among the trends, we emphasize two: the evolution of urban areas as residence places for most Midwesterners, and the turning around of migratory streams.

What happened as millions of Midlanders moved from nonmetropolitan communities during the late nineteenth century and most of the twentieth century? The figures in Table 6.1 indicate that the rural population absorbed most Midwesterners, but at a decreasing rate for ninety years. That era was followed by almost as long a time period in which rural population increased, decreased, or stability occurred.

Demographic change at the regional level gives general information; for specific details one must consider community studies. Galpin (1915) wondered about the "social anatomy" of farming districts that had had declining population. He found village and small town life in Walworth County, Wisconsin, to be viable because their concentrated populations were bases for social activities and organizations. But physically isolated farm families were socially handicapped. Furthermore, commercial relationships that existed between farmers and villagers did not bind the separated populations into a social whole. Indeed, farmers used some village services but did not directly pay for them through taxes. Mutual resentment resulted from the *undemocratic* (Galpin's term) circumstance in which providers and users of services did not coincide.

He proposed that new governmental and organizational patterns should be developed to include farmers and villagers in one community. Galpin had noted that a farmer belonged to a neighborhood, state, and nation but was "a man without a comprehensive community" (Galpin 1915:22). Constructing a community of villagers and neighboring farmers would further democracy, empower farmers as townspeople had been empowered, and involve farmers in helping to pay for benefits they received.

Generally speaking, Galpin considered independence and individualism vices of farm life. The farming occupation was enough of a struggle without adding the burden that nonfarm residents enjoyed many social resources farmers did not. Social development of populated centers left farmers independently marooned, but dependent on villages. That needed a remedy, according to Galpin. Had his idea of a comprehensive community been implemented in public policy, perhaps community development would have kept pace with economic development. Instead, economically developing towns and cities drained people from farms, which caused farming areas to become even more distressed. Depopulation represented more than mere decline; it involved comparative disadvantage. Galpin described the evolving disjunction or contradiction between economic and social change.

Demographic researchers studying the 1920s and 1930s accepted rural out-migration as socially given and then concentrated on describing the larger consequences of these moving populations. A study by Gist, Pihlblad, and Gregory (1941) correlating scholastic records of the graduates (mostly 1923–27) from 97 rural Missouri high schools with their later places of residence was repeated by Pihlblad and Gregory (1954) when they studied 1939–41 graduates of 116 Missouri schools.

In the first study, those with the highest scholastic records had moved to large cities by 1938 and those with lowest records lived on farms. And, the more scholarly a graduate was, the farther he or she lived from the native place. Gist, Pihlblad, and Gregory indicated migration was more typical than stability because two-thirds of the graduates lived in a county different from their high school's location.

Pihlblad and Gregory's study located the 1951–52 residences of the 1939–41 rural graduates, and their conclusions were similar to those of the first study: students scoring highest lived in urban places, those scoring lowest were rural residents; farthest movers had highest IQs; and three-fifths of the graduates lived in a county other than the one where their high school was located. The authors suggested that the more intelligent rural natives search for opportunities beyond those offered in their home areas. They pointed out the obvious urban-rural interdependence; for example, Pihlblad and Gregory indicated that metropolitan residents should be interested in better rural education because so many city dwellers moved from rural areas.

Conclusions from Gist and Clark's (1938) study of 2,544 rural students attending 40 small high schools in Kansas in 1922–23 were similar to those from the Missouri studies. By 1935, 70 percent of the Kansas students lived away from their native place. The drastic rates and selective quality of out-migration specified by authors of these three studies indicate that midwestern rural places retained the least talented native-born. The authors were concerned with the quality of adults remaining in rural areas and not with declining numbers.

Other demographers also studied the qualitative aspects of rural communities. Zimmerman and Smith (1930) found that the most and least educated of the farm population had moved to cities from two small areas of Minnesota and North Dakota that they studied. Because farm areas retained those of average education, migration did not deplete the "native ability of agriculturists, as a class" (Zimmerman and Smith 1930:45). They argued that farming required medium skills compared with urban occupations. Ironically, Zimmerman and Smith's defense of farmers was compatible with the generally negative descriptions of rural communities by Gist, Pihlblad, Gregory, and Clark.

These studies of population change in the 1920s and 1930s portrayed the residual community left behind as industrialization and urbanization proceeded. Even Zimmerman and Smith's apology had the hollow ring that half a loaf is better than none. Three more demographic

137

studies will help us to explore organizational and occupational details of rural life and to understand the interdependence developing between rural residents and the world outside.

Bell (1934) described "Shellstone," Iowa, a small, declining, farm-related town in ways recalling Galpin's descriptions. Out-migration eroded Shellstone just as other farming districts and small towns had been socially depleted. Further, Bell described small town residents as believing that cities had attracted their more talented peers. For example, their colleagues who had moved to cities had more eminent reputations to Shellstoners than remaining residents. Such views simultaneously indicated an urban zenith and a rural nadir of midwestern life.

Perhaps it was practical and realistic to assess one's small hometown that way. Shellstoners described local occupational and organizational opportunities as comparatively unattractive. Longtime residents said occupational success required moving away. The economic unattractiveness was disputed, however, when outsiders moved in to manage a railroad station or chain store. Shellstoners explained that managers moving in resulted from the ability of powerful outside financial interests to purchase success. Either view supported the belief that indigenous resources were limited.

Such middlewestern towns had high social costs for their inhabitants. Those who had resigned from competing with the city acknowledged that their locale was comparatively lacklustre, and accepted their lot as a social residue, left over from the excitement, growth, and change elsewhere. Shellstoners were neither optimistic nor hopeful regarding their hometown. Those economically or financially derived assessments caused them to diminish their community socially. Economic growth elsewhere resulted in a shrinking local environment.

One way Shellstoners maintained social self-respect was to deny outsiders who had moved to town access to local organizations.[2] Perhaps industrialization, urbanization, centralization, and population movement orchestrated such awesome forces that only small social games were left for rural dwellers to maintain a semblance of local control. The developing urban or nationally based mass media daily reminded rural Midwesterners of their limited lives. Bell described Shellstoners as being convinced that decline was more likely than economic or social development. A siege mentality represented by closed organizations appeared to be a trade-off mounted to oppose

138

expected economic decline or stagnation. It seems a small social game was preferable to no game at all.

Roberts (1942) concluded his study of 42 Great Plains counties of Kansas by noting that the vagaries of weather or farm prices resulted in drastic population changes. A few peak and valley annual populations he reported are indicative (Roberts 1942:42): 234,231 (1887); 140,959 (1897); 221,272 (1914); 263,053 (1917); 292,169 (1933); 255,424 (1940). People moved in when good moisture or high grain prices prevailed and away when there were dry years or low prices. Roberts noted that more of the larger population of the 1930s remained in spite of drought and depression than had remained in the 1890s. Perhaps there appeared to be fewer alternative opportunities in the 1930s than earlier. High-risk agriculture—like extractive industries—correlated with fluctuating populations.

Edwards (1939) studied population movement and economic changes of Haskell County, Kansas, (one of those Roberts studied) and found that since white settlement began in the 1870s movers-out were the rule in hard times, but when times were good—with high prices, good weather, or both—some people moved in and others moved out. He described moving population more specifically than did Roberts. Then Edwards compared populations before and after the droughts of the 1890s and 1930s. He concluded that federal programs to buy and store crops, to pay farmers to conserve soil, and to lend money had kept more people in Haskell County during the drought of the 1930s. Reducing agricultural risks reduced population out-movement. Subsidies stabilized social circumstances even though economic difficulty occurred.

Haskell County farmers received assistance from the outside. Their acceptance of governmental subsidies sharply contrasted with Bell's description of the way Shellstoners regarded the outside. Edwards attributed neither seductive attractiveness nor powerful exploitiveness to the outside world. The outside world could benefit rural areas. The contrasting accounts by Bell and Edwards indicate that Midwesterners' attitudes toward outside forces had undergone a change of important dimensions.

Much sociological research published as late as the 1950s repeated Galpin's descriptions of rural living; however, other research indicated a new interest in describing satisfactions to be obtained from rural living. Apparently, finding and describing rural advantages would allow nonmetropolitan community development even if population declined.

139

Among these studies is one by Jesser (1967). He asked all clergy, dentists, lawyers, physicians, and teachers living and working in three rural Michigan counties how satisfying their residence places were. All professionals found larger towns in these counties more satisfying than smaller places. Self-employed professionals had moved less often than clergy or teachers and were satisfied with their life in the larger towns. Some clergy and teachers lived and worked in smaller towns, but many had moved to work in larger places. Though some clergymen had obtained satisfying situations after moving, few teachers had satisfactory situations in spite of having moved. Jesser described self-employed professional persons as less migrant and more satisfied with their communities than salaried professionals.

The millions of Middle Westerners who moved from centers like Shellstone, or from Walworth County farm neighborhoods, populated cities but depleted the places they left. These migration flows point dramatically to the interdependence of rural areas and urban places. But does one area have to suffer because another prospers? Because research on changing communities includes more than population studies, we can go further than just answer that question in the remaining pages.

Changing Nonmetropolitan Communities

Sociological research on changing midwestern communities published from 1930 to 1970 identifies and illuminates social processes more profound than mere motion and conflict. This section surveys some studies of changing communities—instances of gradual change, short-run economic change accompanied by social stability, and, for comparison and contrast, changing metropolitan communities. These changes are much more specific than tabulated data that describe a regional population. For example, Landis (1935) studied three iron range communities in Minnesota from their original settlement by whites in the nineteenth century to the 1930s. With the discovery of iron-ore deposits, individuals moved in to develop that resource privately. Boom town populations were dominated by men involved directly or indirectly in mining ore; everyone succeeded or failed according to iron-ore yields and prices. Landis suggested that cohesive communities resulted because everyone faced the same compelling risks.

The frontier towns evolved by adding businessmen, professionals, women, and children. The population additions tamed frontier life so that gambling, prostitution, and saloons were no longer openly tolerated. Then steel-manufacturing companies purchased ore lands from small holders, and that change of property ownership had social consequences. When a few outside corporations owned the ranges, employees felt free to strike, and local government commenced court actions against the steel companies. Now the cohesive communities contested absentee corporate owners.

Private-enterprise mining was the economic basis of these iron-range towns both earlier and later, but when ownership of iron ranges changed from local individuals to outside companies, residents used local organizations differently. In Landis's account, change of ownership of resources caused social change in the communities.

In another study of a community faced with outside influence, Martindale and Hanson (1969) noted in their study of Benson, Minnesota, that small towns that had been trade and social centers in the last century were losing ground in the twentieth century to outside metropolises, industries, or governments. Those who had founded the town and those who had broken the sod to farm had advocated self-sufficiency occasionally tempered with charity when individual activity was insufficient. The drought and depression of the 1930s shook their faith in self-sufficiency. The authors stated that more than one-half the county's families received assistance some time during the 1930s. Nevertheless, Benson's economy, religion, education, and public services in the 1960s were all focal points for conflict between residents who wanted self-sufficiency and those whose careers were shaped by outside interests.

Martindale and Hanson felt that self-sufficiency had been undermined by dependence on enterprises outside Benson. Schools, churches, retail stores, banks, factories, and the hospital and retirement center mixed local control with outside control. How that mixture influenced preferences of leaders of Benson was one concern of these authors.

They used Benson's high school to illustrate conflicting expectations and purposes. Locally born leaders complained because teachers failed to emphasize Benson's employment opportunities and its occupational needs to students. Also, these residents thought that their school was subsidizing the world outside because most graduates went to college or urban jobs. Many teachers—like managers of outside-controlled

141

agencies—were transients: they taught in Benson only until they could move to a larger system. The old-style leaders were discontented with the education these transients provided, perhaps because dependence on outsiders was the heart of their discontent. For example, standards for employing and accrediting teachers, for curricula and educational content, set by outside agencies, did not consider Benson's interests so much as they implemented the outside interests.

Old-style and new-style leaders of Benson disagreed on community, economic, and governmental issues. Those disagreements were apparent to these sociologists. Martindale and Hanson believed that power and influence were shifting to leaders connected to the outside who were changing the town from the sociable place it had been to a commercial center like a metropolis. It seems the authors preferred the way Benson had been.

The studies by Martindale and Hanson and by Landis each describe communities where economic change led to new social arrangements. The studies differed, however, in important ways. In the iron-range communities, opposition was unified; in Benson it was causing fragmentation since the elite was being displaced.

Two more researches in Plainville, by West (1945) and Gallaher (1961), concern outside influence and provide evidence of long-run and short-run social change. West found that although Plainvillers were involved in the 1940s money economy, they preferred the last century's subsistence economy. Family obligations and neighborly relations changed with the introduction of social security, farm machinery, and automobiles. New ways made it less necessary for families to care for old, infirm members, or for farmers to exchange labor at peak seasons, or to neighbor with near neighbors. New programs and technologies had social costs.[3] Residents disliked the bearers of new technology—the county agent, the state and federal officials, who worked in Woodland County—because their recommendations and their agencies' standards discredited local ways. In that respect, Plainvillers were similar to the old-style Bensonites. West described residents of the community as wrenched and controlled by outside forces and as struggling with competing or conflicting rural and urban ways. He predicted Plainvillers would flounder until the ways of life in small towns and the nation became better coordinated.

West reviewed the origin and development of a local culture; Gallaher's restudy concerned Plainville 15 years later. He agreed with

West that ambitious persons wanting social mobility had to leave Plainville and that education was ineffective and irrelevant to local purposes—just as in Benson. However, schooling was more highly regarded than it had been earlier. West had noted that technology could change Plainville in the future: Gallaher described television, home appliances, and improved farm machines that had changed the quality of life in less than one generation. Among other influences, governmental programs, new highways, and migration and mobility generated by World War II had brought elements of the larger society to that midwestern community. A massive change had occurred. While West's Plainvillers resented their dependence on the outside, Gallaher's Plainvillers acknowledged their dependence and anticipated more modern goods and services from the outside. From Gallaher's description, West's prediction that the small community must become better coordinated with the larger society had occurred.

A community's relationship to the larger society undoubtedly varies with era, with the social institution(s) involved (whether the outside interest is a private or public enterprise), and with the community's internal organization. These four studies indicate that residents who want independence from outside influences behave differently from those who assume a dependent relationship with outside forces.

Research in the Lake States cutover area by Kercher (1941) and by Mason (1940) also involves independence/dependence, but these authors proposed contrary policies for comparable rural populations living under difficult conditions.

Kercher studied consumer cooperatives in Finnish communities to discover what responses a socially isolated nationality group had taken when they experienced unemployment, underemployment, social discrimination, and monopolistic marketing practices. The Finns used ties of language, religion, a socialist political heritage, and their working-class origin to organize cooperatives that gave them some control over their lives. When the Finnish people assumed control by organizing consumer cooperatives, their action reduced the power local retailers, produce buyers, or employers exercised over them. In addition, Finns, who were the last immigrants to arrive in the mining and lumbering areas, were empowered by their cooperatives to confront social circumstances that had appeared to be leading to their cultural extinction. Kercher proposed that Finnish farm and small town residents were able to cooperate because their rural communities allowed face-to-face interaction and planning that resulted in effective organizations. Most important, their cooperatives assured their social and cultural survival.

In contrast, Mason described Koochiching County, Minnesota, a boom area where white settlers moved in to "mine" timber, after which the fewer remaining residents cleared and drained land to do marginal farming. In the 1930s, dispersed residents lived on frequently impassable roads and so far from neighbors, markets, schools, and health services that attending school, shopping, selling produce, or even visiting neighbors was not easy. Mason proposed that high private and public costs of living in thinly populated areas would be reduced if the government relocated households in central places. He regarded concentrating populations to be "imperative" (Mason 1940:221) if residents in cutover areas were to have modern life-styles.

Both of these authors considered new organization necessary, and their proposals both dealt with dependence: Kercher suggested that indigenous action fostered independence as it reduced dependence; Mason suggested that moving dispersed residents to concentrated centers reduced dependence. The Koochiching Countians' ability to organize independently was a mere potentiality, however, whereas the Finns' independence was actual. Stating the difference otherwise, the Finns had already created organizations, but Mason's Minnesotans would have to create a social fabric. In spite of these differences, both authors indicated that economic decline requires social action.

The form of this action constitutes another basic difference in these proposals. Mason used a variant of a conventionally prescribed popular remedy—centralization or consolidation—to improve quality of life in rural communities. His proposal varied somewhat from the usual remedy, bussing students to schools or driving farther for services. Rather, Mason would bring people and services closer by permanently moving the people to the services.

The rationale for consolidating public facilities in fewer centers with larger populations is fairly common. Only mobile libraries and tuberculosis screening programs represent widely used exceptions of bringing services to rural people. Consolidating public services (or, indeed, consolidating church congregations as an illustration from the private sector) is ordinarily legitimized because it reduces financial costs. Reducing financial costs is a good idea. There is an attendant danger, however: only one kind of benefit analysis overlooks costs involved in destroying social networks. A moratorium on consolidating public services should hold until social costs of centralization have been assessed and are compared with their financial benefits.

Kercher's solution is more unconventional, but it offers an alternative to people moving. The Finns instigated their cooperatives when actual or potential decline threatened. He suggests that indigenous organizations can deal successfully with declining opportunities. Apparently, the Finns appropriated control over decision making and policy formulating that had been held by others. Though Mason and Kercher agreed that new organization was needed, they disagreed on who was to construct or control the new arrangement.

Control of Seneca, Illinois, a town whose long-term decline was arrested when a shipyard to build landing ships was located there during World War II, was studied by Havighurst and Morgan (1951). Changing transportation demands caused Seneca's booms and declines: its location on a canal gave it early prosperity but competing rail transportation in the 1890s reduced its locational advantage. Then, paved highways built in the 1920s drained farm trade from Seneca to several nearby larger towns or cities. Still later, its location on a canal connected to the Mississippi River was a reason for Seneca's being chosen as the wartime site for a shipyard.

The boom brought hundreds of daily commuters and 10,000 new residents to work in Seneca alongside the 1,200 people who lived there in 1940. New businesses opened in town and enlarged or renovated older establishments served more customers. Havighurst and Morgan found that retailers who had been Senecans before the war looked forward to the shipyard's closing because then they would again enjoy business as usual. Sudden economic growth and drastic in-migration in the 1940s did not change Seneca socially. The town's establishment, who remained in charge after the war boom, prevented general social development.

Retailers interested in business as usual successfully opposed any new or expanded public works proposed by company or federal officials if these projects required increased local taxes. Federal funds paid for an addition to the school, an enlarged sewage system, public housing, recreational programs, and for salaries of teachers, recreational workers, and other professionals needed by the swollen population. The authors noted that although Seneca's retailers opposed tax increases, they soon learned how to get federal money as a result of the war boom. It seems

145

that economic growth rates and returns realized by businesses far exceeded increased private investments made by retailers. Indeed, private investments appreciated because of public investment.

According to Havighurst and Morgan, being dependent on the U.S. government did not bother Senecans. The authors, however, considered dependence to be an undesirable circumstance. Perhaps one reason why communities are often described ambiguously is because observers' viewpoints differ from those held by residents. In Seneca, economic growth did not result in social development. Local retailers maintained control of decisions and policies. Company officials and federal authorities single-mindedly interested in producing landing ships were concerned with maintaining war workers' morale but not with controlling Seneca. War workers moved in for good pay and then away when jobs ended, without ever becoming involved in Seneca's affairs.[4]

We conclude this consideration of changing communities by discussing middlewestern metropolitan communities for purposes of contrast. The apex of life in the region, from the late nineteenth century to recent times, has been its metropolitan centers. Cities attracted migrants to their commercial, financial, or industrial opportunities and increasing populations offered residents numerous and growing organizations and institutions. In large, sociologists' descriptions of rural and metropolitan life contrast sharply: out-migrating populations, homogeneous residents, economic and social stability or decline have been used to describe rural areas; in-migrating, population increase or change, variety of life-styles, and growing economies and scales of services have described metropolitan scenes. But the metropolitan way of life may have reached a watershed in the early 1970s, and new features, including declining cities, may be used in future descriptions. Nevertheless, decades of published sociological research provide very different pictures of nonmetropolitan and metropolitan social realms.

One difference between metropolitan areas and smaller communities in the Middle West can be seen by identifying the point at which the residents became aware of dependence. By the middle of this century, many nonmetropolitan people had realized that their power to control their destinies had lessened. Imposing consolidated schools on farm families was the first clear evidence of the increased power of outside agencies and the decreased autonomy of local communities. Federal programs from the 1930s to the 1970s provided further evi-

146

dence of increasing outside power and decreasing local power. What was clear early in rural areas, however, did not become clear until much later in metropolitan places. For example, the annual rural crisis experienced by wheat farmers in certain districts when there are not enough railroad cars to carry grain to terminal markets is matched in some cities when gasoline supplies dwindle in the summertime. These episodes that indicate dependence now characterize both urban and rural areas, but until the 1960s they were more common in rural areas.

Nonmetropolitan independence and self-sufficiency probably were really myths that were revealed as fairy tales after World War I. Only now, in the 1970s, do the controversies generated by the energy crisis, ecology, nuclear power, or pollution make it clear that no metropolis or geographic region is independent of others. Proposing that the United States gain national energy independence is a present-day exercise in myth making. However, it is not a myth, for example, that today essentially every resident of this country depends on truck deliveries. Perhaps a "truck fundamentalism" describes today's dependence: we all depend on a rolling machine. None of us could live for more than a few weeks if all trucks stopped moving. Independence and dependence, migration and conflict, and organizing to obtain control—all are factors in any study of the Middle West. All are considered further in the remainder of this paper.

DEVELOPMENT AND ORGANIZATION OF NONMETROPOLITAN COMMUNITIES

Much of the discussion by sociologists on changing communities concerns the role of outside forces and whether Middle Westerners assume an independent or a dependent posture regarding those forces. The authors of this paper have also considered outside influence. Our conclusion is that towns or cities and the larger, enveloping society were and are interdependent. Now we focus on internal arrangements, especially on efforts to organize in nonmetropolitan places in the region. An assumption that has been implicit is now made explicit: people organize to change social arrangements, relationships, or structures.

Community organization occurs when people seek change, whether the purpose is to form a broadly based community development corpo-

147

ration or a narrower civil rights organization. In other words, developers and protestors are alike because both propose to change present arrangements in order to improve life and work in the community. A parallel assumption is that separated individuals are subject to innumerable indignities, but that organized people survive and surmount difficulties and change environments in desirable ways. To illustrate the source of these assumptions, we analyze four studies of community organization. These studies concern indigenous or interdependent organizations that resulted in development.

An article by Hollingshead (1937) considered reasons why organizations persist. Comparing churches organized in southeast Nebraska by Old Americans and by immigrant Americans from the 1850s to the 1930s, he found about 70 percent of the congregations organized by denominations like the Baptists, Methodists, and Presbyterians had been dissolved, but that only about one-sixth of the Evangelical, Lutheran, or Roman Catholic churches had been abandoned. Hollingshead considered the reasons for these drastically different rates of forming and dissolving congregations, and attributed the discrepancy to different organizing procedures and different meanings members and officials assigned to churches. Enterprising, itinerant, individualistic, independent ministers assembled Baptist or Methodist churches among early settlers. They organized too many churches for the population. By the 1890s many churches had been dissolved. In addition, such ministers were interested in "saving . . . lonely pioneers" in a "church that was not an integrating factor in community life" (Hollingshead 1937:190). These denominations, like many farmers and some small towns located on the frontier, experienced cycles of boom and bust. They can be called religious expressions of rugged or laissez-faire individualism.

Many immigrants or migrants from the East moved to Nebraska under auspices of denominations whose officials knew where communicants had earlier settled and where farm land was available. These denominations supplied new congregations with clergy-missionaries. According to Hollingshead, the main concern of these denominations was expanding "the ecclesiastical organization rather than the saving of souls, . . . the church is the center of life . . . and an integrator of community life" (Hollingshead 1937:190). The churches of immigrants were intended to stabilize colonies of landholding farmers whose farms would pass to the next generation. The immigrants' collective approach to the frontier resulted in organizations, which in the 1930s had persisted for three or four generations. Such churches probably were *the* local organizations in the area's farm neighborhoods in 1935.

On the other hand, Old Americans casually formed and dissolved churches and casually bought and sold farms. They had approached the frontier as individuals and joined religious congregations compatible with individualism. Then, they moved easily away from farming and from rural churches. Most Old American farmers and the churches they organized were gone from the farm neighborhoods Hollingshead studied. [5]

Hollingshead's study contrasts the uses made of local and outside resources: Baptist, Methodist, and Presbyterian congregations succeeded or failed on their own resources; far more of the Evangelical, Lutheran, and Roman Catholic congregations succeeded, and probably their success was due to denominational resources from outside the community that could augment local resources. Undoubtedly, these denominations exercised control over the religious as well as the secular concerns of local congregations because they were involved in local affairs from the time of early settlement. One could argue that Old American congregations were independent, and that immigrant American congregations were, in comparison, more dependent upon their denominations.

Hollingshead's study demonstrates that affiliation between local community organizations and outside agencies does not always result in local dependency. Coordination between internal and external affairs does not have to sap the vitality of local groups. At any rate, Hollingshead did not describe immigrants or their offspring as powerless dependents although their churches had long-standing ties to denominational offices. In that regard, Hollingshead and Kercher agree—affiliated local and outside branches of religious or cooperative organizations can be mutually beneficial, and outside ties can, in such instances, strengthen local organizations.

Hollingshead pointed out that independent Yankee farmers were the first Caucasian occupants of southeast Nebraska and even their religion fortified their individualism. They broke the sod but did not establish permanent farm communities. Their individual, independent preferences led them to economic opportunity. Apparently, personal profit was the reason Old Americans moved. When they moved away—and Hollingshead discussed that movement as a general migra-

149

tion—few traces of their sojourn in southeast Nebraska remained. Independence meant freedom to move, and freedom to abandon an enterprise, whether it be a farm or a congregation.

Many permanent rural settlements were established by immigrant Americans. Germans and Czechs settled new land or bought farms vacated by Old Americans. Both economic and social reasons were involved in their decisions to settle in Nebraska. The social auspices of religious organizations enabled their frontier settlements to evolve into permanent farm neighborhoods. Interdependence accounts to some degree for their permanence.

Population movement, a characteristic of the nineteenth-century heartland, was intertwined with economic and social considerations in Hollingshead's account. Old Americans moved in and out for economic opportunities; immigrant Americans moved in and stayed for economic opportunities and for social purposes. We will explore this relationship between economic and social change or development in more detail later.

Another approach to intentional organizing was taken in a small city and its surrounding area studied by Sower, Holland, Tiedke, and Freeman (1957). They described an organization of 700 interviewers who made contact with one-half (10,000) of the families in a middlewestern county to learn about health conditions and health delivery systems at the grass roots. On the basis of this successful community self-study—successful because organizing 700 volunteers who worked long hours amounted to a Herculean accomplishment—the authors predicted that in the future, Independence Countians could easily assemble another successful and effective organization to deal with local issues. Also, the surveying organization succeeded in spite of apathy or opposition from important groups in half of the county. In addition, the interviewers continued their surveying even though three of the four salaried professionals (all were public employees) involved in starting the project left the county while the study was in process. Transient professionals had bothered some of Benson's leaders. Professionals moving through did not affect the Independence project.

The study is unique because, among the studies discussed here, self-employed businessmen were not described as the leaders of the organization, though they were active in local organizations formed to build hospitals in Independence, even while the health survey was being done. Demographically, the interviewers were better educated, more likely to be both middle-class persons and movers to the county than average residents. That last item suggests that people who had lived elsewhere thought Independence County needed improvement. Residents often use outside standards as reasons for changing the place they live. Others resist using those standards because they prefer the locale as it is. As a result of such different viewpoints, Independence County split into two camps.

The medical community, Grange, and county officials sponsored the health survey. Support from those organizations and from organizations the interviewers belonged to helped to recruit workers, publicize, and make legitimate the self-study. Sower et al. concentrated on how the organizations operated. Surveyors were organized with help from some community organizations that sponsored or supported the project, but other community organizations were cool towards the project or opposed it. Their study results in the construction of a sociological map describing social development.

Some towns seem to have a tradition of cooperation. Hoffer (1938) described Howell, Michigan, as a town whose residents had historically used indigenous, intentionally developed organizations to solve problems. A dairy cooperative organized in the 1890s had become nationally known. Since then the cooperative form served as model for several rural and town projects. Hoffer called cooperation a cultural practice of the small town. He discussed Howellites as needing no outside stimulation to develop their community. We can infer from the Sower et al. and Hoffer studies that organizations are necessary for social development. The intentionally formed organization that immigrant churches transferred to the frontier gave immigrants and their descendants a model for organizing churches, neighborhoods, and generations of families. A "descendant" of that pattern was used in Independence to do the health study, and in Howell to deal with different community issues as they surfaced during a four-decade period.

The immigrant congregations of southeastern Nebraska and Hoffer's account of cooperation seem to indicate that local organizations persist even though population moves through or, in net terms, away from communities. The historical characteristic of out-migration from rural areas cannot socially denude such communities entirely. If residents maintain organizations that represent the interests of most families, then persons who remain in out-migrant areas have available actual or potential power.

151

A journalist named Lyford (1965) studied Vandalia and Fayette County, Illinois, in the 1960s. Rising costs of farm production and low farm prices, farm-town conflict, declining small trade centers, and consolidation of schools had characterized the area since World War II. The declining hinterland of Fayette County had been overshadowed by Vandalia's industrial development since the 1940s. Factories located in the small city gave employment to more than 800 workers in 1961. Retailers in the county seat offered more services and employed more persons than ever before. Still an uneasiness prevailed.

The few self-employed Vandalians who led civic affairs worried because their town's fate was tied to farming and a few factories. They worried about the flow of youth to cities. Even though Lyford described a viable economy, many Vandalians felt that their town was teetering on the brink of decline.

Those who led the development in the 1940s continued to do so in the 1960s. But they had tired of spending energy and money to acquire plants, build a library, or retain factories whose managements threatened to leave Vandalia. They could see no younger replacements, and this increased their anxieties. While the leaders regarded these problems as their crisis and as critical issues for Vandalia, other residents viewed the elite as somewhat less than devoted, selfless, or enlightened. Critics complained that the inner circle privately decided for Vandalia. Discussion of new projects or details of development never saw daylight until the projects were accomplished facts. Perhaps citizens feared for the future of the local economy because of this social circumstance: that a small elite could decide the town's industrial fate.

Lyford concluded that Vandalia could fly apart. When private conversations decide public affairs, then local government is weak and ineffective because few private individuals do what public officials ought to do. When there is no forum to discuss plans or to authorize decisions, then critics' complaints become a muted or perhaps, finally, a strident chorus. Lyford suggests that the elite's program of economic growth was achieved at the expense of social growth. A disjunction had occurred between economic development and social development, and Vandalians were uneasy about it, perhaps without really knowing why.

These accounts of organizing or developing communities with the conclusions of demographic change and of changing communities suggest that out-migration will not decimate a community if its resi-

152

dents intentionally organize to gain control over their lives. Additional instances of intentional indigenous organization could be drawn from many sources. The epochal presidential campaign of 1968 provides illustrations; black residents of Ocean Hill-Brownsville sought community control, Students for a Democratic Society advocated participatory democracy, and George Wallace emphasized local control. Even these contradictory, antagonistic elements can be assembled into a collage of groups, all seeking indigenous, intentional action.

Such purposeful action can even change the execution of public programs. For example, Rodgers (1969) described the Amish communities of Oelwein, Iowa, who successfully resisted consolidation of their schools with other public schools in the 1960s. When national television news coverage showed Amish children fleeing from buses into cornfields, state officials rescinded the consolidation order. The Amish demonstrations against consolidation caused officials to rescind a court-supported legal order because they did not want to force citizens to acquiesce to public authorities. The Amish successfully resisted because they were organized to seek their interest even if it went against the larger public interest and opinion. Finally, public officials respected them and their interest.

In the 1970s, citizens still find their personal interest at odds with public policy. Only if patrons of small rural post offices demonstrate and protest against closing those facilities will they gain sympathetic public attention and successfully countermand financially derived decisions to close their high-cost units. The lone individual writing letters to editors or members of Congress will not keep post offices open. Similarly, if farmers want to influence federal agricultural programs or foreign agreements concerning farm products, they must organize and demonstrate for what they want as they oppose policies contrary to their own welfare. Killing livestock, dumping milk, or destroying crops are inappropriate measures to many farmers and nearly all nonfarmers. An alternative form of protest might be convoys of farm pickups on interstate highways, slowing intermetropolitan traffic, but at the same time informing travelers of farmers' preferences and interests. Such an organized demonstration would inconvenience nonfarmers. But they might learn about farming. With knowledge of the farmer-demonstrators, more nonfarmers might support farmers.

Writing letters and petitioning officials did not secure black civil rights. Rather, boycotts, demonstrations, and demonstrators ready to go to jail for their beliefs secured those rights. Today's world requires those who wish to turn their private problems into public issues to organize so as to confront the well-organized powerholders in private or public sectors. The organized powerful can ignore or disrespect the unorganized. Even small populations demonstrating in their own behalf win concessions if they are well organized. More important, the organized seem to gain both self-respect and respect from others.

DISCUSSION

This section focuses on declining communities as they are influenced by the changing national economy and on the necessity that their residents must organize to represent local interests. Before discussing these topics, we consider some demographics. In 1970, this region included 5,054 incorporated places of less than 1,000 population. The nearly two million people who lived in those nonmetropolitan places resided in centers averaging fewer than 400 persons. Possibly another two million lived in unincorporated places. Today, because these people are dispersed in many, and remote, centers, they and their interests can be ignored. We believe that these residents should organize to attract attention.

Several surveyed articles were concerned with the social correlates of a local economy. Similarly, the national economy has social aspects. For example, if the shift from economic abundance to scarcity is permanent for the United States, then there will be enormous shifts in political and social affairs. The source of that hypothesis is Potter's sketch of the historical relationships among economic, political, and social sectors of the United States (Potter 1954:111–27; 189–208). Potter proposed that economic abundance correlates with democratic politics and permissive child-rearing practices, but that scarce economies associate with autocratic politics and authoritarian child-rearing styles. His discussion of the evolving of our national character in an abundant economic context is superb. His brief discussion of economic scarcity helps us understand the 1970s. For instance, Potter regarded scarce economies as producing submissive, deferential, obedient, undemocratic citizens. Economic scarcity and social troubles coexist.

Whether or not nonmetropolitan Midwesterners are submissive and undemocratic cannot be learned from the surveyed articles. Most stud-

154

ies of school consolidation indicate that rural people submitted to closing their schools. Some instances of resisting centralization are known. Further study is needed to test Potter's conclusions.

The abundance of the United States in the nineteenth century is well known. The abundance of the Middle West was more pronounced. The millions of adults moving here to work represented abundant human resources. Farming and manufacturing were based on rich natural and energy resources, and farm and factory products had eager consumers worldwide. The Midlands epitomized abundance in an abundant nation until World War II.

On the other hand, scarcity is a quality of community life many nonmetropolitan Midwesterners have known in recent decades. Declining farm neighborhoods and villages indicated scarce or limited resources. Closing schools and retail enterprises in rural areas were early symptoms of local scarcity that contradicted general abundance. Rural communities were involved in scarce economies years before scarcity overtook large cities. In the 1970s nonmetropolitan scarcity sharply contrasted with metropolitan resources, when kinds and extent of public services available to rural and urban residents were compared. Perhaps city people can learn about living with decline from the country people who have already learned to do so.

Rural-urban interdependence correlated rural decline with urban growth. Another connection between rural areas and the outside is that the abandoned farms and villages of the past abundant days indicated attractive alternatives elsewhere. That the overall economy was thriving does not mean that each part had abundance.

Because resources are scarce, recycling instead of abandoning materials has become popular. Rural people have been recycling for many years, sometimes converting a vacant bank building into a residence, or a school house into a community center. Many villagers could only tighten their belts by staying in their homes after local businesses, churches, or schools had moved away. They could not afford to move where centralized services were offered. Residents have not abandoned villages, but private enterprises and public facilities have abandoned smaller places by withdrawing from them.

Modern living requires resources in addition to those obtainable or recyclable in most locales. Funds, goods, people, or services are transferred between communities or states. Those transfers involve interdependent sharing of costs or benefits. The New Deal began

155

large-scale transfers because the economic depression demonstrated that no place was completely self-sufficient. The Great Depression raised questions about the distribution of resources; New Deal policies changed allocations of resources by transferring funds or services.

When the resources middle western residents of nonmetropolitan places have received are compared to resources spent or exported it is concluded they have been victims of interdependence. Natives move away, leaving fewer, elderly persons to carry on community life. When population losses lead outsiders to close local facilities, then a vicious circle of decline is complete. Farmers and small town Midwesterners have known relative scarcity for half of this century. Even so, although smaller places decline, few disappear. If village and hamlet residents, whose small numbers and physical isolation have allowed them to be ignored, become involved in larger systems to aid their social development, then their interdependent situation can be transformed from negative to positive.

Residents of declining places do interact to sustain themselves socially through participating in informal groups and a few organizations. Their existing social base could be used to develop community organizations expressing local interests. If social development is to occur (few declining places offer economic development possibilities), however, villages will require outside resources from private and public institutions. Maintaining schools, post offices, and churches in declining places will keep some professionals in local areas who could assist social development. Community development will have to be based on salaried professionals, because self-employed persons are not present in most or many declining communities. This need for a source for the cadres to aid organizing is the reason for our proposal earlier that a moratorium on closing public facilities be observed.

Unless residents of declining places are organized, we run a risk that social wastelands of submissive, resigned· inhabitants will characterize the future. Outside resources are required because most residual communities do not enjoy social structures on which organizations may be built. The religious communal faith of the Amish or the social background of the Finns were resources appropriate to organizing, but few declining communities have such social structures. Rather, communities need outsiders who want to work with beleaguered people. Even scarce resources at the national level must not be used as an excuse to allow social wastelands to evolve.

156

Let us close by referring to Bell and Galpin. Bell (1934) described indigenous organizations as enormously important to Shellstoners. Galpin (1915) proposed that the government draw lines to make a political jurisdiction coincide with a trade community. It seems to us that whatever is done to improve living in declining communities will at least require local organization of residents in partnership with outside agencies. This conclusion is cogent today even though it goes back to studies published in 1934 and 1915, respectively.

NOTES

1. This essay is taken from a larger work by the authors. The study involved analyzing novels published before World War II and sociological research published since World War I on the twelve states designated as the North Central region by the U.S. Bureau of the Census. This is Contribution 47-A, Department of Sociology, Anthropology, and Social Work, Agricultural Experiment Station, Kansas State University, Manhattan, Kansas.

2. Among other studies, articles on churches by Louis Bultena (1944) and Lowry Nelson (1943) describe exclusive rural or small town congregations.

3. Midwestern research by Earl Bell, Allen Edwards, and Horace Miner deals with these same topics.

4. A comparable study by Carr and Stermer, *Willow Run*, affirms details of the Seneca case in the Detroit metropolitan area. Indeed, Willow Run, as Carr and Stermer described it, was more of a wasteland for war workers than Seneca.

5. Hollingshead (1938) described the shift of farm land ownership from predominance by Old Americans in the 1890s to predominance in the 1930s by younger generations of the German and Czech immigrants.

7

The Expendable Rural Community and the Denial of Powerlessness

HARLAND PADFIELD

Department of Anthropology
Oregon State University

I dreamed constantly of my home country, of my grandfather's farm, of Pleasant Valley. . . . I would find myself returning . . . going back again to the mint-scented pastures of Pleasant Valley or the orchards of my grandfather's farm. It was as if all the while my spirit were tugging to return there, as if I was under a compulsion. And those dreams were associated with a sensation of warmth and security and satisfaction that was almost physical.

—Louis Bromfield, *Pleasant Valley*

Perhaps the oldest cultural contradiction in the United States is embodied in two ideal images of the pilgrim/pioneer community where citizens were both private investors and communal Christians. The transformation of hoards of would-be agrarian capitalists into a regimented industrial labor force and, ultimately, consumers took place without affecting the popular American perception of reality. The compelling effects of the agrarian past exist to this day—the nostalgia for the childhood farm, the rural school, and the rural community of yesteryear as if nothing had changed and, worse still, as if the social contradictions in the rise of the rural community had not been there from the beginning. This is more than a cliché. It is a fundamental illusion of American culture: the persistent celebration of rural life in the midst of its destruction.

This chapter discusses the culture and sociology of rural communities in economic decay.[1] But before this can be meaningfully discussed, we must discuss what gives rise to communities in the first place. If the natural environment of community growth is economic exploitation, then it must be said that community decline is natural and inevitable. In other words, a community is doomed by the very forces that bring it into being.

My discussion will address two levels of reality: the political-economic structure at large, which enables economic institutions to operate the way they do, and the life circumstances and environments these institutions shape and that in turn shape the behavior and mentality of communities, families, and individuals. Broadly speaking, the political economic structure I am referring to is laissez-faire capitalism. The immediate environment is that set of social conditions created by laissez-faire capitalism that daily confronts the individual and for which local, collective solutions are developed. Thus, when we speak of an economy, we imply a society, and when we speak of an obsolescing economy, we also imply an obsolescing social system. Although our social order gives economic capital the freedom to move all over the world—even to communist countries—this freedom does not extend to workers or communities. Moreover, it can be said that an economy that mines a local resource, or one that establishes a technology with a place-specific life expectancy, thereby decrees both growth and decay for a community. Hence the term *programmed to die*.

Because our political system is geared fundamentally to protect the privileges of private capital, it is implicit that the economic base of the human habitats fostered and used by capitalists will have a fixed life expectancy. But our political institutions require an infrastructure of cultural stability. Also, one of the fundamental purposes of community culture to its inhabitants is to make the world predictable. Therefore it is implicit that the community as a habitat will have a life expectancy that is not fixed. Thus, there is a fundamental contradiction in capitalist societies, and American society especially, between the value the society places on community and the value it places on individual freedom in general and the freedom of capital in particular. Community culture and society by its very existence and reason for being cannot self-destruct. Thus, our system programs it to die on one level and to persist on the other. In more ways than one, the community is the stepchild of our society.

In exploring these themes, it is well to define more clearly the type of community I have in mind as I develop my discussion. I will be thinking about and limit my examples to small communities in a rural (not necessarily agricultural) setting—the kind of community created by laissez-faire economic practices and resultant demographic forces under frontierlike conditions. Such communities also arise under purely colonial conditions. They tend to be one-industry towns linked to the exploitation of natural, exhaustible resources or colonized labor. In historical literature they are referred to as frontier communities. More recently they have come to be referred to as boom/bust communities.

Although I will confine my discussion to the American context, examples can be mentioned all over the New World, and perhaps recently in Western Europe as well. Historically they are cattle, railroad, lumber, mining, agricultural, and plantation communities. Currently they are oil, atomic energy, and light manufacturing communities. It would be a mistake, however, to limit the significance of themes that surface somewhat dramatically under these conditions to this relatively simple set of circumstances. It is an important part of my argument that the dynamics, internal and external, involved in this pattern of experience are endemic to our society as a whole and that they underly problems we are experiencing at all levels of community life, urban as well as rural.

THE FRONTIER EXPERIENCE AND THE CULTURAL CONTRADICTIONS OF LAISSEZ-FAIRE CAPITALISM

My basic thesis, borrowed and modified from Fredrick Jackson Turner (1921), is that not only did the frontier experience have a permanent effect upon American economic values and political institutions, but the frontier community lingers throughout the West and continues to evolve in new ecological settings in much the same way as in the past. Moreover, its persistence continues to perpetuate both naiveté in American political culture regarding the direct relationships between "economic effects" and political power, and the denial of powerlessness even while its consequences are being experienced.

Although agriculture was not the only economic basis of community settlement in the U.S., historically it was the most important. The American agrarian system did not develop along peasant or feudal lines. These institutions were planted but never materialized, primarily because of the abundance of unsubjugated virgin land (Edwards

161

1940:175–76). Although escape from religious and political persecution was an important motive, it is more realistic to regard the European colonists to America as pioneer shareholders in huge land corporations (Webb 1951). Commercial, as opposed to communal, agriculture was established early in the southern colonies. Even in the New England colonies, where land allocation and town settlement were governed by communal principles, land was privately owned. Private allocation of the public domain transformed colonists into private owners, and although these primitive rural capitalists were heavily constrained by early American communal institutions and the surrounding wilderness, their small, albeit self-sufficient, enterprises contained the determinants for the changes that befell agriculture and community settlement in the 1800s.

Moreover, if the American Revolution is to be regarded as an agrarian movement, it should be regarded as an agrarian capitalist revolt against the political and economic domination of eastern colonial absentee landlords and not as a movement aimed at revolutionizing the prevailing economic institutions. The history of the American frontier is replete with the violence of the struggles between contending capitalists over control and ownership of resources. The fact that one set of contestants was composed of farmers in no way sets apart farming for profit from mining, lumbering, or manufacturing for profit. Failure to recognize the basic capitalistic nature of farming early in the history of U.S. political formation is responsible for much of the self-delusion inherent in American political culture.

In 1790 American community settlement patterns could truthfully be called agrarian. The first national census (in 1790) showed over 90 percent of the population engaged in agriculture (Goodwin and Johnstone 1940:1184). The free-land policy that prevailed throughout the westward expansion of the U.S., especially in the trans-Mississippi frontier, led to the placement of more than 32 million people on farms from coast to coast (Edwards 1940:196; Taylor 1940:1046). Opportunity, nineteenth-century style, presented itself to the mass of people, not as jobs in industry, government contracts, or advertising, but as land. So the majority of Americans became farmers, and American society entered the age of popular agriculture. In this way part of the stage was set for the elimination of marginal farmers and rural communities. This began shortly after the free-land supply was cut off—referred to as the closing of the frontier.

162

Commercialization set another part of the stage. This began soon after the opening of the Northwest Territory, where wheat, favored by new soils, became a principal cash crop. The transfer of manufacturing to industry (hence loss of "self-sufficiency") was part of this process. These factors, in combination with westward settlers' encounter with decreasing rainfall and tougher soils, stimulated mechanization. The prairies and the semiarid plains became the cradle of farm technology. The mechanical systems developed here extended the workpower of the farm family and broke the 40-acre barrier. Farms of 80 and 160 acres became common (Webb 1931:385–452). The setting for marginal farmers and decaying communities was complete. All that remained was for the dole of free public land to be cut off, for rural depopulation to reach the proportions it did in the 1920s and 1930s. The southern plantation system was modified during the post–Civil War reconstruction period, from slavery to tenancy, thereby setting the stage for another pattern of emigration and community dislocation. There was a steady decline in the percentage of the national population employed in agriculture, from 90 percent in 1790, to 31 percent in 1910, to 4.4 percent in 1974 (Banks et al 1975). In terms of absolute numbers, however, there was a constant increase until 1910, twenty years after the close of the frontier (Goodwin and Johnstone 1940:1184–93; Rohrer and Douglas 1969:108). The arid-land frontier, which did not really begin to absorb population until after 1900, undoubtedly had some holding effect on rural-to-urban migration.

Although popular agriculture and the rural community is viewed traditionally as an omnipresent institution, it was but an economic episode that waxed during the cheap- and free-land era of the 1800s. Its passing should have been expected from the start, but just the opposite prevailed. The marginal farmer was a cause célèbre for policy makers in the 1930s (Alexander 1940; Maris 1940). Policies like commodity price supports, liberal loans, land diversion, and payments in lieu of production—management of aggregate demand—were adopted. But these, like other previous policies, favored the large producers, widened the gap, and produced more *marginal* farmers.

Other frontier industries must be included with agriculture in terms of the westward impulse toward community settlement and decay. Among the most common are the cattle, railroad, and mining industries. In addition to virgin land, the constant presence of enormous stocks of natural resources combined with low population density made

163

the American frontier in essence an enormous ecological laboratory, in which the competitive economic advantages of certain institutions and cultural systems over others were decisive. Organizational forms, having the advantage, developed and were reinforced with each new stage of westward territorial acquisition (Turner 1921; Webb 1931).

The rural community was the primary socializing environment in this natural milieu. Growth ideology and individualism were continuously validated by objective personal experiences, and therefore, not surprisingly, the rural community was and still is the academy of American frontier ideology. There is irony in all this; the small rural community was extremely vulnerable to the social and economic consequences of resource exploitation and in reality was destined to become a casualty of the very forces that created it. The ultimate irony is that, in terms of its cultural function, it was cast in the role of cultural handmaiden to its own demise. I would argue that of all the values enduring from the 200-year boom known as the American frontier, the two that are the least compatible are belief in "progress" as essential to the good life and belief in the rural community as the ideal human environment. Of the many cultural contradictions creating acute stress in the national society, growth fundamentalism and rural fundamentalism are perhaps the most persistent and profound.

Therefore, when social analysts attempt to enumerate the basic tenets of growth fundamentalism, they should not ignore the role played by the small community and the community's cultural view of its own fragile economic position (see Vidich and Bensman 1968; Stein 1960).

Thus, in addition to identifying the tenets underlying frontier-extractive and natural-resource industries (resource exploitation is fundamental to the quality of life; resources are infinite; and its corollary, a given resource is expendable because another one will be found to take its place), we must identify those that evolved out of the peculiar experience and coping institutions of the small frontier community (social and economic environments are natural; community florescence and decline are inevitable, i.e., like natural resources, communities are expendable).

As these statements imply, an important impact of the frontier upon American culture has been the creation of social and economic naiveté juxtaposed with technological sophistication. Putting it another way, just as the frontier experience was instrumental in institutionalizing extreme analytical capability with respect to the natural world, it has also been instrumental in institutionalizing analytical *incapability* with respect to the social world. The role of the rural community in this cultural process is basic.

Moreover, despite the supportive role rural towns have played historically and continue to play in maintaining nineteenth-century economic values, economic insecurity is, by and large, their reward. In fact, a major portion of the social energy in a small town is devoted to the management of the social and psychological tensions created by the contradictions between their beliefs and impinging economic and political realities. Vidich and Bensman, in *Small Town in Mass Society* (1968: 225–314), provide an analysis of the mechanisms used to accommodate these tensions. They call this process the "Reconciliation of Symbolic Appearances and Institutional Realities," in which local religion, politics, and institutionalized patterns of personal and group interaction play key roles. Important psychological mechanisms are: the repression of inconvenient facts; the falsification of memory and the substitution of goals; the surrender of illusions; mutual reinforcement of public ideology; avoidance of public statements of disenchantment and the exclusion of the disenchanted; the externalization of the self (Vidich and Bensman 1968:292–314).

Although the forces threatening community integrity in Vidich and Bensman's case are the encroachments of mass urban-industrial society, as opposed to the loss of the natural- or capital-resource base in a one-industry town, the conflicts are much the same, as are the dilemmas they pose for citizen and analyst alike.

In sum, I am arguing that we should acknowledge the functional necessity of an additional element in the cultural system of a small community— coping with the threat of resource depletion and human obsolescence by intense dedication to economic growth and laissez-faire ideology. In essence, this posture constitutes a mind set against cognition of the forces impinging upon it, like the denial of death in a dying patient. This situation creates a sharp dilemma for policy science. Whereas rigid belief in the symbols of a decaying economic order impairs realistic adjustment, it has high social-psychological value, serving among other things as an important part of rural, working-class identity.

165

ANALYTICAL APPROACHES TO THE SMALL COMMUNITY

Rather than say rural, small town ideology denies the cognition of political economic realities, it is more correct to say that the beliefs that economically motivate rural, working-class people, and for that matter even poor people (see Lamb 1975:66–78), tend to focus on individual and class as opposed to societal responsibility. Political consciousness in terms of radically altering the circumstances affecting their life situations is not rewarded. Individual achievement is. Opening the cognitive door to a politicized world view brings their life strategies into question. This is not only psychologically painful, it is economically risky.

The question is what role participants' or natives' constructs of reality play in developing objectively valid propositions about reality. For analysts of exotic culture, the difficulty is to discover native propositions. For analysts of our own cultures, the difficulty is to have scientific skepticism with respect to our own culturally imbedded and politically sanctioned propositions. In other words, social scientists enjoying privileged social status are not the best people to develop coherent concepts of power and powerlessness. The natural strain toward recognition and honor in academic disciplines predisposes us to accept the national structure of economic and political power as given and to concentrate on theoretical issues of topical interest to our respective disciplines (see Merton 1973). One decade it may be assimilation, another time cultural evolution, cultural ecology, cultural cognition, human capital, input/output models, returns to education, and so on—seldom the big picture. This is left to poets, playwrights, and philosphers.

The problem is that partial phenomena, though necessary to understand broader and more complex phenomena, are almost invariably perceived as closed systems. Thus, enormous blind spots develop when closed-system theories are applied to natural-life situations. These scientific blind spots tend to be filled by social stereotypes and other concepts used to rationalize the prevailing social order, and nothing much changes. The rules of effective action simply shift from one arena to another. In fact, if anything, partial, closed-system (especially *apolitical*) explanations simply imply another set of techniques and resources, which the politically economically dominant institutions and classes can generally easily and quickly turn to their comparative advantage.

An example of closed-system analysis particularly subversive of common peoples' interests and having particular relevance to the topic of this book is what I call "descriptive symptomatology." Broadly speaking, it is the concentration of scientific interest on the characteristics of people and communities experiencing natural problem situations as opposed to the study of those groups and institutions *not* experiencing the problem situation but making up the environment of those who are. By this approach, problems are at worst defined in ways that imply that the attitudes and behavior of the inmates, patients, unemployed, or disadvantaged are responsible for their circumstances. At best, problems are defined as emanating from historical legacy, natural forces, or the "invisible guiding hand." In the area of community studies, the literature abounds with such fatuous concepts as "weakening of traditional restraints," "conjuction of differences," "location preference," "proclivity to migrate," "proliferation of alternatives," "susceptibility to new life-styles," "deferred gratification," "achievement motivation," "fatalism," and so on, ad nauseam.

At best, descriptive symptomatology simply trivializes life situations. At the worst it becomes subversive of local community and individual interests, since many symptomatological problem definitions are not trivial, particularly when researched by imaginative and disciplined scientists. The concept of IQ is perhaps the most notorious example. Sophisticated studies of "attributes of success," "indicators of employability," and "indicators of community economic viability," like IQ, quickly become screening criteria used by potential investors, creditors, and employers as well as teachers, welfare workers, and government agents. The pursuit of this kind of "useful" knowledge results in the replacement of the pursuit of academic recognition by the pursuit of recognition from bureaucratic managers of research. It capitalizes on local and national predicaments while implicitly accepting the continued rationing of sacrifice among the powerless.

To develop a truthful theory of community decay, we must think in terms of open systems. We need to develop the conceptual capacity to see such social categories as personality, institution, or community as interactive processes rather than as autonomous entities. And most important, we must examine social problems in the context of our macrosocial order.

167

ADAPTATION AND NATURAL ENVIRONMENTS: THE LIMITS OF THE SOCIAL/CULTURAL ECOLOGICAL PERSPECTIVE

Adaptation and environment are hyphenated concepts and derive from the general premise that personality, social institutions, and culture are environmentally specific. The general concept of behavioral environment (Hallowell 1955) is fundamental to more recent concepts like "cultural ecology" (Cohen 1968; Bennett 1969), "human ecology," and "social ecology" (Moos and Insel 1974).

The usefulness of the social ecological perspective to understand a community has long been recognized: namely, that a small community is an interdependent network of institutions shaping the lives of its members. I have two points to make relative to my thesis: first, applying the principles of social ecological theory and method to participants in small social assemblies (like communities, gangs, labor forces, and small businesses) perpetuates the illusion of autonomy of the unit, just as the study of a public school as an ecological unit affecting the behavior of teachers and students perpetuates the myth of the school as an autonomous social entity. Second, although methodologically the small ecological unit is more manageable than transregional and national ecological units, ecological theory carried one step further implies that the forces impacting upon the community resident are simply in part the ripples of forces impacting upon the community. Hence, the community must be seen as a component of larger ecological units. But at this level the utility of social ecological theory diminishes. This is where culture ecology enters the picture.

In anthropology, the concept of culture as an adaptive system dates well back in both American (Kroeber 1923; Wissler 1914; Steward 1955) and British (Forde 1934; Evans-Pritchard 1940) schools. More recently, it has received renewed emphasis (see Cohen 1968; Bennett 1969, in the Aldine-Atherton series Worlds of Man: Studies in Cultural Ecology, edited by Walter Goldschmidt; Bennett 1976). Most cultural ecology studies, however, including Bennett's (1969), treat their subject societies in the context of environments that are implicitly, if not explicitly, natural. Where external, manmade features are recognized, they are for all intents and purposes indistinguishable from features such as climate, topography, soils, minerals, and other natural endowments. To be sure, macrosocial environmental features, like natural features, are recognized by most cultural ecologists as important determinants of adaptive behaviors and strategies. However, the emphasis is on the equation

Culture in T_1 + Natural Environment in T_2 = Culture in T_2.

It is also recognized (Bennett 1969) that competing societies constitute important environmental components vis-à-vis one another. Within the culture-ecological framework of anthropology, however, the primary interest is upon adaptive processes of societies in a man-versus-nature setting. The primary interest is in instrumental systems such as hunting, farming, mining, lumbering, or cattle technologies, which are seen as resource manipulative, and while these technologies may adversely affect the welfare of competing groups in the same habitat, they are not seen methodologically as manipulative of the social environments of competing individuals, groups, or societies. Thus, when Bennett (1969:161–69) discusses economic adaptations of Jasper Indians to the Canadian plains milieu, it is clear that he perceives the non-Indian settlers as integral resources of the northern plains Indians' environment. Although he makes occasional references to the exploitation of Indians, Bennett's study is clearly not centrally interested in such questions as the white settlers' system of control and manipulation of Indian social environments through Canadian schools, law enforcement, and social welfare; or the impact of corporate control of the grain market on the plains farmers' economic environment.

I am not saying that the man-versus-nature focus is not legitimate or instructive. Small units are easier to comprehend, and a dominant natural resource base in a stark environment like the Northern Plains and the Great Basin reduces the variables in such a way that direct interrelationships emerge that are scientifically instructive and, in an elemental way, valid for all societies globally.

Politically and economically, however, such high levels of generality are naive. Intertwined with local adaptations are pervasive mediating political and economic institutions. Control of natural forces implies control of social forces. Just as technical control of specific natural resource systems has become a deliberately manipulative process, so has the control and manipulation of the social and economic environments, including communities, in which vested capital must operate. The struggle for the control of the institutions and public processes that regulate access to natural resources is where the action is. Only the powerless any longer stand guard on the banks of diminishing streams with six-shooter and rifle.

In addition to the bias of perceiving controlled and manipulated habitats as natural systems, there is another bias we must guard against in adaptational theory. That is the tendency to obviate hierarchal structures.

Although adaptational theory could logically lead investigators step by step to the discovery and scrutiny of the political and economic institutions dominating the environments of their communities, it is hard to see how the concept of coping, which figures prominently in adaptational definitions, would get them there. Whether one calls it instrumental or strategic, coping is implicitly passive or adjustive in orientation and internal in focus. It implies adjustment to, or, at most, the manipulation of, constraints as opposed to breaking them. It is implicitly apolitical in terms of being either vague about external power relationships or accepting of them. Coping can be anything that enables one to survive, including invalidating the experience of oppression and identifying with the oppressor.

Moreover, the coping concept of adaptation is one-sided. It implies strategies devised from a position of vulnerability and weakness, not those devised from a position of strength and power. The inmates of mental institutions cope. The caretakers administer. It is naive, if not self-serving, to say that the upper hierarchies of centralized government and monopoly capital cope. To place the private, centralized deliberations and global actions of General Motors, ITT, Tenneco, and the agricultural subsidiaries of Standard Oil in the same category as the disarrayed responses of marginal farmers, unemployed workers, and small town officials[2] is to obviate fundamental political differences. I am not arguing that social science must be an advocate but that it invariably is. I am arguing that without political consciousness, adaptational theory, just like neoclassical economic theory (Ford 1973:8–14), handily reinforces the moral authority of the existing political and economic institutions that dominate if not totally control social environments.

I close my argument with a reflection on an observation by Nisbet in *The Quest for Community* (1969:22):

It is impossible to escape the melancholy conclusion that man's belief in himself has become weakest in the very age when his control of environment is greatest. This is the irony of ironies. Not the most saturnine inhabitant of Thomas Love Peacock's *Nightmare Abbey*, not even the author of the nineteenth century dirge, *The City of Dreadful Night*, foresaw the Devil in the guise he has taken.

On deeper reflection, it would seem there is not irony but profound consistency in all this. For when man's control of his environment is greatest, man's power to manipulate man is the greatest. Indeed, the latter is prerequisite to the former. Intuitively and objectively, people can see that the average individual and the average community are still powerless to do either, while experiencing increasing control over their lives by powerful, organized entities. Confronting one's powerlessness in the midst of this situation is far more devastating than confronting one's helplessness against nature.

ADAPTATION AND CONTROLLED ENVIRONMENTS: THE POLITICAL ECONOMIC PERSPECTIVE

Political economic theory keeps adaptational theory in proper perspective. It penetrates rather than reinforces the mystique of *constraints* like land value, economies of scale, depreciation, and surplus labor constituting the social environments in which communities of low paid, underemployed workers and small entrepreneurs are forced to operate. Adaptation to decline is simply one aspect of an environment created and sustained by a system of economic privilege and political power.

In the book *Political Economics of Rural Poverty in the South,* which includes Appalachia, Arthur M. Ford (1973) examines the problem of persistent, low-income poverty and depressed communities among sectors of the southern agricultural economy. In so doing he systematically examines and critiques neoclassical economic theory in terms of its inability to account for low-wage poverty except in terms of market imperfections brought about by "human" aspects of labor. Drawing upon *political* economic theorists of the Cambridge school (Ford cites Robinson 1971; Neil 1972; Harcourt 1969, among others), he constructs an alternative explanation with principles applicable to predicaments faced by declining sectors and communities in general:

> The very operation of capitalism as a functioning system results in a pattern of wealth and income which in reality is a structured

171

system of privilege. Similarly, Rothschild [1971:7] has reminded us that people are not indifferent to the factors that affect their economic condition. Consequently it should be expected that "individuals and groups will struggle for position; that power will be used to improve one's chances in the economic game, that attempts will be made to derive power and influence from acquired economic strongholds."

The important idea here is that in viewing the factors of production as a system of privilege [as opposed to being neutral] one is also setting out a structure of economic and political power that groups can bring to bear to protect and/or improve their economic position. (Ford 1973:78)

Ford in particular attacks the "value judgments" in neoclassical economic theory whereby the constraints of technology and market conditions are regarded as given:

Ignored in such formulations is the fact that groups may use power to change their constraints and in effect alter the outcome of market operations . . . [and] that market operations *will be more significantly altered the more unevenly power is distributed.* (Ford 1973:78, italics added)

Pointing out that the *consistent* pattern of economic and political inequality in southern agriculture and, one might add, in American agriculture generally, has been due to the ability of the upper-income farmer to exercise *control* over federal farm policy, Ford generalizes to all manifestations of socioeconomic inequality:

The key to understanding a socioeconomic transformation that has differential impact on the various classes [and communities] in society lies in unevenly distributed economic and political power, in which some groups have sufficient power to protect their position while others do not. (Ford 1973:79)

Ford calls for a new paradigm, explicitly incorporating a theory of political decision making, to replace neoclassical economic theory, which is limited in its ability to explain increasing unemployment (in the midst of increasing per capita income), persistent poverty, profit inflation, and so on.

To Cambridge critics such matters as corporate power, unions, structure of industry, and politics should be included in the new paradigm. What the analysis in this study of agrarian transformation in the South points to is the *overriding necessity of beginning*

172

a new paradigm by first coming to grips with power, particularly political power. (Ford 1973:79, italics added)

In terms of the relationship of political to economic power, Ford clearly considers political power primary. Although he acknowledges the fact that Marx considered political power to be derivative of economic power, Ford, bolstered by Heilbroner (1970) and Neumann (1968), argues that Western capitalism has undergone a massive transformation since the nineteenth century, changing from a relatively disorganized, competitive economy to an organized, controlled economy. Although he considers economic and political power to be interdependent, he follows Neumann in contending that political power is evolving into a separate and independent base for the acquisition of economic power.

Returning to my central argument, power to control social environments is basic and the behavior of the inhabitants of these environments is secondary. For instance, the question of who controls agriculture, mining, or lumber in the West is more basic to community death and decay in that region than the question of "location preference" of migrants, or how the unemployed cope, or how sacrifice is rationed among the underemployed. But political economic theory takes us one step beyond the general notion of political economic linkages. It puts the emphasis on *political* relationships and activities by means of which economic control is gained. Therefore, to the question of *who* controls an economy from which a community derived, must be added the question of *how* they control it. What land, mining, and tax laws, what regulatory agencies, and what special legislation give capital the privilege to create communities, extract the wealth from them, and abandon them on the public doorstep? In what political context are the decisions of such corporations as Tenneco, Food Machinery Corporation, and Weyerhaeuser made? What say do the local communities have in these decisions?

Clearly, *local* applies to the boundaries of small communities' political power and not to the boundaries of the political ties enjoyed by the industries who dominate them. The effective environment of industry, all industry, has grown continually larger, while the effective environment of the local community, if anything, has grown smaller. Clues to the mystery of the small community's demise are not to be found locally, but in faraway places, like the central headquarters for multinational corporations, and regulatory agencies.

173

IMPACTS OF LOSS OF ECONOMY:
THE EXHAUSTED COMMUNITY

Certain social forms evolve under conditions of growth; under conditions of economic decay, other social forms evolve, as opposed to the original social forms simply disintegrating. This is the essence of the concept of impact. Resource and economic exhaustion, even in such traumatic cases as the decimation of North American bison, did not mean that every single Blackfoot, Assiniboin, Sioux, and Cree would suddenly die. Ecosystem changes, whether subtle or cataclysmic, *impact* upon habitants. New environmental conditions elicit adaptive behavior and ultimately social institutions. These in turn impact upon the social environment, forming in time relatively more stable interactive systems.

A basic distinction must be made between income decline and loss of economic or ecological *position*. A person, family, community, or society's loss of ecological position has fundamental impacts. The loss of a job in and of itself does not necessarily mean loss of ecological position for a person or family. Persistent underemployment does (see Padfield and Williams 1973). The closing of a mine, a mill, or a plantation in a one-industry town, the amalgamation into huge corporations of small farms surrounding a rural town—all mean loss of ecological position for the local businesses in that town. The destruction of a natural resource like the North American bison, the Columbia River salmon, the grasslands of East Africa, the soils of Texas and Oklahoma plains, the forests of the Northwest, constitute loss of ecological positions for entire social systems. The broader the scope and the more complex the social order resting upon the ecological base destroyed, the broader and more complex the ramifications of the loss. Depending upon the size of organizational unit involved, entire assemblies of socioeconomic institutions are invalidated by loss of ecological position. At the social-psychological level, social identities are invalidated with profound implications for the mental health of individuals and families (Komarovsky 1940; Bird 1966; Levin 1975).

In terms of social-evolutionary process, two facts must be recognized. First, the loss or extinction of social forms, like the loss of genetic forms tends to be permanent. Lack of general appreciation of this fact is another instance of a cultural myth sustained by the American frontier: namely, that social institutions will persist independently

174

of economic foundations. Putting it another way, the fact that resource-specific communities and entire social systems could reestablish themselves as the cattle, mining, and lumber frontiers moved westward (Webb 1931; Jensen 1945) provided a culturally impressive but sociologically naive object lesson. But as resources became exhausted and economies obsolete, community forms themselves began to disappear, and despite town celebrations of the frontier, they do not reappear. Second, new adaptive strategies, whether at the individual or community level, imply new institutions. And simply because these new behaviors and institutions provide the benefit of survival for the individual or population does not mean that they have functional value for the society as a whole. In fact, quite the opposite is often the case.

Impacts may be observed at various organization levels, including the individual, firm, and community. Impacts at the community level to loss of ecological position usually mean depopulation and/or radical changes in population composition. This means making a transition to another kind of ecological environment because continuous demographic shifts have cumulative economic consequences for the local environment. Trends in age composition are perhaps the most fundamental in terms of the biological continuity of the community. As Morrison cogently explains (1974), relatively small decreases in the percentage of childbearing (adults aged 24 to 44) families over time lead to diminished replacement capacity. When replacement capacity has diminished to the point that more people die than are born, then the community, demographically speaking, passes a threshold. Barring a dramatic rise in fertility or a massive influx of child-bearing families, it is in a situation of natural decline.

With respect to trends in the composition of classes or income groups, thresholds are also involved. Since a community by definition is identified with a place, it has a fixed political boundary. This boundary then sets a limit beyond which the community cannot collect revenue from individuals who have benefited from its human resource investments, but the boundary cannot stop the out-migration of its human capital. Conversely, a community's political boundary cannot stop the influx of disadvantaged people; i.e., people who need educational, health, and employment services in excess of their ability to pay. Such an influx has the tendency to drive out people with high income potential. Thus, with respect to the flow of human resources, a community may be dying *without* a net decrease in population, the outflow of resources in essence indicating a transition to a depressed community.

Trends in racial composition closely approximate trends in class composition because of the tendency to maintain economic privilege. Racial differences make it easy for advantaged groups to monitor settlement patterns affecting their economic and social interests, and immigration of racial minorities in and of itself tends to become the symbol of economic deterioration of a community.

A brief look at a timely economic analysis of community and regional decay in the context of Appalachia and the agricultural South adds additional strength to the insights of demography and sociology on this subject (see Ford 1973:59–68, 79–92). In a chapter on labor market perversity, Ford takes a hard look at the popular policy contention that migration response to regional inequality is a desirable phenomenon. The assumption has been that migration reduces poverty, raises income for migrants, and has favorable effects on the job opportunities of those who stay behind. In other words, in a free society, as labor demand fluctuates geographically, so should labor supply. People recognizing their own self-interest respond by "voting with their feet."

Ford matched the 1950–60 data on the consequences of migration in Appalachia against this popular assumption and found that rural (agricultural and mining), low-income communities lost their young (15–29) males who were the most educated. He concludes that there are three important economic consequences to this kind of migratory pattern, each of which contradicts the conventional wisdom. First the region or community experiencing the loss is accumulating a population with high economic dependency; i.e., the aged, the juvenile, and the uneducated. Second, local investment in education is lost by out-migration of its graduates. And third, the community experiences severe income constraints, reducing the community's already limited ability to take effective action on its own.

Each of the above demographic consequences has economically regressive ramifications. For instance, the national ratio of dependents per thousand workers in 1960 was 872. The regional average for Appalachia was 928 with specific counties as high as 1,113—almost half again as high as the national average. The rising age composition increases the percentage of residents on welfare and fixed incomes.

176

Skill selective out-migration depresses the income of an already disporportionately small work force. Finally, the community tax structure becomes regressive, eroding its tax base further and forcing the community into retrenchment.

In response to the question "Where must retrenching occur?" Ford concludes that it is in the public sector and that the causal chain is as follows:

1. Local government can either raise taxes to provide essential service, reduce service, and/or raise prices.
2. Given an inability to raise taxes, service reduction and/or price change are the only alternatives. However, such action results only in further reduction in utilization of the services, necessitating another round of price change and service reduction. The end result is either abolition or extreme curtailment of services offered. Other services, such as public education and health, deteriorate in quality via low salaries and general inability to obtain staff and to maintain equipment.
3. The consequences of this for a community is at first a relative deterioration of infrastructure and public sector capabilities in general. But industry does not prefer to locate in communities with inadequate systems of power, water, transportation, and education, and where the work force is primarily semi-skilled.
The retrenchment process thus becomes a cumulative process of stagnation and eventual decay. Unfortunately, death is lingering rather than instantaneous. And in the long process of decay the community turns out each year a new set of poorly educated, poorly socialized young who are unprepared to take part in modern industrialized society. (Ford 1973:64–65)

Hence, age, class, and race composition do not merely make up descriptive indicators differentiating a dying from a growing community; they are indicators of processes at work having irreversible psychological and economic consequences within their existing political frameworks. In addition to income and tax disincentives, community residents' cognition of the indicators themselves tends to increase the trend toward out-migration, thus increasing the rate of natural decline. Conversely, adaptive responses on the part of those left behind, although rational from the perspective of maintaining their institutions, may themselves contribute to the demise of the community and the worsening of the very environment or those aspects of the environment with which they are attempting to cope. For instance, this can be seen in the way public institutions, such as schools, respond. Such institutions in the process of responding rationally—i.e., cutting costs and reducing services—contribute ultimately to the death of the community. The final autopsy could well occur when the crisis-oriented human resource institutions, such as law enforcement, welfare, social security, and unemployment, become the main channel of allocation of public resources. Thus, the vital institutions of the community are forced by the macrosystem to become executors to the community's demise.

TRANSITION TO THE DEPENDENT (MARGINALIZED) COMMUNITY: AN EXCURSION INTO THE CULTURAL DYNAMICS OF CAPITALISM

The assessment of economic disability, whether of individuals, ethnic groups, or communities, becomes an extremely sensitive ideological issue for two reasons. First, it has the potential of diverting and mobilizing the social energies of the disabled from the pursuit of economic solutions to the pursuit of political solutions. Second, and perhaps more important, it confronts the economic definition of reality upon which our social order rests, precisely at the point of the greatest evidence of ideological fallacy. The potential for threat is a real one.

Returning to the central theme of this chapter, the denial of powerlessness in response to economic frustration, we cannot develop a proper understanding of this process without directly coming to grips with the issue of the cultural and social infrastructure of capitalism. I have argued in terms of the historical past that, contrary to popular belief, American culture has had a fundamental, secular economic cast to its development. If anything, this economic cast to our way of seeing the world and developing solutions for our predicaments has increased rather than diminished its dominance over our lives. This bent in our private and public thinking has led to an enormous creativity for technical and economic change, but it has also led to an enormous resistance to political change. Our recent history has been one continuous struggle to work out economic solutions to basically political problems. It is more than a tendency. It has become a national compulsion. As the consequences of political provinciality become more critical, the search for economic growth becomes more frantic. My

178

purpose is not to develop this generalization into a political scientific dissertation, but to dwell on the predicaments this compelling institution creates for the cultural imagination. It creates unique opportunities for the politically powerful, artificial puzzles for social theoreticians, and cruel dilemmas for the powerless.

The basic necessity underlying all strategies for action in this society is to convert political realities into economic realities. Even social action of militant political groups has this cast to it. The strike, the boycott, the class action lawsuit; all implicitly recognize the equation: social and political disability equals economic redress. In this way the mantle of economic legitimacy is placed upon efforts to correct political inequality. Direct political confrontation, like political ideology that fundamentally challenges the prevailing political institutions, is rejected. Cloaked—one might say subverted—by "economic" objectives, social action has moral authority.

This necessity for the laying on of economic hands presents unique opportunities for social scientists and practitioners in all disciplines. Sooner or later anthropologists, sociologists, psychologists—even political scientists—become amateur economists. And, needless to say, those community developers who are recognized and rewarded tend to be applied economists.

The basic instrumental mechanism for access to and participation in the capitalist democratic system is economic status. It is the program that activates democracy or the sharing, albeit minimally, of power. Even attorneys at law operate in the economic realm. And the courts, which are preeminently political institutions, function as arbiters of the last resort in mediating economic conflict—or more correctly, political conflicts *defined* economically. When courts are forced to deal with political conflicts that cannot be defined economically, as in the case of military justice versus civil justice or executive power versus legislative power, judges and justices quake in their chambers.

Sooner or later every individual and institution, to be effective, acknowledges this dominating cultural constraint. Therefore, ingenious strategems, both psychological and social, become an acquired skill of every American, rich and poor. The problem is that the political content of social circumstances not circumscribed by the economic interpretation—i.e., the political remainder—must be continually dealt with. In other words, political questions can be avoided when economic solutions work. To the extent that they do not, or in those social sectors and persisting circumstances where they do not work (such as in decaying cities and dying communities), the political "residue" becomes an acute ideological problem, especially for those experiencing these life situations. It becomes especially necessary, therefore, for analysts of these social circumstances to reappraise their economic definitions. Let us begin by reappraising the dying community in the context of the inconsistency between political problems and their economic solutions. The logical place to begin is phase one, the rising or boom community.

Community growth begins as the aggregate effect of individual economic decisions to escape dying communities prior in time and space. Or putting it more correctly, it begins with the decision(s) of capital to establish new locations. Growth, not necessarily in the national aggregate, but in the local sense, is the proper beginning, first, because growth environments provide the economic incentives for capital to relocate. Both depreciation in the old setting and investment in the new can be written off against income. Labor is unorganized and cheap. Land is cheap, and so on. Second, growth situations are a logical beginning in our quest for understanding of the dying community, because at the popular level, economic growth constitutes the behavioral environments in which economic definitions of social reality are reinforced. It is in growing communities that economic viability most effectively perpetuates the illusion of political autonomy. They provide an environment where economic solutions work. When these solutions cease to work, the most natural thing for the economically viable to do is leave in response to capital-created opportunity elsewhere. In this manner, their instrumental strategies are rewarded and their ideological constructs of reality maintained. Solutions, especially solutions to the ideological predicaments for those who remain, or for the economically frustrated who return, are more difficult—again for reasons basic to the culture of capitalism. In contrast to growing communities, dying rural communities, like dying urban neighborhoods, are sore spots. They constitute the ideological Achilles' heel of laissez-faire capitalism. Intuitively, the residents know it; practical political theoreticians know it; and local, state, and national police know it.

In phase two, the end of growth or the beginning of decline, the conflict in public ideology begins to appear. The appearance is subtle because it presents itself largely in terms of private-versus-common economic strategies. Despite private doubts and the search for private options, public hope in *the* economic solution is steadfastly maintained by local businessmen. In the local political arena, autonomy, always a sensitive issue vis-à-vis state and federal entities, becomes acute because of loss of income, decreases in the ratio of industrial employment to public employment and welfare, depreciation of the tax base—all of which cause increased reliance on federal dollars, and political interference. I would argue, however, that erosion of autonomy is more illusory than real, because surrender of authority to state and federal entities simply represents the transfer of autonomy from one outside entity to another—from monopoly capital to the state.

The transition to the administered community or rural ghettoization (Bender et al. 1971) is an example of the cumulative result of economic as opposed to political problem solving. The power lies with monopoly capital and centralized government. In response to the political position of weakness in which communities and local institutions like families find themselves, and having been socialized from birth in the sanctity of private enterprise and the economic perception of social reality, people respond up and down the class structure, not politically but economically. Shopkeepers, small farmers, and entrepreneurs sell out, die out, or declare bankruptcy. The professional classes take their services to better markets. The skilled workers "vote with their feet" *against* the declining community and *for* a growing one, or, using another sociological cliché, suddenly become aware of a "preference" for a new location. But the low-wage worker, the young, and the aged remain, where they too use their economic imaginations to survive.

The question of why radicalization and political mobilization don't occur arises. The question is both a deductive and an empirical one. Empirical studies and journalistic accounts of current events show that it does occur at times and under certain conditions (see Lamb 1975: 105–40). Studies of the temper of the American people during the Great Depression also indicate the capacity for radical action (Hallgren 1933; Simon 1967). Just as clearly, the Great Depression also showed the capacity of the state and monopoly capital for brutal political repression (Hallgren 1933:47–161; Smith 1967). But in terms of sustained political action, even on a small scale, to effect transfer of power from the traditional sectors of power—from monopoly to small capital, from centralized governmental units to small governmental units, and from the middle to the lower classes—is impossible. The prosperous

1920s did not see it (Hallgren 1933:13–31), the Roosevelt era did not see it, the post–World War II boom did not see it, nor did the OEO era see it. In fact the OEO experiment was terminated precisely because it *did* stimulate effective political action and the impulse toward decentralized, local power (Lamb 1975:29–53).

Arguing deductively, the lack of political consciousness among those suffering the most from powerlessness—small capital, small communities, and rural low-wage workers—is rooted to the experience of equating economic viability with power. In other words, the very strategies used historically to cope with their political situation operate to mystify their existing circumstances and negate a politically meaningful class consciousness. Therefore in the encounter with their economic disability, they do not seem themselves as politically alienated, but as economically frustrated. Are they marginalized? Politically and economically, yes. Culturally, no (Padfield and Young 1977).

When economic disability becomes an established fact, individual as well as community powerlessness becomes a very strategic ideological issue. The denial of powerlessness and loss of autonomy is not simply a stage a community passes through. It is a studied cultural strategy. The price people pay for blaming themselves instead of the social system for economic failure secures a vital part of their cultural and class identity. But, in the final analysis, the denial of powerlessness has value because it is indispensable to a more important symbolic quest—the quest for the past. This brings me to the fourth phase of rural community decline—the nativistic community.

THE RISE OF A RURAL PROLETARIAT:
THE NATIVISTIC COMMUNITY

In response to white oppression generally, there arose among North American Indians what anthropologists call nativistic movements (Linton 1943; Wallace 1956). These were symbolic rituals that assured cultural survival by glorifying selected cultural elements of an earlier and happier age. Also these rituals assured the participants that the white oppressors would be swept away and that Indians would be invulnerable to their military power. Not all nativism was symbolic.

Numerous movements and numerous features of movements studied by anthropologists had ideological themes that were political.

In contemporary rural America, it is becoming common to see pickup trucks with gun racks and bumper stickers that say such things as "Register Communists, Not Firearms," "America: Love It or Leave It," "Eat Lamb—100 Million Coyotes Can't Be Wrong," or "Sierra Club Hike to Hell." A gun rack, a bale of hay, or saddle may be added paraphernalia.

These sights indicate symbolic demonstrations of power against intruders in general and against the political ideology of powerlessness in particular. In part this is a reaction to growth, but an unfamiliar type of growth, which is now taking place in previously declining rural communities. The rural citizens' intuition of what is happening to their habitats is being confirmed somewhat belatedly by demographic analyses. Instead of economic and population decline, census data are beginning to reveal significant urban-to-rural migration trends in most rural counties, especially in the western U.S. (Beale 1975). This does not mean every rural county in the U.S. is now growing. Beale cautions that depopulation is still the trend in the Great Plains. But in the western region, the average percentage gain of rural counties between 1970 and 1974 was over 10 percent, whereas western U.S. metropolitan counties increased by only 6 percent. In the 1960s, the rural-urban trends were the opposite.

Part of this increase is due to the continuation of the flight to the suburbs, now the "rural suburbs," especially in rural areas adjacent to cities. Retirement and middle-class, commuter neighborhoods would fall in this category. Part of the rural turnaround is due to the bohemian element looking for an artistic setting amidst relics of the past. Part is due to the restless search by counterculture utopians for remoteness and isolation. And only a small fraction, I suspect, is due to the return of a rural person of the same class, ethnic, and occupation type that predominates in the host community.

Demographic revitalization, however, does not in and of itself mean the revitalization of the rural habitat. Unless the population movement is in response to a resurgence of the original economy, there are bound to be radically different social-ecological implications. As I have repeatedly argued throughout this discussion, the typical dynamics for the social perpetuation of conservative political ideology in the rural environment is economic growth. In decline this ideological posture does not change. It simply becomes defensive. Moreover, in the context of economic decline, the influx of culturally different people without increased job opportunity for the natives produces an experience not unlike the Indian experience with white invaders. For one thing, it implies competition by different occupation and class groups for the economic opportunities, if any, associated with the immigration, and competition for the social-psychological benefits of the rural habitat, including use of land, space, air, and water. For another, it implies ideological conflict. This can be especially threatening in the case of newcomers whose political ideology invalidates the defensive, economically oriented ideology of the rural inhabitants.

Given years of adaptation to social diminution and economic insecurity, ideological reaction is inevitable. This includes flamboyant displays of symbols of a potent past depicting: the supercowboy, the superlogger, the super country patriot, and the superindividualist. Moreover, there is not symbolic activity exclusively, but local political action directed against intrusive elements. Informal as well as formal vigilante groups, such as the Minute Men and the Posse Comitatus, take direct action against individuals and institutions that symbolize ideological deviance. They also take action against what they frequently call "conspiracies." Almost weekly one can read newspaper accounts of this kind of action.[3] In rural areas one hears about it firsthand, and occasionally witnesses it. This spontaneous resurgence of American frontier radicalism is one of the more extreme manifestations of the quest for the power and identity of a bygone era. While it may not constitute a pervasive social movement, I would argue that it is an impulse toward modern rural proletarianism.

"The true hall-mark of the proletarian," Toynbee warns us, "is neither poverty nor humble birth, but a consciousness—and the resentment which this consciousness inspires—of being disinherited from his ancestral place in society and being unwanted in a community which is his rightful home; and this subjective proletarianism is not incompatible with the possession of material assets." (Nisbet 1969:21)

NOTES

1. Research for this chapter was made possible by Grants—GA SS 7404 from the Rockefeller Foundation, and 516-15-44, 616-15-58, and 701-15-77 from the U.S.D.A. Cooperative Research Science and Education Administration—to the Oregon State University Agricultural

The Denial of Powerlessness

Experiment Station and Western Rural Development Center. The author also wishes to thank Courtland Smith for helpful criticisms of earlier drafts.

2. The following is an example of numerous newspaper accounts bearing on small town officials. Taken from the *Corvallis Gazette Times* (August 20, 1976).

> LA CENTER, Wash. (AP)—This little town about 20 miles north of Portland is coming apart at the seams. Soon it may cease to exist, at least in legal terms.
>
> The school system is in disarray, with the superintendent in the process of being fired and a recall drive under way against the school board chairman.
>
> At least one Clark County official, asking not to be identified, says locals are hostile to outsiders. Residents complain about taxes and vandalism. Some town officials have resigned, and the mayor is leading a petition drive to disincorporate the community of 400 persons.
>
> Disincorporate? Throw in the towel after 67 years as a recognized governmental jurisdiction with its own taxing, bonding and police powers? Yes, says Mayor Marion G. Brashear, 78.
>
> "The town is just not equipped for self-government," he said Thursday in a telephone interview. "I think we'd be better off under the county government."
>
> Brashear says he started circulating disincorporation petitions this week and plans a public meeting next week "to explain it to the people."
>
> If he gets the signatures of more than half the registered voters in La Center, the issue will go on the ballot—perhaps at the same time as the general election Nov. 2.
>
> According to Brashear, the issue is "big town problems and small town income." He says he got the disincorporation idea after the town council voted in favor of a controversial $350,000 water system overhaul. . . . He claimed that most older residents favored disincorporation but conceded that many younger townspeople are likely to oppose the move.
>
> Brashear says there's only enough money for a half-time town marshal despite "rampant vandalism." La Center's "bonded indebtedness (is) almost equal to New York City" per capita, he adds.
>
> Brashear said the town can't cope with the red tape and strings attached to federal and state funds. "We're practically bankrupt now, getting this 'free' money," he grumped. . . .

3. An example is the following, taken from the *Corvallis Gazette Times* (August 28, 1976).

> Posse Group Gives Up to Real Police. Stanfield (AP)—A group of armed men claiming affiliation with the Posse Comitatus has peacefully surrendered the potato packing shed that it occupied for 11 hours Friday.
>
> No injuries were reported in the incident.
>
> The men occupied the shed in support of a claim by . . . that they own acreage on three large ranches in northeastern Oregon.
>
> . . . filed a suit last month in U.S. District Court in Portland in an effort to get title to the $70,000 worth of land. . . .
>
> Some 15 members of the Oregon State Police and 10 officers of the Umatilla County sheriff's department seized two dogs, handguns, rifles, Molotov cocktails and baseball bats when the men were arrested.
>
> Members of the right-wing Posse Comitatus believe a conspiracy exists in the United States to subvert individual rights. They profess their right to get involved directly in enforcing their interpretation of laws. . . .
>
> All were charged with conspiracy to commit first-degree burglary, criminal mischief, unauthorized use of a motor vehicle and criminal trespassing. Bail for each was set at $65,000.

8

Ethnic and Social Class Minorities in the Dying Small Community

ALVIN L. BERTRAND

Boyd Professor Emeritus
Department of Sociology and Rural Sociology
Louisiana State University

INTRODUCTION

Recent years have seen the unrelenting hand of change move with a swiftness that has forecast the demise of many small communities in the United States. Calvin Beale (1974:3) observes that since World War I we have had the paradoxical situation that the faster our national population has grown, the faster our small communities have declined. Those of us in the social sciences have a clear responsibility to help in the design of program strategies that will dull, if not completely repel, the probe of economic and social inequality, which is the dread hallmark of communities "left behind."

In this chapter I shall develop a perspective for contemplating "what it means to be a minority in an economically stagnant or declining community." By virtue of my experience and my sources, I have interpreted the task at hand to apply primarily to the United States. A discussion of minorities in a declining community can best be put in perspective by a review of certain features of small communities and by

187

clarifying minority group identity. These and certain other orientations I have followed are outlined in the first sections of this chapter. The remainder of my discussion then will attempt to explicate the situation of minorities in declining communities.

SPECIAL FEATURES OF SMALL COMMUNITIES

Since the concept of community and what is meant by community growth and decline has been addressed in the first chapter of this volume, there is no need for further elaboration of those points here. Suffice it to say that, in the sociological tradition, a community is construed to have a manifest nature as a social system. Certain special features of small communities thus serve the purpose of providing a conceptual framework for a consideration of minorities in declining communities.

1. *Communities are open systems.* That is to say, they are linked in many ways with the outside world. The schools, many of the churches, and even local governments have direct ties to regional, state, or national centers. Thus, to a certain extent, the well-being of a community depends on the well-being of the region and society to which it belongs (Warren 1975:12). It is possible, however, for a community to stagnate while a regional center prospers.

2. *Communities are not tightly controlled formal organizations.* Because they include many groups and complex organizations that are in competition (some may be in conflict), small communities often are poorly equipped to take concerted, community development action. There is no strong overriding government that controls all aspects of the community in the interest of an objective of growth.

3. *Informal controls dominate in interpersonal relations in small communities.* Intense face-to-face interaction characterizes almost all activity in small communities. It is thus that informal controls function through custom, public opinion, praise, blame, and gossip to maintain social distance and the patterns of segregation and discrimination that are characteristics for minorities.

4. *Challenge of the power elite is infrequent and abortive on the part*

188

of minorities in small communities. The distribution of social power is so skewed to the majority that confrontations by minorities are likely to fail. This fact discourages overt attempts to bring about a redistribution of power.

5. *Prolonged deterioration in a small community fosters an attitude of defeatism.* When such attitudes crystallize, the prospects for rejuvenating the community are virtually nil (Williams 1974:98). Community members especially affected are likely to exhibit pessimism and despair.

6. *The leaders (elites) in small communities typically are not enthusiastic about change.* This tendency is a function of conservatism and proindividualism on the one hand, and a fear of upsetting the existing power structure on the other hand. There may be especial resistance to programs promoted by outsiders that are designed to help improve the lot of minorities.

The above features of communities provide, to my mind, a clear perspective from which to consider the condition and lot of minorities in small communities on the decline. I turn now to a description of these minorities.

ETHNIC AND SOCIAL CLASS MINORITIES IN U.S. COMMUNITIES

There is an unsettled debate surrounding the concept *minority*, a fact that leads me to be cautious in my use of the concept. In an operational sense, I am interpreting ethnic minority to include racial groups such as Negroes and Indians, as well as culturally distinct groups such as Spanish or Mexican Americans and other nationality distinguished groups. This interpretation is not technically correct since Negroes are racially distinct, but there is a rationale for its usage in the common social distinctions implied in the concept of *minorities in the dying community*. Also, the organizers of the seminar that gave rise to this book asked that racial groups be included under this rubric.

The term *social class* obviously relates to the phenomenon of "structured inequality," which exists in community and larger social systems. The social positions individuals hold are arranged in definite strata, on the basis of relatively stable patterns of inferior-superior relationships in a given community. A person's class position not only determines what groups he or she will be identified with, but also, more pragmatically, it determines what one gets and when and how one gets it.

Three observations are in order before descriptions of minority characteristics in United States communities can be reviewed meaningfully. First, the use of the term *minority* does not necessarily imply an inferior numerical relationship. It does, however, connote people treated as subordinate in a social distance sense. Such groups may well include a greater percentage of the total community population than the higher status or dominant groups do. In fact it is not unusual to find towns in the southwestern United States that have more Spanish-American and Indian than Anglo residents and many southern communities that have a large percentage of blacks.

The second observation I have is in the nature of a well-known fact. It is that in typical situations there is a conjunction between ethnicity and social class (Vander Zanden 1966:269). In fact, it probably is more correct, in the context of the topic under discussion, to use the inclusive concept *ethclass*, as some writers have done. This term clearly underscores the association of ethnicity with class (Griessman 1975:8–9).

The third observation I wish to make also relates to a phenomenon commonly known in social science circles. It is that ethnic and class positions have definite human interactional connotations. The members of a community will look for and perceive clues relative to the ethnic and class positions that an individual holds and adjust their role enactment accordingly. Such a pattern is amply illustrated, for example, by what goes on at a communitywide school. Research that I have done in small Louisiana communities shows clearly that students of lower-class origin seldom get elected or appointed to class or school offices, or invited to off-school functions sponsored by middle-class students (Bertrand and Smith 1960).

One final point completes the perspective I wish to provide for the remainder of my discussion. It is a fact that virtually all small communities in the United States have some type of ethnic and/or class minority. Yet, the pattern of minorities varies immensely as one travels from one locality to another. And, it is safe to speculate that there is considerable variation in minority patterns from one community to another within a region. It is risky, therefore, to generalize or to stereotype as must be done in a statement as short as this one. The only defense that can be given is that general pictures tend to emerge from past studies of minorities. It is these general patterns and broad tendencies, then, that provide the undergirding for our discussion.

Ethnic Minorities and Their Features

The point has been made that the individual members of a community typically and deliberately form patterns of association with their fellow community members and that these patterns give some persons social advantage and others social disadvantage. These patterns, as noted, are arbitrarily structured on defined categories, including ethnic background. In the United States, three ethnic (or race) groups have received much special attention. They are Negroes, Indians, and Spanish or Mexican Americans. Various smaller ethnic groups, such as Chinese, Japanese, Italian, French, German, Polish, and Swedish have also been studied, but to a lesser extent.

It is not inaccurate to state that blacks represent the most commonly found minority in small U.S. communities, followed by Spanish and Mexican Americans. It is also easy to defend the notion that all ethnic minorities share certain characteristic patterns of social relations in their communities with the so-called majority group. I have identified and listed these characteristics, so that changes as a consequence of community decline and decay might be highlighted in a later section of this paper.

The first feature of an ethnic minority in a small community is that it almost always will represent a highly visible component of the community. Said another way, although its members may participate in all facets of community life, they will always be recognized by skin color, speech, name, or religion. It is interesting that even the "ethnics" who have achieved high status seldom completely escape identification and differential treatment. A black doctor or a Chicano mayor, for example, is likely to be reminded, subtly or not so subtly, of his ethnic status.

A second characteristic of ethnic minorities is that they are conspicuous in the ranks of unskilled and semiskilled laborers, and appear frequently in the personal service industries. Elaine Burgess (1964:36) gives a vivid description of the jobs held by members of the lower class (mostly black) in a southern city more or less typical of many communities throughout the nation.

191

Employment is less certain, and temporary employment is common. The men are found in the dirtier manual and unskilled jobs, being employed as cutters and sweepers in the tobacco factories, janitors, night watchmen, ditch diggers, and handy men. The women work as domestics, cooks, cleaners, and unskilled factory workers.

The latest U.S. Bureau of the Census reports (1975) show some degree of occupational upgrading for minorities, but blacks, Spanish Americans, and other minorities still predominate in low-skill, low-paid jobs, wherever they are found. Those minority members who do succeed in business, the professions, or in politics generally form special elites exempt from some, but not all, of the disadvantages of the rank and file of the minority group.

Burgess identifies black elites (leaders) in the community she studied as successful businessmen, prominent educators, influential religious leaders, physicians, dentists, and lawyers. While these individuals controlled political and participation decisions in their subareas of the community, they accommodated to the larger community power structure (Burgess 1964:25–75).

The third generally recognized feature of minorities is their tendency to stand apart as a subcommunity in all social-action matters. Programs of one kind or another—street, welfare, school, health—always consider them differentially. This correctly suggests little formal political power. There is a coordinate voting action on certain issues, however, which at times commands attention and concession. It has been observed that one is more likely to see evidence of concern over the welfare and opportunities of minorities just before election time. With regard to this phenomenon, political scientists have recognized the importance of what has been termed ethnic politics. Perry Weed notes, for example: "At all levels of government, politicians practice ethnic politics" (Weed 1973:132). Ethnic politics can be exploitative of or beneficial to minorities. It is exploitative when minorities are scapegoated in an attempt to get majority vote support or are made promises for their votes in bad faith. Benefits accrue to minorities when concessions to their needs are made to obtain and keep their support.

A fourth characteristic of ethnic minorities is unequal participation in the social systems that support the institutional structure of the community. While it is true that schools, some government functions, and many economic activities may be shared, the participation of

192

ethnic minorities tends always to be marginal. This marginality may diminish into a state of complete separateness, especially during times of economic and social stress. The latter development in turn may give rise to formal groups organized around action goals—to reduce inequalities in the social structure.

The fifth common characteristic of minorities is residential separateness. They tend to live in certain parts of town, and to have less available to them in the way of housing and related accommodations. The following account of a black family's home in a rural community describes lower-class housing common to many times and places.

> As you approach the dwelling, you see an unpainted, rather old house with a porch across the front. There are no screens on the windows and an old front door remains halfway open because the house is no longer level after years of use. There are several holes and cracks between the floor boards. Attempts have been made to patch these cracks with tin, yet the cold air still flows freely throughout the house. The center room is very dark and the wall board, painted in years past, is now dark in color and well stained. One light hangs from the center of the room by a single wire. (Crosswhite 1970:13)

Social Class Minorities

It is appropriate to note that social stratification is a universal phenomenon. Despite much ado about classless communities and societies, such remain in the realm of the abstract more than in the world of reality. With this thought in mind, it is possible, as noted, to conceive of the lower class in a given community as a minority class, even though it may well include larger numbers than the middle and upper classes. Lower-class minorities share most of the characteristics of ethnic minorities, because the latter usually are in the lower socioeconomic levels.

By way of review, it may be stated that the lower class in a small community inevitably includes employees rather than employers. Seldom are individuals found who fall outside of the semiskilled and unskilled rank of workers. Although the members of this class do not necessarily have physically distinguishing features, they have family names and occupations that set them up for easy identification by local persons. Like ethnic minorities, they have little opportunity for input into community decisions; and when present, they are mere bystanders in affairs of school, government, and business. Although lower-class persons may appear at meetings called to address community concerns, the middle-class dominate attendance at such affairs, and the formal procedures followed tend to intimidate and discourage the participation of lower-class persons. Like ethnic minorities, the lower-class also tend to live in special areas that connote inferior status identity.

Two particular features set members of nonethnic class minorities apart from those with ethnic identity. The first is the competitive advantage of being a member of the dominant group, regardless of socioeconomic level. Vander Zanden points out that skin color is definitely a prestige factor among lower-class individuals. He cites typical statements that lower-class whites make to indicate their willingness to take advantage of their skin color for competitive purposes. "I've been a white man all my life and always will be." "We may not have the prestige, but we aren't Negroes! We're members of a 'God-given superior race'—the white race!" (Vander Zanden 1963:124). It is for this reason of status that lower-class persons from a dominant ethnic group sometimes tend to settle in areas apart from other ethnic minorities. The second distinction between the two classes of minorities is the lack of a complete class hierarchy in the nonethnic lower social class. Whereas ethnic groups may well have some members who are influential and affluent, this is not possible, by definition, among the lower-class, nonethnic groups.

The likenesses that ethnic and class minorities have, that is, their interstructural overlaps, decree that they share certain social limitations. It is now appropriate to review these features of community social organization.

The Social Organizational Limitations of Ethnic and Class Minorities

Within any community there are essential social functions or tasks that have to be performed. Not all of these tasks are equally challenging or pleasant, so it is customary to assign different rewards in terms of money, power, and prestige for given assignments. In this regard, almost everyone associates the "place" of everyone else with the positions they hold and the roles they play. Community life is subtly geared to those who belong and those who don't (Irelan and Besner 1966:2–4).

The first social organizational limitation of minority classes is that they are made up of persons who have only limited, if any, access to the more rewarding positions in a community. One consequence of such limited access is that it poses a barrier to the opportunity to learn the new roles that qualify one for higher social status. At this point it is appropriate to cite the linguistic problems of minorities, which often serve to block access to higher status positions. Blacks and nonethnic, lower-class whites tend to speak what is referred to as nonstandard dialects of English. Saville (1970:125) describes the characteristics of black speakers of nonstandard English as follows:

> The most diverse variant found in nonstandard black speech is in its verbal system. Usually a verb is not inflected differently for simple past and present in this system. *He throw the ball* may mean either, "he throws the ball" or "he threw the ball." A past perfect is used for example, *I seen it,* . . .and there is a form to express action completed earlier, *I been seen it,* that has no equivalent in standard English. *I be busy* refers to habitual activity and is also unique to black speech.

Ethnics with a language background besides English tend to have phonetic, syntactical, and semantic problems that tag them as poor speakers. As Saville (1970:118) notes, "A child raised in a Spanish-speaking household will distinguish sounds the English speaker learns to ignore and will disregard some sound differences vital to English word meanings. He will, for instance, hear *share* for *chair* . . . but distinguish between Spanish *pero* and *perro,* which are heard as the same word by most speakers of English." For social mobility, one must receive invitations to participate in places that make him or her socially visible in a positive manner. Such invitations are seldom received by persons who have not had the opportunity to learn good English.

A second limitation characteristic of minorities is their lack of access to social power. In an operational sense, social power emanates from the control of things and services others want. About the only source of power the lower classes have is in their value as workers and their worth as voters, and in these cases power is not exercised to the fullest because of too little sophistication and a dread of the consequences of failure. The feelings developed around this perceived impotence will lead to alienation, that is to a cynical, fatalistic view of life as meaningless and under the control of unmanageable forces.

The third social limitation of minority classes is manifest in their relative lack of visibility as a worthy and contributing component of the community. Whatever their accomplishments or distinctions, they seldom enjoy display in the mass media. By contrast, negative incidences, such as crime or illiteracy, receive disproportionate coverage. Bodine illustrates this point, for example, in his analysis of a small town in New Mexico. He notes that whenever anything happens of a criminal nature a finger is pointed first at the Spanish-American minority in the community (Bodine 1969:206). Bodine goes on to explain that the Anglos (the majority ethnic class) imperfectly understand the stresses and strains facing many of the Spanish Americans. Since most of the latter are lower-class, they bear the problems such a predicament carries. Their behavior, which is stereotyped as immoral, deviant, and so forth, is a manifestation of the futility and frustration they feel in facing the conditions of their lives. It is hard to assess the full implication of the derogatory visibility minorities receive. In this regard, it has been pointed out that concern over "trouble" is a dominant feature of lower-class culture. "Trouble" refers to involvement with employers, officials, or agencies in a negative way, and generally implies an economic or physical sanction (Ferman, Kornbluh, and Haber 1965:263).

A final social limitation of minority classes is manifest in their constant insecurity. Their jobs tend to have more temporariness than those of the majority, they are more susceptible to problems related to housing, health, and education, and they are always subject to one-upmanship when interacting with members of the dominant class. The insecurity that minority status evokes has been associated with psychological or mental health manifestations, which is a commentary on the grave importance of this limitation. In this regard, a number of psychologists and psychiatrists have documented the debilitating effects of poverty. Polanski, Borgman, and De Saix, for example, have written a book on poverty as the root cause of futility and alienation. They describe the characteristic affect of the apathy-futility syndrome as a "deep sense of futility, accompanied by massive inhibition, giving rise to a far-reaching anesthesia or numbness" (Polanski, Borgman, and De Saix 1972:54).

In sum, the life or life-style of minority classes is likely to be one that is vulnerable to change, which comes with the decay of a community. I turn now to a look at this phenomenon.

THE SOCIAL STRUCTURE SYMPTOMS OF
A DYING COMMUNITY

As shown by others contributing to this volume, there are many specific causes or reasons to account for the decline of a community. By way of summary, it may be noted that new technology may outmode industries that support a town, as happened in railroad "shop" communities when diesel locomotives replaced steam engines (Cottrell 1951). Interstate highways may bypass and deal a death blow to a community depending on tourists for customers. Or, the natural resources that sustain an economic base may play out, as when coal mines and oil fields become depleted (Beale 1974).

Whatever the cause, the social organizational consequences generated by a trend toward decline are similar. Together they spell a decay in the opportunity structure. It follows then that probably the most dependable social indicator of decline is population decrease and change. This is caused by young adults leaving the community soon after high school, seldom to return. As a consequence the average age in a community begins to rise, and at some point in time the number of persons over 50 years of age overtakes the number below 30 years. When the median age of the community reaches approximately 35, deaths begin to exceed births, and decline becomes a function of low birth rates as well as out-migration (Beale 1974).

The general pattern in a declining community is for economic functions, such as employment and services, to be transferred from local establishments to regional trade centers (Wilkinson 1974). This means that the larger region may actually undergo growth at the same time that the local community undergoes decline. All in all, a substantial and persistently high rate of unemployment and underemployment is symptomatic of a depressed community (Hauswald 1971). Such a community tends to lose control over its destiny as its members become more dependent on external sources for survival needs. It is illustrative to note that the businesses in a small community are highly interdependent. The restaurant depends on the grain elevator and the local plant and the banks depend on both operations. If the elevator or the plant closes, the position of the remaining businesses is immediately precarious. Pierce Lewis (1972) describes how a thriving county seat town in Pennsylvania lost its economic base when the production of

197

pig iron no longer remained profitable. Gradually its services and functions were taken over by a more viable nearby town. Thus many residents now travel to the second town to work and to go to the hospital, and they find it to be better for shopping and for securing professional services, such as dental and medical care and legal advice. When vital services are no longer available, as in the example cited by Lewis, the degeneration of a community proceeds to the point where it is no longer a bona fide community, but rather becomes a neighborhood.

The key sign of decline at the level of local government is a lessening of participation and competition. Whenever fewer persons become involved in community issues and elections, and fewer candidates seek office, there is an unmistakable sign of a diminished viability. In dying communities it is typical to find leadership-political systems effectively closed. Officials move almost automatically into positions because of titles they hold, families they belong to, or, as Eugene Erickson points out (1974:78), because they fit the community. Such officials seldom have knowledge of resources beyond the boundaries of the community, nor are they motivated to push development schemes, since they generally have security, economic and otherwise. The description of the leadership picture in a declining community given by one researcher of a small town is illustrative:

> Insularity and alienation, compounded by more than a decade of economic decline, have blunted social awareness and induced languor in _____'s local leaders. And the usual corrective replacement of the old and disenchanted by the more daring and vigorous young has not been available, because the young have departed in droves, and continue to do so. (Dean 1967:50)

The schools in a declining community also exhibit characteristic patterns of organizational atrophy. Since school financing is a local matter to a considerable extent, reductions in the tax base are reflected immediately in salaries, supplies, building repair, and extracurricular activities. Younger teachers are hard to attract and hold; at the same time, course offerings begin to lose diversity and trend toward the traditional. Buildings and grounds soon develop a worn-out, run-down look. When enrollments eventually begin to drop, school administrations become apathetic and the formal educational function becomes more of a token effort than anything else. Little wonder that the more ambitious families leave the community or send their children to schools elsewhere.

The decline of communities is also manifest in church support, programs, and attendance. Churches first lose members, then they lose their most experienced and capable leaders. Ellenbogen reports that the decline of churches is manifested in several ways: the outright closing of a church, interdenominational consolidation in order to provide enough attendance, and the resort to itinerant or less than full-time ministers (Ellenbogen 1974:83). When such changes occur, the sophistication of the church is likely to decline to the point that its appeal to youth and more progressive adults is lost. It is a rather common occurrence for individuals living in distressed communities to drive long distances to fulfill their needs for religious expression.

Families also undergo changes in declining communities. The first structural evidence of change is found in the composition of family groups. Older couples and single surviving spouses increase their relative numbers. A second clue to family change is the increasing number of women who enter the work force to supplement family income. This pattern leads to changes in family decision making and in the way all husband and wife roles are played. In this regard, it is typical in small communities to define "earning the money [as] the man's responsibility." This provider role entitles the man to certain authority and gives him a definite feeling of being responsible for the family's destiny. If and when he loses his job or fails to provide sufficiently for the family, and the wife goes to work, his basis of authority is eroded. And it is not unlikely that he will be strongly encouraged to take on some of the "house chores" formerly performed by his wife. It is thus that employment of wives must be seen as affecting existing family ideology regarding man-woman relations, including their status and power. Families may also lose some of their effectiveness as the basic structural group supporting the community and perform less efficiently in support of businesses, school, and church—especially if one or another parent has to leave for extended times in the interest of employment outside the community. Margaret Bubolz, in light of her studies, asserts strongly that a declining community atmosphere has a debilitating effect on its resident families, impairing their ability to socialize the young completely (Bubolz 1974:63).

In concluding these comments on the structural symptoms of a dying community, it may be noted that there is a chain relationship between the groups and organizations that make up a community. When a community begins to deteriorate, there is an easily detected constricture of the social structure, which in turn is reflected in the quality of life. This leads logically then to the question of what such a development portends for minorities.

THE IMPACT OF COMMUNITY DECAY ON ETHNIC AND SOCIAL CLASS MINORITIES

There are numerous studies that document the deterioration in the economic base, the lessening vitality of local government, the drop in efficiency of schools, the decline of local churches, and, in a general sense, the lowering of the quality of life in dying or declining communities. There are not any, however, that focus directly on the impact of community decay on minorities as such. The typical research project treats the community in holistic fashion, with offhand statements about minorities at best. For this reason, the discussion that follows is to a large extent speculative. However, for each observation an attempt is made to interpolate, from the known facts about change in declining communities and about the social organization, patterns that are generated under such conditions.

The first observation I wish to make is that both ethnic and lower-class minorities are likely, by virtue of their places in the social structure, to be more firmly wedded to their communities than are dominant groups. This is especially true of those individuals who have no special skills and who have reached middle adulthood. The latter have neither the sophistication nor the training and experience to enable them to break out of their situations either in or out of their communities. In fact, dying communities effectively reject in-migrants with higher level skills at the same time they lose their younger, more employable members. The phenomenon referred to here is what Doeksen, Kuehn, and Schmidt call the ghettoization process. They state:

> The style of life in a declining region screens out certain classes of potential in-migrants and encourages out-migration of these same classes within the region. The out-migrants are the highly educated and the in-migrants are the unskilled workers with similar

values, attitudes, and characteristics to those of the people left in the region. (Doeksen, Kuehn, and Schmidt 1974:31)

Further, Hauswald (1971:99) concludes that unemployed workers in an economically distressed community may resist out-migration for "reasons of community affinity, inadequate retraining opportunities, inadequate economic wherewithal to effect geographic and skill transitions, and lack of knowledge as to opportunity elsewhere."

In view of the above patterns, it is my conclusion that minorities in a declining community are "locked in" to the community to a considerably larger extent than members of the dominant group. The point here is that the positions and roles they are qualified for leave little in the way of an alternative. Such fate apparently is shared more or less equally by ethnic and social-class minorities.

The second impact of community decline on minorities that I see is hard to assess in a comparative manner. It is the effect of the economic stagnation, which characteristically typifies dying communities. The evidence I have accumulated seems to indicate that minorities may not be as adversely affected, at least in a relative sense, as the dominant classes. In this regard, it is clear that a major symptom of dying communities is a decline in the demand for goods and professional services. Bert Adams (1969) points out that the first to leave a dying community are the specialized professionals, such as dentists, doctors, and lawyers. Next to go are dry goods dealers, auto dealers, and appliance dealers. Beauty shops, television repair shops, laundries, and paint stores follow close behind. While some members of minorities are affected by these closures, they suffer less than the persons who are owners and managers, or who render professional services. Members of minorities are more accustomed to losing and/or changing jobs and have routines with unemployment compensation and other types of welfare assistance that tend to dampen the impact of adversity. The remark of a local merchant interviewed about the problem of unemployment in his depressed town illustrates this point.

> I know lots of men who are out of work, and it doesn't bother them at all. They just go on collecting unemployment compensation as long as they can and after that runs out, they collect relief. (Dean 1967:63)

Ethnic minorities probably experience more unevenness in this sense than do lower-class minorities. This is because some members of ethnic groups will be professionals or own business establishments, and thus will experience this type of vulnerability as well.

Another probable development in a dying community is increased crystallization of patterns of discrimination and social distance. Such tactics are ploys to provide advantage in the increased competition for available jobs. The members of the dominant class are likely to guard their status and class rank against all minorities. But, nonethnic class minorities will also encourage behavior on the part of their members that accentuates social distance from ethnic minorities. A white unskilled worker who finds himself in competition with a black or Chicano will not hesitate to use his ethnic identification for whatever advantage it may bring him. The remark of a white, lower-class worker relative to lower-class blacks in his depressed community area is illustrative. "I'm poisoned toward 'em. I've seen . . . the way they live—dirty diapers, messed up yards, tin cans—and they smell" (Dean 1967:53–54).

Still another organizational change that seems to come to minorities during times of community recession is stronger family and/or brotherhood associations. In this regard, a study conducted by the national Welfare Administration indicates that the poor, in comparison with the nonpoor, receive substantially more help from their relatives (Besner 1966:16). Another author reports evidence of more extended family relationships and kinship support systems in counties with ethnic enclaves and experiencing population decline (Bubolz 1974:60). This phenomenon is allied to the trend toward greater cooperation and mutual aid, but has an added connotation. It may well be that as life becomes more uncertain and insecure, there is a psychic need for shared experience, which makes the adversity more bearable. At any rate, the sincerity with which minority members support each other and their neighborhood organizations in depression periods testifies to the comprehensibility such participation gives to the economic and social woes they have.

In final essence, it is apparent that the quality of life will deteriorate for minorities, whatever their status, during times of community decline. Needs such as health care, housing, food, and education, even though utilized previously at minimum levels, will become increasingly harder to satisfy. Doctors and hospitals move down the road to the next city or town; needed repairs to dwellings are hard to get from landlords;

meals become scarcer and more monotonous; and schools deteriorate to token existence. Ellenbogen reports that many small communities studied in the upper midwestern states could well be "no physician" towns in the future. Doctors in these localities were found to have a significantly higher median age and were quite skeptical about replacing themselves.

Yet, one is forced to wonder if congruity in life-style does not remain greater for minorities than for those who were socially and economically more advantaged prior to a distressed community situation. Minorities probably experience less of a relative loss in their levels of living than those who were more fortunate, and thus experience fewer problems of adjustment. In simple terms, the poor and the disadvantaged always appear in greater relief during times of growth and prosperity than they do in times of depression. To acknowledge this is not to condone the difficult lot of minorities in dying communities. It is simply to suggest they may be better prepared to cope with the inherent lack of opportunity because such is indigenous to their stations. When this is said, the question of dying communities comes back into a total perspective and inspires a concluding contemplative thought.

IN CONCLUSION

I have described the symptoms of dying communities, with especial emphasis on the implications for the quality of life of ethnic and social-class minorities. My conclusion is that the lot of minorities does indeed worsen when the communities they live in decay, but not to so great a relative extent as might be expected. The real tragedy of minorities in dying communities is that they may well have no escape, and be bound to a fate of poverty and social disadvantage through a lack of community development effort. The attitude of a banker residing in a declining community illustrates such a situation:

> Well, the population has been going down over a long process of time, but that isn't too serious in itself. In fact, it's a good thing those people did leave since there's nothing for them to do *here*. We'll eventually hit our level. (Dean 1967:59)

To improve the lot of minorities (and of all classes) in depressed communities requires that something be done to increase the oppor-

203

tunity locally to achieve a more rewarding life. This obviously means creating more jobs and providing more services—that is, improving the quality of life of community residents. In other words, change is in order, which by definition refers to alterations in social relationships (Bertrand 1967:118–19). From a community development perspective, social change has to be induced or instigated in the interest of desired goals. The question that must be pondered is, Who bears the responsibility for such action programs?

It is in keeping with American ideals and values to espouse "self-help" approaches to community development. In fact, projects imposed solely by external agencies are almost always resented if not rejected. In this tradition, the rational and ideologically consistent answer to the question of community development responsibility lies in the people of the community themselves. I subscribe to this view, and elaborate briefly in support of my stance.

It is true, as I have stressed, that local leaders in decaying communities are not apt to be interested in change. It is also true that local people, as volunteers, seldom have the energy, skill, or time to devote to long and involved projects of improvement, even if they have the sophistication to comprehend them. Furthermore, some outside resources normally are necessary for the implementation of projects. Without belaboring this point further, I will reiterate that the initiative for improvement programs must come from the community itself, despite these awesome hurdles. This fact literally pervades the literature I have consulted on community development efforts (Bennett and Nelson 1975). It is the theme of the excellent monograph "Approaches to Community Development" by Huey B. Long, Robert C. Anderson, and Jon A. Blubaugh (1973). Once an initiative is manifested, there is usually access to planning and development assistance from various government agencies and some private organizations. Communities whose leadership does not make sincere attempts to improve the economic base and social amenities are doomed. It is illustrative to quote Carl E. Annas of Burlington Industries, who explains his company's policy relative to locating plants in small communities, by asking and answering this question (Annas 1970:18):

> Does the community leadership really want industry? This is a legitimate question and one that has considerable significance for us. Often . . . the broader leadership may be less than enthusiastic.

I end my discussion on a note that is a bit sad, but sociologically realistic. Minorities in dying communities are constrained to a future that is dependent upon the efforts and ability of the leaders in their communities. In those communities where leadership is lacking, they will remain at the height of disadvantage as measured on a relative scale in the United States. Where a sufficient leadership effort is available to reverse the declining trends in their communities, minorities will fare proportionate to, but seldom in greater measure than, the positions of inequality they inhabit in the social structure.

9

Growing Up in a Dying Community

DAVID H. LOOFF, M.D.

Child Psychiatrist
Lexington, Kentucky

For more than two decades, the writer has had a variety of clinical experiences in serving people as a general physician and child psychiatrist in several cultural settings. Several of these settings were in dying, or partially dying communities in Alaska and in the Southern Appalachian region. From the very beginning of these experiences, one could see how adolescents and adults, particularly, coped—or failed to cope—with severe and protracted stress in these regions. And one could see well just how their coping efforts successfully—or unsuccessfully—reared younger children. Thus, these clinical experiences have been with child development in a variety of regional and ethnic cultures in the context of prolonged social and economic stress. Following the telling of the life stories of people from these particular communities, the writer will summarize the inferences he has drawn from the developmental data the stories provide.

EXPERIENCES IN ALASKA

During the two-year period between July 1955 and June 1957, the writer served the U.S. Public Health Service–Alaska Native Hospital in Juneau, Alaska, as its medical officer. At the beginning of this

207

period, the medical care being provided for various American Indian groups was transferred from the Bureau of Indian Affairs to the U.S. Public Health Service. With this transfer, general medical officers of the Health Service's commissioned corps, like the writer, were stationed for tours of duty at hospitals and clinics that provided health-care services for American Indians at locations throughout the continental United States and in the Territory of Alaska.

In those years, the Juneau Alaska Native Hospital was a 58-bed general medical facility, which also operated a busy outpatient service and an annex, in which 28 additional long-term patients lived while they were undergoing chemotherapy for tuberculosis. On an average, the facility had 2 or 3 general hospital admissions each day, and 8,000 outpatient visits and the delivery of about 200 babies during the year. The staff consisted of the writer as the sole general medical officer, a dentist, 12 registered nurses, and a variety of aides, secretaries, cooks, and janitors as support personnel. For this staff, those years were exceptionally active ones with regard to the provision of symptomatic, crisis-oriented general medical care.

EXPERIENCES AMONG THE THLINGIT INDIANS

The Juneau Hospital served the Thlingits, whose six thousand members or so were scattered throughout the upper portion of the southeastern Alaskan panhandle. This area lay between the towns of Yakutat and Skagway to the north, and Wrangell and Petersburg in the south. As members of one of the four Indian ethnic groups—the others were the Eskimo, the Aleut, and the Athapascan tribes—in the Territory of Alaska, the Thlingit people were unique in that they were bound economically to the local salmon-fishing industry. This industry was at that time the only one of any size, since lumbering was not yet on the ascendency in the region. Moreover, the fishing industry was a purely seasonal one. Accordingly, those who worked within it, like the Thlingit people, were required to live during the summers, when the annual salmon runs and the canning seasons were on, in small villages (among them Hoonah, Angoon, Kake, and Kluckwan) that had been built up as part of the widely scattered canneries in the area.

These salmon canneries were owned by continental United States-based firms like the Atlantic and Pacific Company, the Pacific Ameri-

208

can Fisheries, and the Alaska Packers Association. Administrative personnel who ran the canneries, and those who provided skilled technical services (the machinists, welders, foremen, and the electrical plant operators), were white men who lived primarily in the Pacific Northwest and came north only as seasonal employees of these firms. The Thlingit people from the canning villages provided the unskilled laboring services for the canneries during the summers. And when the canneries closed down in September, the Thlingit people moved away to winter as groups in such larger towns in southeastern Alaska as Sitka, Skagway, Yakutat, and Juneau itself. Annually, beginning in late April, whole families of them closed their winter homes and moved back to the canning villages for the summer fishing season.

In the communities like Juneau where the Thlingit families wintered, however, there were in those years very few seasonal laboring jobs— ones for which they were best suited since they had been trained in no other salable skills—available for the adults. There were a few exceptions among individuals, of course. These were ones who had finished high school and were working as clerks or secretaries in territorial government offices, or who owned small stores serving primarily the Indian communities in these towns. But most of the Thlingit people had only a few years of formal elementary education. And most of them had not had any vocational training beyond the on-the-job apprenticeships provided them as they had grown up and worked in the seasonal salmon canneries, in those few small plywood mills existing in the area, and on local road crews. Moreover, none of them were in a position of being themselves employers: the firms in which they worked, and the canneries, the mills, and even the fishing boats were owned throughout the area by others. Thus it was that the Thlingit people were bound inextricably to the unskilled laboring positions provided within the canneries during the summers. And since they lacked any winter-season employment, their families were in great numbers supported by welfare payments during the winters while they lived in the towns where their children attended the local schools. In the Juneau area, for example, there was in 1955–57 an annual exodus to the summer canneries and return of over 1,500 Thlingit men, women, and their children. And of this number, perhaps 1,000 were on welfare rolls during the winters. If the Territory of Alaska had not been eligible at that time for federal welfare payment aid, the 8,000 other residents of Juneau would not have been able to support so large

209

a welfare program. In the other towns where the Thlingit families wintered, the figures were much the same in those years.

Several more or less summary observations about the Thlingit people impressed the writer as he spent those two years working with them. The first had to do with the very sharp regional economic decline prompted by a slowing-down within the salmon industry. For many earlier years, the fjord waters of southeastern Alaska had been overfished, and few conservation and propagation measures had been practiced with regard to the annual salmon run. During the years the writer practiced in Juneau, catches of salmon were said to be then only a third of their earlier level throughout the area. Some canneries were forced to close; others operated on only part-time schedules with small work crews. And for the fishermen themselves, smaller catches meant smaller paychecks. For the Thlingit people throughout southeastern Alaska in those years, the net result of this decline in the salmon industry was that their community was partially dying economically. Nor could relief be provided by other industries then, for no new ones had as yet arisen to provide additional unskilled laboring jobs for these people in the area.[1] As a result, more and more Thlingit families were forced to subsist on welfare payments throughout the year. In time, subsistence living became the general mode for a great majority of families. And the impact of this economic decline and resulting forced idleness of the work force upon the general health and adaptive living skills of these people was one of considerable negative effect. Just how damaging this impact was on peoples' lives will be reviewed shortly.

The second observation was that the Thlingit people, provided one could apply the concept of a group life-style for them, were in the writer's estimation singularly ill-prepared to cope with the blow brought by the salmon industry's decline. Just how their life-style was formed, and what characteristic traits it entailed for this group, are issues to be taken up at this point.

Throughout ancient times and to the present day, the Thlingit people, like the three other Indian ethnic groups in Alaska, lived by extracting both their food and a means of livelihood from the land and its surrounding waters. What we have of Thlingit tribal dances, songs, and myths depict this well (De Armond 1975). Gods and evil forces were personified in them in natural animal forms. These lived within the remote fastnesses of the rugged fjords, mountain ranges, and icefields of the area. And from these sites they were once believed to intervene

210

directly in the daily lives of the Indian people. The tales and dances the writer heard and observed not only depicted the Thlingit people as inseparably bound to the land and its bounty, but also showed how swiftly and often sternly godlike forces moved to affect their lives in action-oriented ways. Furthermore, few of these tales contained particularly pleasurable or humorous themes. In none of the Thlingit legends, for example, do the actors—gods, evil spirits, or the people affected by them—laugh at themselves. Nothing in these stories is ever taken lightheartedly, a frequently effective way many other people have of putting troublesome events and the feelings aroused by them into an assimilatory perspective. Instead, so many of the tales have a gray, pervasively brooding, affective quality about them not unlike the hanging mists and drizzling rains that so often hold the area in their grip.

Moreover, the Thlingit people as a group seem to have expressed their propensity for direct action in other ways besides projecting and embodying it within their folklore. Reference here is made to the fact that, in ancient times, they were a marauding, aggressive people whose war canoes ranged as far south as the coasts of present-day British Columbia and the state of Washington. Much of this pillaging stopped after the coming of the Russian fur-trading colonists to the area in the mid-eighteenth century, both because the Russians suppressed warlike activities in the area they now controlled and because they opened up the trapping of furs to the Indian people as a new means of livelihood. From that time on, however, even though their wars had ceased, Thlingit tribal dance masks still bore brooding, rather menacing countenances, and many of the dances still celebrated, and from among other themes, the forays into battle the forbears of these people once had made.

From such antecedents, and probably brought about by social modeling or patterning for generations as the writer would conjecture it to have occurred, there was developed a life-style for the present-day Thlingit people whose traits are strikingly similar to those depicted in their ancient legends and in actual history. With few exceptions, the writer found both young and old Thlingit people alike—though this was more true for older adolescents and adults, those whose personality traits were more fully formed through development in time—relatively nonverbal, brooding, distance-promoting, and sullen individuals. If these same traits were more markedly held, as occurred in some persons, they were taciturn, morose, suspicious, vindictive, and sometimes vengeful people. Of course, there were the exceptions among them— people who were more verbal and who shared their hopes and fears with others, and who seemed to trust others more openly and to cooperate with them. But even these persons had a stoicism and seriousness about them that often left them humorless in most situations that would ordinarily produce mirth among people.

Even visitors to the wards of the hospital where the writer and his staff worked were struck by the evidence of the Thlingit group life-style in this setting. On the wards, or within the crowded waiting room on general clinic days (during which between 40 and 60 patients of all ages would be seen, on an average), one observed little of that jocular noise and confusion created in other, but similar settings by kaffee-klatsching mothers and their exuberant children. Instead, the waiting room of the Juneau hospital was, so often and in spite of staff attempts to change its emotional tone, a depressing place in which to work. Thlingit people waited there quietly—too quietly—and the sense of futility and personal despair that pervaded the room so often became, as one nurse put it, "so thick you could cut it with a knife."

Earlier, the point was made that the economic decline of the area's fishing industry had affected primarily the Thlingit people. But what made it even more devastating, much more of a stressful blow for them, was that their life-style had left them peculiarly and particularly vulnerable to the stresses attending unemployment in the area. As a brooding, sullen, silent people they were ill-equipped to cope with the problems that were created, as they viewed it, by their conquerors. It was no wonder, it seemed to this writer, that so many Thlingit individuals talked so often of disliking intensely the white race. The facts of history at the time interacted with the Thlingit traits to produce among these people chronic despair and tense, sullen ways of relating with others, themselves as well as whites. As a white physician among them, the writer felt these events and forces daily, and it could be observed how these same traits operated in other ways to affect the Thlingit people.

It was striking in those years how the same life-style that made it difficult for them to cope well with these stresses—leading to the general feeling of futility and despair among them—was at the same time a major factor in causing difficulties in individuals' personality growth and development along the entire span of the life-cycle.[2] Viewed as an overall pattern, it could be said that many of these chronically depressed people were not able to raise their children fully effectively, nor could they function well among themselves as adults.

Among the Thlingit infant population, for example, the writer and his staff were struck by the many newborns who failed to thrive during their first year of life. Most of these particular infants were healthy at birth in the hospital. But even before this, during their mothers' pregnancies, difficulties first arose that continued to affect the youngsters' lives after birth.

These problems began with the fact that the majority of these mothers were unwed adolescent girls between the ages of fifteen and nineteen. Most of them had dropped out of formal schooling in the area, were unemployed, had consequently been idling around the community, and were now pregnant through really nonintimate, rather casual relationships with young, white U.S. coastguardsmen stationed in Juneau. Occasionally, the fathers of these babies were older white men, or adolescent Thlingit boys or young men. What created the initial problem for these pregnant girls was the fact that Thlingit custom at the time, which was reinforced by the general feeling of futility pervading the group, was to ostracize these girls if their pregnancies were brought about by contacts with white men. Even the girls' own families were generally overreactively dismayed and emotionally nonsupportive toward them. As a consequence of this loss of community and family support, the girls themselves were quite tensely depressed throughout their pregnancies, and no amount of personal counseling could change their outlooks when the harsh realities of life outside the clinic were as they were for them.

When their infants were delivered, many of these unwed mothers were forced by their families to move elsewhere. Although those who kept their babies (and a majority of the girls did keep them) and were forced to move were supported financially by aid to dependent children, it was the impact of the social stigma of having borne a biracial baby and the loneliness forced upon them that affected these girls in continuing ways. They remained significantly tensely depressed, and in this state they could not comfortably care for their newborns.

Thus, during the critical first months of their infants' lives, at a time when mothers everywhere are called upon not only to respond to their babies' needs in flexible ways but also to serve as a stimulus barrier for them (screening out noxious stimuli from the environment, which their immature perceptual capacities cannot as yet sort out and cope with adaptively), these Thlingit girls failed very often in this role. Tense and depressed themselves, they handled their newborns as frustrating burdens. There was little of that cuddling, soothing cooing, and comfortable handling while bathing, feeding, or diapering their infants one sees with other mothers. Instead, tense and sometimes bitter handling of their babies was frequently observed among the Thlingit girls.

Consequently, their newborns often failed to develop regular cycles of sleep and wakefulness, of digestion and elimination, and of satisfied exploration of themselves and their nearby environment when they were awake. Instead, they were tense, fretful, irritable, crying babies whose irregularity in nearly every function only reinforced their mothers' feelings of frustration and hopelessness. And, not only were these infants reacting directly to their mothers' tense ways of handling them, but also their fretfulness was a sign of perceptual flooding—of sensory stimuli of all types impacting in full force because their mothers were unable to screen out the more noxious ones from among them.

Every few days after these infants' births, their young mothers would bring them back to the hospital's postnatal clinic with the complaints that the babies were unconsolable in their crying, were vomiting many of their feedings, were wakeful, and were losing weight. Some, on examination, were found to be so dehydrated through vomiting that they had to be readmitted to the hospital. There, under the more relaxed handling of the aides, the babies slowly began to thrive again. In time, they were again released to the care of their own mothers, who, unfortunately, were still tensely depressed. Thus, the conditions were still there that made for a repetition of the troublesome clinical cycle. The mothers would come back again complaining that they felt completely inadequate to care for their babies, and it was obvious in time that no amount of counseling and demonstrations of infant care in their homes by the public health nursing staff was reversing these trends.

By the time many of these infants were six months of age, it was obvious that they were failing to develop truly need-satisfying relationships with their mothers. Instead, these Thlingit babies were by now reactively depressed; they had apparently established sufficient relationship with their mothers to continue to react fretfully when their mothers were emotionally unavailable to them. Attaching behavior on the infants' parts was noted in that they had developed normal following responses at about two months of age; at four months, social smiling toward the aides and nurses in the hospital could be observed. Nonetheless, they could only rarely be consoled by their mothers—a continuation of the neonatal pattern previously mentioned. Indeed, some of these older infants were so tense that they developed patterns of cyclic vomiting, and were failing to gain weight on this account.

By this point in these infants' lives, the staff together were forced to conclude, after repeated but unsuccessful attempts had been made to assist the young mothers with their troubled feelings, that many of these babies would have to be removed to other caretaking settings if they were to thrive. Accordingly, recommendations were then made to the Alaska Department of Child Welfare to begin the legal process by which these infants were placed in individual or group foster care homes in the area. Many of these new homes were already caring for preschool and even early adolescent Thlingit children at the time the infants who were failing to thrive were placed; indeed, some of the older foster children were ones who had been placed in these particular homes as infants and had grown up there. But, regardless of their ages, these foster children seemed to be growing up fairly satisfactorily following their placement. It seemed to this writer, who with his staff continued to provide medical care for these foster children, that these children subsequently met and mastered the essential tasks of development relatively well.

By contrast, many of the preschool children and the children of middle childhood age who continued to live with their own Thlingit Indian families began to reflect in their lives the despair felt in varying measure by their adolescent siblings and by their parents. These younger children were becoming mildly suspicious and mildly withdrawn in their ways of relating with people, and they were frequently morose in their moods. This depressed withdrawal of the children was noted by the writer on the occasion of his frequent home visits to care for their physical needs. And it was noted as well by these childrens' teachers, who contrasted sharply these childrens' emerging lifestyles with those of the community's white children. The Thlingit children, as a group, were developing varying degrees of overly inhibited (shy), mistrustful, and depressed traits in their personalities. In the classroom, many of them were silent, morose children who withdrew from visiting strangers and seemed to mistrust the teachers themselves.

Furthermore, in time, such reactive, negative traits as they were developing began to invade or influence the intellectual-cognitive functioning of these children. They daydreamed frequently in class in worried or despairing ways and failed to complete their assignments; or they adopted an oppositional pattern of procrastinating, blocking-out, and failing to hear their teachers and the other children in classroom discussions, with the overall result that, in time, they were falling farther and farther behind in their lessons. Indeed, these experiences of failure only reinforced the hopelessness and growing mistrust of others they felt and exhibited. And, by the time they were twelve years old or so, and sensitive to their failures—and to the overall socioeconomic differences between themselves and the white children—many of these Thlingit children dropped out of school to begin a pattern of drifting idly around the community.

Concurrently, the extension of a pattern of school failure, unemployment, idleness, and living with troubled parents and grandparents together took its toll on the adolescents in the Thlingit community. As emancipating youth, they frequently coped with the harsh problems of family life by rebelliously throwing off what few parental injunctions, limits, and supports remained. Many of them became drifters in the community, engaging with each other in spree drinking, sexual promiscuity, and in varying antisocial activities ranging from minor vandalism to stealing and malicious cutting and wounding of others.

In the hospital clinics and on the wards, most of these Thlingit adolescents were found to have strong underlying identity diffusion problems, in that they were developing no positive identities, no settled sense of themselves, no feeling of power in and of themselves. Consequently, as a group these adolescents felt defeated, harbored feelings of anomie or of not belonging really anywhere, and experienced deeply feelings of estrangement from others. In a diagnostic sense, many of them under increased stress ranged from having reactive anxiety and depressive disorders that were more transient, situational clinical states, to exhibiting behaviors indicative of such severe personality disorders as mistrustful and impulse-ridden life-styles.[3] It was of interest, too, that as a group under frequent stress these adolescents generally failed to develop psychoneurotic disorders or borderline psychotic states, which might have developed it they tended to internalize their problems and troubled feelings. Instead—and the writer feels this was true because of the prominent action-oriented

216

trait in the general Thlingit life-style—these youth more often acted out their negative feelings without delays, or inhibitions, or, often, any regard for the consequences of their behavior. The end effect of this tendency, as it has been mentioned, was to produce more acting-out disorders (the personality disorders) than other forms of psychopathology among them.

Inevitably, the psychopathological problems many of these sad, angry, disillusioned, impulsive adolescents were having made it very difficult for them to remain on their jobs—if, rarely, these were available to them—or to continue the training some of them were undertaking at the regional vocational school provided at that time in Sitka, Alaska, for Indian youth from throughout the Territory.

Understandably but unfortunately, these same Thlingit adolescents brought real personal problems and many maladaptive ways of coping with them into their later marriages as young adults. Unemployment, running hand in hand with that same pervasive sense of futility and despair, continued to plague their lives in this later stage of development. Indeed, it came to be experienced even more acutely as they grew older and attempted—and often failed—to establish intimate relationships with spouses and with acquaintances, or to relate well with fellow employees and to accept the direction of employers. As the writer experienced it, only a few clinic and hospitalized Thlingit young adults were not tensely depressed to some degree. And many of them, particularly the women who had been deserted in marriage by their husbands and left to care for large families of young and burdensome children on welfare support, made occasional suicide attempts. Although the actual suicide rate among Thlingit women and men was somewhat higher then in the area than among whites, the attempts at suicide were alarmingly higher in the Indian group. Even more striking, however, was the high incidence among them of such self-destructive acts as recurrent acute alcoholism; the several chronic brain syndromes frequently connected with extended alcohol abuse; broken marriages and homes; instances of actual child abuse; job failures; and acts of violence directed against one another, ranging from malicious cutting and wounding to occasional murder.

Of further interest to the writer was the fact that, from among the middle-aged and even the older Thlingit men and women, there were many who were equally as despairing as the young adults in the community but who, unlike them, had overly dependent or overly inhibited

217

life-styles. These particular older individuals did not act out their futility and despair against others as the younger and impulsive men and women would do. Instead, they "acted in" their troubled feelings, as it were, by suppressing and failing to verbalize them with others. As a direct consequence of not verbalizing their most troubled feelings, many individuals from among this group developed such psychophysiological disorders from time to time as neurodermatitis (hives), bronchial asthma attacks, and bleeding duodenal ulcers. At times these individuals, too, by turning despair and anger (engendered by harsh circumstances) against themselves, only deepened their depressive feelings.

Many of these more dependent and shy older individuals had been raised in families who had turned inward, upon themselves, in response to harsh living circumstances. Adults in these families generally tightened limits, and overprotectively hovered over and infantilized their children. These parental practices produced compliant, shy, dependent traits in the children, traits that remained as significant ones in their own adult life-styles. As the writer talked with them, many of these older individuals characterized their families of origin as attempting to "live in peace with the white man, to tolerate but not be a part of his ways, and to maintain dignity at all times."

Indeed, the comments like this one made by these older men and women pointed up another aspect of the Thlingit Indian group's functioning throughout southeastern Alaska in those years. To put it simply, their culture was dying. The colorful legends, the active dances, the tribal councils and their injunctions were all rapidly dwindling to the point of being mere parodies of hollow forms of customs. By 1955, the once-powerful traditions that had guided the Thlingits for centuries were becoming ineffectual in the lives of the community, the family, and the individual. It had taken years for this decline in the old belief system, of course. It began, as it has been noted, with the coming of the Russian and the American colonists to the area and the previously marauding Thlingits' subjugation. It was hastened, too, by their necessity to ally their economic life chances with those who now possessed not only the territory, but the authority and the capital to exploit and to extract its riches. And it was reinforced in shameful and self-demeaning ways, through the failure of those who now occupied their former lands to accept the Thlingits on a more egalitarian level.

In just several generations in more recent times, the Thlingits, once a proud and conquering people, were relegated to the shameful posi-

218

tion of being treated as second-class persons. They did make an attempt to adapt to these new circumstances by accepting the only jobs—low-paying ones involving primarily manual labor—offered them. But the changes wrought in their lives failed to maintain their self-acceptance and self-esteem as a people. Despair began among them, as well as reactive anger. And as these feelings persisted and deepened, it became natural for many of the action-oriented adolescents and young adults among them to project the blame for the overall decline of the Thlingits' fortunes on the old tribal ways and traditions. As one young Thlingit adult man, whom the writer frequently treated for acute alcoholism, once expressed it, "I don't give a damn about those [dances]; and you can shove the tribal [council], too; none of that will ever get me a job today, or my respect back!"

Obviously, for traditions of any type to continue to be accepted by rising generations of any people, they must be viewed as valid forces contributing to the overall adaptive development of the group. Other-wise, they are often cast aside as ineffective in the face of present circumstances by those who, like the younger generations of Thlingit people, do indeed face harsh lives and times and who possess as a group a life-style that makes it very difficult for them to "roll with the punches."

Simultaneous with the events just described, there was another fac-tor entering in to diminish further the Thlingit peoples' ability to cope with changing circumstances in southeastern Alaska. Reference is made here to the fact that they—like the other three Indian ethnic groups in the Territory—were decimated by the various forms of tuberculosis. Host factors and accompanying immunologic systems were very differ-ent and ineffective among the Alaskan Indians at the time of the coming of the Russians and the white Americans to the Territory, it would seem, and they were stricken with pulmonary and bone-and-joint tuberculosis for many years. Only now is a reversal or slowing of this chronic disease trend becoming noticeable. For several genera-tions of Alaskan Indians, the death toll and debilitating chronic orthope-dic and cardiopulmonary problems among them were literally appalling.

To sum it all up, one very fine Thlingit gentleman, an eighty-two-year-old man who, with his wife, came frequently to visit the writer in those years, once sadly shared these words:

Our people in many ways are no more. They must fish to live, and the fish are dying. The young people are angry and sad, and they

219

want no more of our old ways. So our ways, too, are dying. And we die so much so often from the sickness. Where are we going? And when will it all end?

EXPERIENCES AMONG THE ESKIMO

The characteristic traits outlined for the Thlingit people as a group, many of which made it difficult for them to cope with changing circumstances in their economically, culturally, and emotionally impoverished community, were in direct contrast to those traits possessed by the Eskimo men and women who during 1955–57 were hospitalized in the annex of the Juneau hospital for long-term chemotherapy for pulmonary tuberculosis. There were 24 Eskimo men and women there in all, who ranged in age between 22 and 64 years. They had been sent to the Juneau hospital from villages far to the north, some as far away in Alaska as 1,000 miles. And when the writer first came to be their attending physician, many of them had been hospitalized there for many months. In fact, some of them were to spend an average of a year and a half in the annex before they were well enough to return home.

As a group on the annex, the Eskimo patients were warm, personable, altogether friendly people who sang and laughed and talked openly among themselves and with staff personnel with no hint of personal mistrust, sullenness, moroseness, or fear. Moreover, whenever any one of them was situationally concerned (a letter from his home village might contain news of another family member's becoming ill, for example) the Eskimo patients quickly talked about these circumstances and openly shared their troubled feelings with one another and with the staff. In the words of one hospital aide, herself an Eskimo woman who had been trained in a southeastern Alaskan program and who remained close to her people and therefore knew them well, "Our people share whatever it is we have, and how we feel, with each other; and, afterward, we sing and laugh or play a game together."

Certainly, this young woman's words found frequent expression from among the Eskimo patients in the annex. Every one of them seemed to know every other person's life story and circumstances in accurate detail. This was true, it seemed to the writer, because they had both an immense capacity for empathy and an objective capacity for self-observation. As possessed by any people anywhere, these two

220

capacities are important aspects of anyone's integrative personality functions; and, taken together, they often enable the person possessing them consciously to make very adaptive choices for action for himself based on the feeling-oriented accuracy of his self-observations and the observations of others.[4] Time and time again, the Eskimo patients demonstrated how well they knew themselves and others, and could plan their actions according to these observations.

Just how sensitive this capacity for emphatic and accurate observation of self and others was for these people was demonstrated one day for the writer on one of his ward rounds in the annex. In the open ward, in full view of the other eleven men there, a twenty-nine-year-old Eskimo man gave the writer one ivory die he had made. This man, an ivory-carver from the northern village of Shismaref, who spoke very little English, ordinarily on the ward made pairs of such dice to sell to local tourists through a crafts clearinghouse in Juneau. Puzzled as to why the man would extend him *one* die as an obvious gift when he customarily made *pairs* of them, the writer discreetly inquired through the Eskimo aide as an interpreter about the matter. In reply, the ivory-carver warmly, but somewhat shyly and certainly diplomatically, told the aide that he guessed "the doctor was a man who didn't gamble." The man clearly had no way of directly knowing this one, highly accurate aspect of the writer's own personality functioning other than through his own careful observations of the writer's behaviors on the ward and the inferences he had so carefully drawn from these data. At the same time that he obviously intended his gift to be pleasing to the writer and to be of a type that would not risk offending him, the man also embodied in it his very real pride and self-sufficiency as a craftsman. No more clear vignette of one Eskimo man's highly adaptive personal functioning could have been provided for the writer than through this experience.

Moreover, this was not an isolated instance of mature personal functioning on the part of one man. For he himself, as well as the other Eskimo men and women in the annex, demonstrated again and again how maturely and adaptively they functioned in all manner of events and relationships while they were hospitalized. Furthermore, it was easy for the writer to conjecture that they related among themselves in very similar ways in their home villages. In fact, this was confirmed for him later in that period, when other U.S. Public Health

221

Service physicians, who were stationed at small hospitals in the north among the Eskimo people themselves, relayed to him how well these people did function there on the whole. These other physicians pointed out how well the Eskimo people coped with economic life circumstances that were as difficult at times for them in their own villages as events were for the Thlingit people in southeastern Alaska. *But what seemed to distinguish the two Indian groups along coping lines was, first and foremost, the differences between their group life-styles.* The Eskimo people were a warm, outgoing, trusting, friendly people who welcomed strangers as equals and, as a consequence of this way of relating with them, made it easy for others to treat them as equals in turn. This relationship capacity was also reinforced by their capacity for empathy with others; through their capacity for accurate self-observation; by their unfailing interest in talking over events among themselves; by the ability to neutralize troublesome feelings and events in stories, songs, and games in which they laughed at themselves; and through their immense respect for their traditional belief systems embodied in legends (these were futuristic and growth-promoting in themes), which were carefully preserved among succeeding generations. Thus, unlike the Thlingit people, the Eskimo possessed a group life-style that enabled them to "roll with the punches."

Furthermore, and of great interest to the writer with regard to regional child-training themes, was the evidence then that the Eskimo people really cherished their children; they did not apparently consider them a burden, but welcomed them into their lives and trained them through succeeding stages of growth in ways insuring that they, too, would function well as adults. The data for this conclusion were provided through the observations made of Eskimo family life, structure, and functioning by those other public health physicians mentioned earlier with whom the writer had continuing contact.

Thus, the Eskimo parents were observed to be actively participating with their children in the evolution of basic relationships to each other as differentiated, trusted, cherished individuals. These parents and their younger children were capable of evoking satisfying action from each other in terms of need and displaying mutually responsive communication and affective exchange. The children seemed to be developing autonomously with the appropriate mastery of motor-muscular skills in the toddler period and basically sound foundations of sex-role differentiation in the later preschool period. Closely related to this satisfactory emotional-personality development were observed age-appropriate language and intellectual-cognitive skills. And, last, the adolescents from among the Eskimo families seemed to have few identity problems, even though they were passing through hard economic times, as were the others, and changes were coming about in the ways older individuals were making their livelihood.

On many occasions in later years, the writer was again to observe the importance of peoples' regional life-styles to their coping skills as he began his work among troubled children and their families in the Southern Appalachian region as a child psychiatrist. And these experiences led him, frequently, to compare and contrast the life-styles of these mountain families with those of the Thlingit and of the Eskimo people among whom he had worked earlier in his clinical career.

EXPERIENCES IN SOUTHERN APPALACHIA

For well over a hundred years, the people living in the southern Appalachian Mountains have presented some striking differences in the ways they function as individuals and as families when they are compared along socioeconomic class lines. Throughout the region, the stable working class (although they are generally poor by federal income standards), the middle, and the upper classes generally succeed remarkably well in providing for their health, education, and welfare needs. The most important developmental force accounting for this success is regional familism—close, interdependent family functioning, of which the most obvious expression is the extensive kinship system in the mountains (see T. Ford 1969; Weller 1965). By ensuring that even limited resources will be shared among the extended family, particularly at times of crisis, familism stabilizes family life, structure, and functioning. This positive side of familism provides a steady state even for very poor families. In this respect the Appalcahian very poor, unlike the often socially disorganized families raised in urban slums, possess a strength that often can be tapped for redirection of their lives in many areas (Looff 1976a). Nevertheless, one finds the manifold problems of the very poor to be the most vexing in the region.

Throughout Appalachia, many of the very poor are clustered together, living in small, dying communities, like those found at Granny's

223

Branch and in Muddy Gap.[5] There, amid the squalor surrounding the shacks in which poverty-stricken people live out their lives, one can perceive why this aspect of Appalachia has been a thorn in the side of the United States for so long. In the rough coves and hollows of the region, locked in by geography and bypassed by a rapidly developing country and economy, these small, dying communities in Appalachia became synonymous with destitution and backwardness.

The term *very poor* in these dying communities refers to those families who live at the bottom of the socioeconomic ladder, as distinguished from those poor who are one rung up this ladder—the generally self-sufficient and at least moderately successful working-class families. The very poor include individuals who have extremely limited employment skills. They are usually unskilled, casual laborers who remain chronically unemployed (many are on welfare support) or severely underemployed. They are apt to have less than a fourth-grade education; many are illiterate or only barely able to read and write. For the most part, they come from families in which lack of education, and lack of adequate income, have tended to be the rule for several generations. These families in Appalachia, as elsewhere in the nation, are often referred to as the "hard-core poor"—and this hard core seems to be the axis of the "cycle of poverty." The situation underlying the terms *cycle of poverty* (poverty that extends from generation to generation) and *culture of poverty* (the distinguishing folkways of the very poor) have been the subject of Appalachian regional writing for years.

These writers have pointed up one aspect of these dying communities of the very poor in the region—the feuds, the inadequate agriculture, the harshness of despairing lives, the shocking illiteracy rate, the poverty, the squalor, and the chronically high incidence of disease. Overall, the Appalachian very poor in these communities could be described as the product of initial backwoods intransigence followed by generations of isolation, poor schools, and governmental neglect.

But as one looks more closely at the lives of the very poor in these communities, one finds that there are two general attributes of their functioning as families. The first of these attributes is the severe stress under which such families must operate as a result of their chronic exposure to a great number and variety of severe problems. The second is the limited number of alternative solutions to these problems that they perceive as being available to them.

The mental health implications of this severe and chronic stress

224

suffered by very poor families in Appalachia have been traced out in the writer's earlier book, *Appalachia's Children*. Certainly the very poor living in these communities do seem to have more than their share of mental retardation and mental disorder. Taking the matter of protracted stress broadly, however, one can examine the characteristic ways by which these very poor families attempt to cope with such stress. How do they try to handle their problems? Which techniques available to them seem adaptive, and which do not? We have much empirical evidence to suggest that in the past, on the whole, the very poor in the region have coped with stress only partially or have not been able to cope well at all. In fact, their failures to cope leave the anxieties and strains raised by stress largely raw, unbound.

The relatively rigid, fatalistic, nonverbal, antiintellectual life-style of the very poor in Appalachia is closely associated with unbound, raw anxiety. Lacking, on the whole, adequate ways of relieving anxiety, the very poor in the region characteristically bow down under the sheer weight of it. They develop an apathetic, resigned, careworn appearance; helpless-hopeless inner feelings; and silent personal withdrawal from tasks and from other people. Such a state, called "the poverty syndrome" by many, can be conceptualized as a chronic psychological depression. Lacking the defenses against their anxieties and this depression, a great number of the very poor find temporary escape in such expressive activities as fantasy, dramatic behavior, psychophysiologic and conversion reactions, impulsive acts, and alcohol abuse. Quite often, the writer has found, the behavior and emotional disorders of the very poor in Appalachia can be interpreted overall as depressed surrender to failure that is perceived by them as inevitable. Like an animal caught in a trap, the very poor tend to lie still, in quiet, withdrawn, conservation-of-energies patterns; at other times, they, like the trapped, kick out in desperate, futile attempts to escape.

Inevitably, the adjustive techniques and failures to cope with severe and protracted stress, characteristic of the very poor in Appalachia, effect how they train the rising generation of their children. As we look more closely at Appalachian family life, structure, and functioning, we find that the adjustive techniques of the very poor used in their relationships with each other and with their children are themselves an outgrowth of the unique life-style of these individuals.

This life-style of the Appalachian very poor involves the interacting traits of individualism (whatever the mountaineer does, he has himself

225

in focus; group activities are engaged in only to the extent to which his private ends are served); traditionalism (he is bound to the past, and to its traditions, ideas, and values); fatalism (the mountaineer feels his life is right, even though it is discouraging); and action-orientation (he is episodic and impulsive, as opposed to routine-seeking); stoicism (silence and denial cover intense inner anxieties) in manner and speech; and an intense person-orientation (a major life goal of the mountaineer is to be accepted as an individualist by others in his group).

These interacting traits of the life-style of the Appalachian very poor give characteristic color to their interpersonal relationships. In particular, they permeate the interactions of lower-class parents and their children, producing the strong familistic orientation families have in this region. Through familism, a major dynamic characteristic of these families, individuals are markedly close and interdependent. They are primarily inner-directed, and hold an overriding sense of obligation to extended-family members. Within such a family system, children are taught from birth in both verbal and nonverbal ways to maintain this family closeness. They are taught to do so even at the expense of an individual family member's personal-social maturation. In such a context, the individual's own growth and development are clearly subordinate to the prime task of maintaining the family as a tight-knit unit.

The writer has elsewhere speculated that this intense familism is trained into Appalachian children; it begins with an observable pattern of parental overemphasis on the infancy period itself. This early pattern is strongly reinforced by later events. The families persist in employing infantile modes in the course of relating with their children through subsequent stages of child development. Moreover, as development proceeds, there is a consistent parental pattern of underemphasis on children's autonomy, initiative, curiosity, exploration, and adequate sex-role differentiation.

Another prominent theme in Appalachia emerges from the lower class families' inability to supervise their wandered-off toddlers, preschoolers, and even older children appropriately. When the children are close by, parents generally display the overprotective, indulgent, permissive behavior characteristic of the children's infancy. The children's response to such treatment is typical: they run free, following any impulse when they are away from adults. And they react with varying degrees of infantility—clinging, whining, demanding, basking with pleasure at being babied—when they return. As they begin to use

226

the autonomy that the development of motor-muscular skills makes possible, sooner or later these children will actually get out of sight of the parents. At this point, they are often treated by these same parents as though they no longer existed. As a result, they frequently get into situations of real or potential danger.

It may be that Appalachian lower-class parents see the child's emerging autonomy as a threat to their complete domination and possession of him that familism demands; they deal with the threat simply by denying it. When the child does come to them, this is taken as a sign that he wants them in their familiar caretaking role.

Inevitably, these lower-class children continue to grow, and then, for the most part, the adults simply stop playing with them. they supervise them inappropriately, and furnish no positive models or training in setting limits on impulse. They establish no disciplinary controls, and they give no preparation for age-appropriate relating to or talking with other adults. These patterns are most evident in families in the region from the very poor and the working classes, but, in an attenuated way, they hold true for the middle and upper classes as well.

Another prominent training theme in the region emerges from conflicts around sexual development, maturation, and functioning. Although present in all socioeconomic classes, again the conflict seems most acute in lower-class and working-class families. For them the open overcrowding necessitated by poverty serves in itself to create numerous tensions, sexual as well as nonsexual. It is also true that the prevalent strict Protestant ethos is a powerful force in maintaining a conflicted view of sexuality in the region.

The life-styles of their parents, the closeness and inner-directedness of the extended-family units, and the operation of the several training themes mentioned above act collectively as a powerful shaping force on the development of many very poor Appalachian children. Just how these children do grow up, measured in terms of the psychopathology to which many of them are subject, and the special personality strengths they all possess, are issues taken up at this point.

Regional Psychopathology

Clearly related to the training theme of close, interdependent family functioning (regional familism), the writer has found from his clinical data over the past twelve years, is the great frequency with which

227

separation anxiety is a major emotional conflict faced by Appalachian children and by their parents. Actual, threatened, or symbolic disruptions in parent-child and other family relationships cause great concern. Separation anxiety was the most prominent causal conflict in children coming to the writer's field child psychiatry clinics with the following psychopathological disorders: acute and chronic schoolphobic reactions, overly dependent personality disorders, deviations in social development, symbiotic psychosis, various psychophysiological reactions, and the consolidated-school syndrome. Furthermore, these clinical data suggest a strikingly higher incidence for such dependency-related disorders in children from Appalachia than in largely urban children. Thus, these field data suggest that this particular type of dependency-related psychopathology is a regional problem of great frequency. And nowhere is it more in evidence than among the children of very poor families who live in the small, dying communities of the region.

As the writer and his staff examined the current interactional patterns and earlier training patterns of families having a child with one of these disorders, we found marked evidence of training in obligatory closeness, coupled with rigorous training in avoiding separation that would disrupt the close family system.

Equally striking to us as we worked with children having various dependency-related disorders was the absence of certain disorders (particularly primary behavior disorders) based wholly or in large part on emotional deprivation in infancy. These disorders simply did not appear in our clinic children.

What the field data, therfore, seem to suggest, is the following hypotheses: regional familism, when overused by families in training their children, is a strong, specific force in shaping those later psychopathological disorders in the children based on dependency themes and related separation anxiety. Furthermore, the same regional familism precludes the formation of those specific types of children's psychopathology based on extreme emotional deprivation in infancy.

And related to a pathological exaggeration of the regional sexual conflicts among the lower class, were children having the following disorders: hysterical or conversion and dissociative reactions: hysterical personality disorders (in adolescent girls); and various other types of personality disorders (as in adolescent boys with underlying psychosexual identity problems).

228

Earlier it was mentioned how frequently verbal communication is a problem among very poor Appalachian families. What amounts to regional taciturnity for them grows out of the characteristic functioning of these families. The family's ties of obligatory closeness to one another, the continuous presence of severe stresses of all types, and the need to ward off situations viewed as potentially disruptive of close family ties, place severe strain upon all family members. This strain may help to explain some of the intensive internal conflicts as well as some of the striking lack of verbal communication inside families. An example of this lies in the observation that the most severely strained families have the greatest lack of sharing such troubled feelings in words.

Thus it is that individuals raised in relatively strained, silent families were prone to develop certain disorders, ones that depend for their development upon the person's inability to express himself adequately. Among these disorders in children were psychophysiologic reactions, conversion reactions (which depend for their genesis as much upon nonverbality as upon sexual and aggressive conflicts), and elective mutism. Among the very poor Appalachian children, this group of problems were viewed primarily as disorders of communication.

Another prominent training theme mentioned earlier has to do with the failure of Appalachian lower-class families to train their young children in acquiring a capacity to store tension. These children very frequently grow up to be wild, impulsive (albeit warm, personable, outgoing, and friendly) older children, adolescents, and adults. They are not trained to acquire inner controls on their impulses. As a result, they present problems that arise from their impulsiveness, problems for themselves and, primarily, for others. For example, as older individuals they abruptly might wander into and out of marriages, jobs, and other major life tasks. They often strike out at others aggressively or steal what they want, acting on the sudden whim of the moment. Should they marry and have their own children, their impulsiveness often presents a problem for their families. Their employers, the courts, and other social agencies typically find themselves coping with similar difficulties.

These four child-developmental patterns—training in dependency, training in psychosexual conflict, training in nonverbality, and training resulting in poor impulse controls—are prominent in Appalachia among very poor families, and together form the basis for the great majority of psychopathological disorders found among the region's children.

Regional Personality Strengths

To emphasize that certain regional training forces among very poor Appalachian families can lead to psychopathology is to present only half the developmental picture. Actually, as these specific regional training themes are examined closely, they are found to be two-edged swords. One edge clearly has to do with the cultural shaping of mental disorders. But the other edge is also of critical importance. It involves the cultural shaping of healthy aspects of personality functioning. These are basic ego strengths possessed by the very poor in Appalachia, as well as by those in the region's middle and upper classes.

One aspect of the culture that has already been mentioned is regional familism, which stabilizes many aspects of Appalachian family life. It makes for coherent family structure, and provides a model for its functioning. This positive side of familism is clearly seen in the traditional tendency of the individual to cope with stress of all kinds by turning inward upon his close family system. Hence, in time of need or crisis, people in this region will share themselves and their often meager resources with one another. Such a turning to each other provides a very real basis for continued emotional and economic support of many individuals. More than that, it also engages the extended family in delightful reunions and other get-togethers. These are of enormous importance in assuring the individual's place in a person-oriented society. Moreover, regional familism accounts for two further strengths in the Appalachian individual's personal functioning.

The first is a marked capacity for essentially trusting relatedness. Although many of the very poor Appalachian adults and children one meets are initially shy, reserved, and even somewhat suspicious of outsiders, they soon drop this guardedness, and relate in ways that are quite personal and often very intense. They begin to involve themselves in discussions with remarkable warmth and candor, and with no sense of personal isolation (anomie). In fact, their relatedness often combines such warmth, openness, and earthiness that it suggests the traditional spontaneity of young children.

It is of considerable interest to note that this basic capacity for related-

230

ness crosses socioeconomic class lines in Appalachia. For example, the often grubby, ragged children of the lower class we saw in field clinics were frequently wild, impulse-ridden, and manipulative. But along with these traits was a warm way of reaching out to others that had the quality of an essential relatedness.

A review of the developmental background of many of these very poor children led to the conclusion that they are well trained in basic relatedness from infancy on. They are not trained nearly as well, however, in acquiring controls over their aggressive and other impulses. As babies and older children, these lower-class children are well liked; but in many areas they are allowed to do just as they please. Beyond infancy, appropriate developmental supports involving a balance between gratification of need and capacity to delay, along with the achievement of limits and controls, are not readily maintained by the lower-class families in the area. This seemed to account for the difficulties that beset many of the older lower-class children; they had trouble with perceptual skills needed for orienting to a new environment, with communication skills, and with capacities to delay gratification and to establish inner impulse controls. But during infancy, the lower-class as well as the middle- and the upper-class families freely gave of themselves to their children. As an outgrowth of this, the children retained a considerable measure of the ability to relate with others in spite of the difficulties with other capacities.

There is a second strength that is also a positive derivative of regional familism. For both Appalachian adult and child, an unusual feeling orientation emerges from this background, a capacity to experience deeply and to differentiate exquisitely the feeling content of one's experiences. The early training in family closeness and relatedness seems central here. An outgrowth of this early training is the skill in observing and correctly interpreting the often subtle behavior of people who are often relatively silent. Early in such training, the child learns to pick up feeling-oriented cues from the behavior, rather than from the words, of adults.

These capacities for relatedness and feeling orientation, which are also a part of the personal functioning of the very poor Appalachian adults and children, are frequently helpful to those who attempt to assist them. Since giving and receiving help proceed in an interpersonal context, this factor of feeling-oriented mutual relationship becomes a powerful one in the undertaking.

DISCUSSION

The children described thus far from three quite different cultural groups are in a real sense not "all children." Since no child grows up in a vacuum, the children of these dying communities cannot be understood apart from the historical, geographic, and socioeconomic characteristics of the areas in which they grow. Knowledge of these children also requires some knowledge of the lives of parents, teachers, and the many others upon whom they are dependent. Moreover, the behavior of any person over his life-span is more complex than any of us can imagine. Given this as a fact, the best the writer feels we can do is to muster confidence that developmental order is to be found in our study of these communities; that from the facts we gather we can discern relevant forces and factors that enable us to compare the early and later life relationships of these children. Here the writer's own clinical work in child development and general mental health in several of these communities complements what has been observed in the past about the structure and functioning of local family life and about forces in the development—and subsequent decline—of the regions themselves.

The National Picture

There are dangers in generalizing from the traits of families of one particular dying community to all others. Nonetheless, there are points of data on which the several communities presented here can be compared with the others elsewhere in the nation.

Initially, we are all aware of the influence of geographic location on dying communities and of the phenomenon of clustering of physical and social pathologies. Most of these communities, in time, become poverty-stricken areas, which, like those elsewhere in the nation, are usually marked by disease, substandard housing, inadequate education, broken homes, and chronic unemployment. Poverty and disease 0are often inseparable: abundant statistical data indicate that the poor have higher death rates for tuberculosis, cancer of the cervix, cardiovascular-renal disease, influenza, pneumonia, and home accidents. In the writer's experience, the poor within the Thlingit Indian and the Appalachian groups—like the poor elsewhere—also have more mental disorders and mental retardation, more births per 100,000 inhabitants, more illegitimate births, more pregnancies with little or no prenatal care, an infant mortality rate two or three times as high as that in more affluent sections, more orthopedic and visual impairments, and a host of other preventable and correctable conditions.

However meaningful these general statistics may be, they cannot reveal the suffering, despair, and apathy that we know exist in unmeasured quantity among many families in dying communities. Such helpless and hopeless feelings are a powerful corrosive force on family life, structure, and functioning as a child-rearing environment. Thus, in time, the interaction between the socioeconomic circumstances afoot in dying communities and the suffering they bring produces many kinds of improverishment for these families—economic, physical, emotional, cultural, and intellectual.

But what is so striking is that these combined forces produce quite different effects on given groups of people. Despite some promising investigations of causal relationships between environmental circumstances and disturbances in human development, there is much in that whole area that is as yet unclear. *We do have evidence, however, that economic decline within communities in combination with social disorganization is frequently psychopathogenic, in contrast to groups where various others social conditions prevail.* Accordingly, the psychosocial (developmental) and psychopathological correlates of socioeconomic decline within communities rest on a tremendous number of variables.

Indeed, we are, in general, perhaps ill-advised to lump thousands of people within dying communities together—at least psychologically. A better approach—and one demanded by the data provided by the two Indian groups and the very poor Appalachian whites presented here—is to recognize that *analysis of families in dying communities is best directed through appraisal of various subgroupings rather than through speculation about them as a whole, or any common denominator thereof.* This point is certainly confirmed by the three groups of people presented here. For them, *the most important factor accounting for their relative successes or failures in coping as families within their beleaguered communities was their varying regional life-styles.*

Effects of Regional Life-Styles

The psychological strengths and the degree of emotional health reported by others (and observed to some extent by the writer himself) from their observations of impoverished Eskimo adults and children

233

living under conditions of severe environmental stress were in sharp contrast to the kinds of serious lapses in child-rearing practices and subsequent psychopathology observed by the writer among Thlingit Indian and very poor Appalachian families. In addition to a life-style of reasonable maturity—one that equipped them well to cope with all kinds of severe and protracted stress—the Eskimo people possessed a psychological mobility that enabled them to move from place to place within their region to offset local decline. Furthermore, their culture came equipped with a futuristic belief system that was basically optimistic and growth-promoting. It was no wonder, then, that among such families child-rearing practices were eminently adaptive, enabling their children to mature generally normally, becoming in time adults themselves who could adapt to change and make reasonable choices for their lives.

By contrast, many of the Thlingit Indian and very poor Appalachian families faced handicaps beyond the severe stresses imposed by poverty, ill health, inadequate education, and the others confronting them in their dying communities. Each of these groups, through generations, had become psychologically locked in to harsh lands that in many ways had limited and defeated them. But what studies of these two peoples clearly point up is the amount of social disorganization within their lives. Much of this came about because the personality patterns or life-styles of the adults were ill-equipped to cope well with stress. Adults in the two groups shared inner-directed traits of pessimism, fatalism, stoicism, and individualism, which, from generation to generation, locked in their inner forces and led them to perpetuate self-defeating attitudes among their children. These regional life-styles, combined with the problems of economics and geography, provide the basis for the resistance to change that has marked the attempts at intervention to modify the attitudes and even the life-styles of the two groups. This developmental process ends with what could be described as the pride and privatism of people unable to compete outside the ancient kinships of the fjord and the hollow.

What is so impressive and yet disheartening is the evidence we have from this report about how early this process begins in the life-cycle. The problems among the Thlingits and the Appalachian very poor begin long before their children reach school age. For example, the children of the many socially disorganized Thlingit families the writer observed did not develop basically trustful relationships in infancy.

Their chaotic, impulse-ridden parents frequently rejected them or related in intensely ambivalent, inconsistent ways. The children grew up to be hypersensitively alert to rejection and to real and anticipated dangers in the environment. Many of these children became immature drifters later on as adolescents and adults. And paralleling this personality disorganization were lags in their language and intellectual-cognitive development.

Yet, even as we compare the very real problems adults and children share from among the Thlingit Indian and Appalachian very poor, we see some differences, too. The point has been made that, although the Appalachian lower class shared hard lives (which give rise to maladaptive attitudes) with the Thlingit people, they, nonetheless, retain basic relatedness, a capacity for basic trustfulness in relationships with others. Thus, in this important way the Appalachian very poor are not as socially disorganized as many of the Thlingit families. In Appalachia, familism was pointed out to be the force accounting for this particular influence; as a result of familism, many very poor Appalachian children retain a good capacity for basic trustfulness, although, like the Thlingit children, they have difficulties with other capacities. And these shared difficulties produced another characteristic by which growing children in the two groups can be ultimately compared: the interacting, reinforcing factors of physical, mental, and cultural isolation operate to hold them in disadvantaged areas, frequently resisting changes that would bring them into effective contact with the outside world.

It all seems to add up to looking back to where the problems begin. This is what comparison of the three impoverished groups outlined in this chapter attempts to do. When we look at the information provided, we eventually wonder about ways for solving the tough problem of assimilating and bringing many Thlingit and lower-class Appalachian families into the mainstream of American life. The implication of these studies is that we must start at the beginnings of the problems, with the very young children. We would like to have a blueprint available for reaching the problems of these particular dying communities—and of others— where they start, in the fundamental child-rearing patterns that close in the individual and make it difficult for many to accept change. The Thlingit children of the fjords of Alaska and the children of the very poor in the Appalachian mountains are born with potentials that are too often never realized. Ultimately, we are challenged to try to see to it that they develop into individuals who can make choices and accept change.

The process of redevelopment being talked about here does not take place overnight or even in a few years. The implications of these studies are that we can have hope for people in these dying communities, but we must also have patience—and multidisciplinary diligence.

NOTES

1. During the past two decades, rapid growth in the lumbering industry in southeastern Alaska has provided additional employment for Thlingit Indians as well as other families. This labor market, coupled with a strong comeback in the salmon canning industry brought about by improved fisheries management, has fostered economic resurgence in the region. Consequently, the Thlingit community is no longer partially dying economically. Concurrently, the community has begun to give careful attention to their cultural legacy in various ways. In time, observers will be able to determine what effect, if any, this reversal in the Thlingit's socioeconomic fortunes will have on their families as child-rearing environments. Personal communications from health professionals in Alaska to the writer in recent years have indicated that the Thlingit regional life-style, however, has not changed. This being so, the writer would speculate that very few changes will be seen over the community's earlier child-rearing practices as reported here. If this is borne out by later observations, then regional life-styles of people remain the most significant variable accounting for child-rearing in dying (or viable) communities—the writer's central thesis.

2. The central tasks confronting any individual in the various stages of development are presented by Erikson (1963).

3. These and other diagnostic categories used in this report are discussed by the Group for the Advancement of Psychiatry (1966).

4. A discussion and list of the major personality functions as the writer conceptualizes them is in Looff 1976b.

5. These two small, dying communities are in Clay County, in southeastern Kentucky. For a description of a family living in Muddy Gap, see "Family Portrait," in Looff 1971.

236

10

The Dying Community as a Human Habitat for the Elderly

MARY WYLIE

School of Social Work
University of Wisconsin-Madison

What is it like to grow old in a dying community? Do the convictions of social gerontological or community theory truly reflect an understanding of the pleasures and sorrows, the expectations and resignations, the day-to-day activities, and the plans for tomorrow shared by the elderly residents of such a community? And would aging persons in a dying community have similar or different perspectives on growing old than their counterparts in a growing, thriving community, or perhaps, than their counterparts in another culture where old age is differently valued?

Although, as others have demonstrated, the dying community is a natural phenomenon, a predominant American value set oriented toward youth, achievement, and progress leads us to view the dying community as an undesirable environment in which to live. Social gerontological theory provides a needed corrective by suggesting, although weakly and tentatively, that a dying community may provide an environment in which the elderly can and do thrive. The major attempt here, based on a study of the aged in one community, is to convey what it is like to grow old in a community that is dying.

Before presenting the data, the state of the art in social gerontology and the relationship of that discipline's theories to community theory needs outlining. What quickly becomes apparent is that social gerontology is fully preoccupied with psychological or social-psychological variables at the expense of examining macro-level structural features that might impinge upon the aging process. At the same time, community theory has developed in the absence of comparative community research or without specification of community properties with which community relations may vary (Reiss 1959:118). There is very little systematic empirical evidence to support a hypothesized relationship between community environment and age (Taietz 1975:357). Taietz quotes Lawton as suggesting the environment is merely the screen against which the dynamic aspects of human behavior are played out.

Aging as a field of inquiry for social scientists was almost nonexistent until the 1950s. As a relatively recent addition to the social sciences, social gerontology has few analytic models. Brown's (1973:3–27) review and critique of social gerontological theory stands as a major comprehensive statement on the state of the art. Her analysis, included here, provides a framework for hypothesizing a relationship between a dying community and the lives of its elderly residents.

Social gerontology's theories can be classified into three major categories: developmental theory; continuity theory; and transition to role loss perspective. Before the development of those three approaches, there was a common sense "activity" perspective on aging, which maintained that individuals should compensate for the inevitable loss of family, friends, and employment opportunities by remaining active and assuming new interests. Essentially the aged person was viewed as relatively unchanged as a result of age, maintaining the same social and psychological needs as other adults. The activity perspective has been criticized conceptually as well as empirically, particularly by Rosow (1963), who highlighted the middle-class bias of the perspective and noted major class differences in participation. The perspective also avoided the issue of meaningful activities, suggesting as it does that any activity will substitute for role losses.

Characteristic of developmental theory is the formulation of psychosocial tasks or stages for various phases of the life cycle. These tasks are presented as universal, sequential, and irreversible. Drawing upon Erikson's (1950) work, Peck (1956), for example, hypothesized a number of developmental tasks appropriate for middle age and old age.

238

The first specifically gerontological theory of aging, presented by Cumming and Willing (1961), is the "disengagement" theory, which posits a mutual and synchronized disengagement between the individual and society, a necessary prelude to the individual's and society's preparation for the individual's death. Withdrawal is not an adaptive response to a hostile world, but rather an intrinsic developmental stage desired by the elderly. While the findings in the disengagement study are of questionable validity, the theory nevertheless has been the focal point of extensive debate for the last decade. The original model was later modified to suggest that the individual's personality mediates the process and thus healthy aging may be found in either engagement or withdrawal. This revision effectively reduced the theoretical power of the model: given an unspecified process of personality mediation, no specific predictions logically flow from the theory. The model thus is an argument for the functionality of the status quo—the burden for adjustment rests with the individual, and the social order is spared the necessity of structural reform.

In an attempt to reconcile seemingly contradictory data, Rosow, in 1967, presented a criterion theory, which recognized that "healthy" aging can be seen in either activity or withdrawal. The key element is in the continuity of an individual's life-style. Adjustment derives from maximum continuity and minimum discontinuity between the pre- (middle age) and post- (old age) criterion periods. The theoretical model does not specify the realm or realms in which continuity must be maintained. In asserting that healthy aging is contingent upon continuity, the model must make one of two assumptions: that disadvantaged persons, unable to maintain continuity due to conditions such as insufficient finances or decreased health status, are doomed to pathology in old age; or that there are insignificant interindividual differences in accessibility to resources necessary to maintain continuity. Additionally, in postulating that continuity must be maintained, it is necessary to assume that the integration of the individual with his social milieu is relatively stable. Work by cohort theorists (Ryder 1965; Carlsson and Carlsson 1970; Eisenstadt 1956) concludes that norms, values, and community constellations change dramatically during an individual's lifetime. Thus, discontinuity may be a function of changing community characteristics that are no longer appealing or accessible to the individual.

Whereas the continuity model posits the necessity of maintaining

239

relative stability, the accommodation perspective directs attention to an array of variables that determine *how* continuity is maintained in the face of dramatic role losses. Recognizing the impact of a constricting social world on the aging individual, Kutner (1962) suggests that changes in social roles accompanying age require a redefinition of self and the development of a new series of roles with which one may become engaged. He identifies the new process as one of redifferentiation and reintegration of social roles and functions. The individual's resiliency becomes the key determinant. To account for the fact that certain role losses do not necessarily create crises, Neugarten (1970) advanced the notion of an "internal time clock"—a mechanism that allows people to prepare for or rehearse transitions by observing others going through crises. Her acknowledgment of the interactive aspects between biological and social time clocks suggests that accommodation is not solely the result of an individual's personality traits; rather it is affected in part by the social context. Nonetheless, but suggesting that the determination of the outcome rests with the individual, the ongoing effects of the environment are minimized.

All of the theories of aging advanced to date acknowledge the enormous impact of society in the form of role losses. The theories tend to stress prescriptions of healthy aging by taking as a given the constricting social world and then going on to offer strategies for successful accommodation to this unhappy state. It is clear that the paradigm is one of individual pathology with the concomitant quest for formulas for accommodation rather than an integrated social-psychological model.

Taken together, the three major theoretical models do suggest that the dying community, with all its resource disadvantages, may indeed provide a compatible environment for growing old. The desired withdrawal suggested by disengagement theory may be enhanced in an environment that is itself withdrawing from society, continuity may be more easily achieved in a familiar environment, an environment in which one's roots run very deeply and which itself is besieged with terminal decline. Finally, the dying community provides considerable opportunity to witness and prepare for the major crises of human existence—loss of family and friends through out-migration, depletion of financial resources as economically productive opportunities dwindle, and a diminished vigor in community life.

Only two studies stand in the literature that take communities as the unit of analysis to elaborate the relationship among aging, status, and community. The Bultena-Wood (1969:209– 17) study of retirement communities suggests that the elderly residing in the age-homogeneous setting fare better than the elderly in age-heterogeneous settings. The Burby and Weiss "New Communities Study" (1977) noted that community inducements for the elderly are quite different than those identified by younger population groups, regardless of race or social class. The elderly attracted to America's new communities valued such features as climate, availability of shopping and health and medical services, safety from crime, and ease of getting around the community. Younger populations prized the community as a place to raise children, for its convenience to work, and because of the quality of the public schools.

Small communities, especially vulnerable to decline and death, can provide services and goods within pedestrian capability; residents are relatively secure from crime; and where medical services are available, they may be characterized by long-standing personal relationships. When the dying community is characterized by a disproportionately high density of elderly, age-homogeneity in the environment becomes a fact—a community feature thought to provide special opportunities for successful aging.

We are continually warned of the perils in treating the aged as a homogeneous group. Perhaps more than any other age group, the aged, with their accumulated life experiences, are vastly heterogeneous. Education, social class, race, marital or health status, all render them difficult to capture and understand as a group. It is true that in America, proportionately more elderly are ill, isolated, and poor than is true for other age groups. It is also true, as Clark points out, that throughout the life cycle, human invention embroiders existence: language, rituals, patterned social relationships, symbolic understandings. In one society, old age may be defined in functional terms, the waning of abilities necessary to perform tasks associated with active adult status. In another, old age may be defined in formal terms whereby status is linked to factors such as the birth of a grandchild or attaining eligibility for social security. Depending on the culture, old age may be revered, ignored, or scorned. What promotes good morale among the aged in one culture, may be devalued in another. Clark and Anderson (1967) show that the values associated with successful aging in the United States (acceptance of withdrawal from productive roles, positive engagement with leisure activities) are the opposite of those characteriz-

241

ing dominant American culture, posing a dilemma for most aging persons. Their studies demonstrate that continuity in values throughout the life-span are conducive to successful aging.

In summary, social gerontological theory does not carry with it sufficient explanatory force to predict with clarity the relationships between community environment and the aging process. Community research has not yet specified the properties of community that affect the aging process.

Given the above, I sought to understand what it is like to grow old in a dying community by locating one that is dying (admittedly in the absence of specific criteria defining such a community) and interviewing thirty older men and seventy women who live there. I asked them to communicate their perspectives on everyday living, their hopes, their joys, and their pains. Whether their impressions differ from those of younger residents in the same community, how the community environment influences the articulation of those impressions, and whether their needs and attitudes are common to aging people everywhere, are certainly open to question. I hope the approach will be a start toward identifying more precisely the important mutual relationships between the community and its elderly residents. Data for this study were secured in a tape-recorded interview using Tobin and Neugarten's Life Satisfaction Rating Scale (1961:344–56) developed on the disengagement study of aging. The open-ended questions were directed to the individual's perceptions of community, daily activities, and attitudes toward those activities, likes and dislikes about life, and plans for the future.

A word about the community in which these men and women live is in order. It is a small, rural community, located in the midwestern part of the United States. If one criterion of a dying community is an eroding population base, then this community is dying. Over the past five decades, for example, what was once a thriving agricultural center has suffered a severe loss of population as young people have moved off farms to seek employment elsewhere. The proportion of age 65 and over residents is approximately 45 percent. Another criterion (suggested in Warren's presentation of El Cerrito, 1963:97–104) is a minimum number of ties with extracommunity organizations and public agencies. There are no branch offices of chain stores—the few commercial establishments are locally owned. There is a welfare agency—none of the other publicly supported services headed by a state agency have

242

representatives in the community. The one high school in the county continues to prepare students for agricultural roles—very few enter college. There is no transportation system capable of moving the residents to larger, more affluent population centers. The physical environment is punctuated with boarded up structures, deteriorating dwelling units, and neglected yards.

I first asked respondents to identify for me the advantages and disadvantages of living in the community. Their answers revealed a number of interrelated themes. Small towns offer advantages that larger communities do not, providing opportunities for meeting with friends and acquaintances, easier access to community life, and a sense of security.

A 72-year-old widowed housewife commented:

> This is a very nice town to live in, there are some lovely people here. I like a small town—people are more friendly and you really have a larger acquaintanceship and you get away from the fact that you have to have a car any place you want to go.

An 83-year-old widowed male agrees:

> I like the people here. I would like to live here for another eighty-three years because it is a pleasant place to be and less expensive than some places for people of limited incomes, and we all know each other.

A single woman in her 80s commented:

> I don't think I would like to live anywhere any better than right here. It is a good town. Everyone was so good to me when I was sick. They just brought all kinds of food, and it was just wonderful.

An elderly husband also cherishes the support of friends:

> I certainly would like to live just right here. Here are our friends, and we have a good many friends who have been good to us since my wife has not been able to get out a lot. We have no notion of going any place else.

So does a widowed housewife:

> I like my home very well here. My neighbors are all so nice to me. I think so much of all my neighbors. I would just as soon live here as any place I know of. I don't know any reason why I would not like to live here.

An elderly married housewife prized the personal relationships that extend even to the town's business community:

243

My friends are here. My church is here. When I go out, there is usually somebody that says hello. Yesterday I went to the store to get a piece of meat. I did not have to tell what I wanted. He got it out for me without any questions, and I like that.

And she adds:

I don't think we have the terror or worries that you would in the larger city. You just feel safer.

One elderly lady, new to the community who had moved from her farm said:

I never had it in my mind that I would care anything about the town. I was born a farm girl and of course, you know, it is pretty hard to tear a farmer off the farm and put him in the city. But I love the churches here. I really have nothing special "agin" this town. I would not care to leave now. My children are located or situated in a position that I have them handy, and I would not want to go anywhere where I would be away from them.

A retired executive, in his 90s, just prefers a small town to a large city:

I really prefer a small town, and I am very fond of country and we have more of that atmosphere. Of course there are some things to go to in a larger city, but I don't have the strength and time or ability to do that. I think that with the television and things like that coming like they have nowadays, people in the country have advantages equal to many other places. I don't find any desire for changing.

There is a strong sense, as in Cantor's study of the elderly living in a disintegrating neighborhood in New York City, that "most people (especially the old) are more favorably inclined to the place they presently live in—to what is familiar and known; what they can navigate and encompass." Here, too, that theme is repeated over and over again. A widowed housewife said:

It just seems like home to me because my parents were here before me.

Another woman said:

This is just home. I never thought too much about it one way or the other. I don't think I would want to live anywhere else. I have my roots down here.

A housewife explains:

244

I think it is a nice town to live in and I never lived in any other town, so all my friends are here, and I like them all. When I go anyplace else, I get kind of homesick and want to come home. This is all the home I ever had, and I don't crave to live any place else.

Two elderly gentlemen, both in their late seventies, put it succinctly:

I think this is a good place to retire, it's been my town for over 40 years.

I don't know anything about any other town, so I'm satisfied here.

On the whole, the elderly in this community prefer a small town. Although many may not have now, or have had in the past, the financial resources to relocate, rootedness and familiarity strike the observer as an overriding reason for continued residency. Indeed, those persons who envision a better environment are almost exclusively retired farmers who moved to town from the farm. For example, many farmers would have preferred to remain in their familiar surroundings:

I would sooner be on a farm. I don't like town, never did. I would sooner be on a farm riding a horse.

I next asked the elderly people in this community to describe a typical weekday, activities undertaken on weekends, and to let me know which of their activities were enjoyable and which were less enjoyable. Again, a number of themes emerged. Their activity agendas reveal the community can and does accommodate a wide range of interests and life-styles. Women continue to devote energy to, and derive pleasure from, maintaining their homes, just as they did in earlier years. Reading, gardening, watching television, or being with family and friends are also valued activities. A typical day is described by a housewife:

Well—mostly outside of our meals and the straightening up of the house and things for the day, I generally do just whatever comes up. I read a lot. Try to read something everyday—that is something that I feel like is educative or instructive. And I generally put in most of the forenoon preparing my meals, preparing my dinner and preparing my supper at the same time. And in the afternoon, sometimes I go out of an afternoon, something like that—whatever there is that is going on that I think I would enjoy. In the summertime I spend quite a lot of time working with my flowers and in my garden because I like to see things grow and I

245

really like to dig in the dirt. We did have a bridge club a few years ago, but I don't know, we kind of lost interest, and then I think as much as anything else, four of the very fine ladies that belonged to it passed away, and it kind of closed that. We get together once in a while of evenings and play pitch or some cards, but since practically all the people have television, they are not interested in visiting so much any more and they are mostly watching the television and growl about the things on it that don't suit them. We have relatives and friends in the neighboring towns, and there is a few people we really call back and forth—maybe on Sunday afternoons and Sunday evenings. On Saturday I try to get my baking done, things that I want to prepare for Sunday. I was always raised not to work on Sunday and I generally try to have my Sundays. The thing I like best is getting out in the country, and I like to get a little time to sit down and do a little fancy work.

A widowed housewife continues to "care" for her family as in earlier days:

I can't say that I have had time hang heavy on my hands. I enjoy sewing and I had eight children. I do some sewing for them and many mornings I spend all forenoon letter writing. My mother is ninety-six years old, and she expects to hear from me at least once every two weeks, if not oftener. So I just have not had much time that you could call leisure time. I do some fancy work, and I have a yard and a little garden to take care of in the summer. I read a great deal when I'm not sewing, I read too late at night most every night. I think if a person is busy and you are interested in what you are doing—any part of the day is all right. On weekends, I'm usually with some of my family. I often go with them on week-ends. I can't say I enjoy going out to clubs or places of that kind like many women do. It has been too hard for me to get around, I think, and I have never been able to do much of that all the time I was working for my family.

Another also maintains activities of an earlier period, even though widowed:

I sew and embroider and keep up the house and do my day's work. I still do fancy work and make a garden. I used to help my husband all the time to plant things. Of course when he was alive I didn't have to do very much of it, and now that I'm alone, I guess I shouldn't do it, but I do. It takes up my mind. It kinda eases ya cuz he was a great gardener. I have the television and I listen to that and read. I just start in and keep on doin' and keep on until I get it all done. Bake and clean and that's about all.

246

What is perhaps most valued by the women is freedom from the pressures and responsibilities of earlier days when families were being raised. A retired schoolteacher describes her day and the sense of luxury that comes with fewer responsibilities:

> This might sound rather foolish, but we both have been hounded by schedules practically all of our lives. When we were first married, we had a business that required early morning til late at night attention, and I had a teaching schedule that was very severe and two children to raise. I can say for myself, and I believe I can speak for my husband, when I say that we enjoy a departure from schedule more than anything else. We are glad we don't have to get up at a certain time of morning, and if we don't want to eat breakfast until noon, we don't have to. And I don't have to wash on Monday morning, or if I want to start a project and lay it aside, I can take it up again whenever I wish. And if we want to stop in the middle of the morning and play two or three games of cribbage and watch for the news—just doing as one would like to do . . . When I was 12 years old, I began working actively in the church, and throughout all the years, until just the last few, I have been regular in attendance at church and choir. Now it is difficult for me to get up and go to church, so I listen to my favorite sermons over the radio. I would say that I have put in at least 60 years of active church service, and I feel that that is enough.

Another elderly woman, a widow, explains her days as follows:

> I put in most of my time here at home. I never was much of a hand to go. I take my work and sit here in the house and have my television on, and the day goes as fast as if I was having lots of company. Now that I'm so crippled up, and just can't go, television is my main entertainment. Sunday afternoons really means a lot to me because I always look forward to some of the children coming home.

An 85-year-old widow, even though confined to a wheelchair, manages a considerable household regimen and friendship activity, much of which consists of providing support and assistance to other elderly persons:

> There is a lady stays with me at night, and she gets up and does everything she can in the morning for me, but I always wash my dishes and then get dinner for her. I study up what I want to cook and I begin to think of things all forenoon—different vegetables that I want to have for dinner. I have mending to do. In the afternoons I have some stories on the television that I listen to,

247

and I set and watch them, and I generally have different neighbors drop in and visit a while. I call an awful lot on the telephone—call up people to cheer them up because I can't get around so good. . . . There is an old gentleman that goes to church and he never hears anything. I call him nearly every Sunday afternoon of my life. I tell him what they have said at church that he did not understand.

Another also enjoys assisting her friends and neighbors:

I have lots of company and I like to go and call on the sick when I am able, and I also like to do things for older people and the shut-ins. I use the old Christmas cards and I cut these cards apart and tie a bow of ribbon at the top and then I write my own verses, so I like to send those out. I always have to take a rest every day, that is lie down, usually after dinner. I try to read, but I have trouble with my eyes. I like to have company—it just brings new thoughts and new ideas from other people. When I am well enough, I like to do baking and share it with other people. There is not many people that make their own bread and cinnamon rolls now.

The retired men in the community have a more difficult time filling their days now that occupational activities are no longer available. Said a retired farmer:

Now that I am here in town, I just don't do much of anything, but when I was out in the country, why then I would have something to do. On Saturdays I generally go to the store, get our groceries, and run around up there a little and set on the corner and watch the people and then I come home.

His wife comments:

Well, now if we were still on the farm, which we were up 'till four years ago, I could just tell you all kinds of things that I did, but now our time is a little heavy on our hands. I have my housework, and I do some ironing. We visit friends once in a while, but television is our main thing. On Saturday we usually go shopping. I'll visit with a lot of the ladies that I've really just learned to know down there. I've got real friendly with them, we even invite each other for dinner at our homes and all, just through visiting at the store.

Another retired farmer said:

About all I do since I quit work is make these braided rugs. To tell you the truth of it, I don't enjoy very much of my time because I

248

would like to be out of here. You know when you work hard all your life and have to just quit and can't do anything, then you don't enjoy it.

One retired laborer developed a new business activity:

I have a workshop up here in my garage, and I take in and I sharpen scissors, saws, and I also sharpen anything that is got to be sharpened—lawn mowers and corn knives and axes. I do all that kind of work. I don't do any automobile work or anything like that, but I do sharpen stuff for people, and I make maybe $1.50 or so, or $2.00 a week and that helps out on our expenses. I do the same thing on the sixth and seventh that I do all through the week. I do go to church and Sunday School and sometimes in the afternoons on Sunday we go over to our daughter's lives here on the west end of town. I like to set around and talk to somebody and watch T.V., that is about all. If I have someplace, a right good place, and there's plenty of time, I like to go afishing.

A gentleman, who formerly worked in the town, maintains ties with his former fellow workers:

I usually make the rounds of where I have worked. I may go up and drink coffee with the boys and most of the time I go down and see my sister who also has retired and has had a heart attack. I look after her. I enjoy going to church and just visiting with friends and family.

A 94-year-old retired executive laments the limits on his activities caused by increasing physical disabilities.

I have about 50 percent eyesight. So I'm able to go about my house and about town without any fear of danger. I do my own cooking from choice, and do a good job of it, I'll say that. But I had to give up driving two years ago, and that is one of the greatest deprivations that I have come to, because I'm sort of a prisoner in my home and have to be taken places. I've tried to accept it rather philosophically. Then on top of that, my hearing is about half efficient. I must admit there's no acute enjoyment left in anything, but I do enjoy having my family come occasionally and visit me, and I like to get baseball on the T.V. and some of the educational features.

An elderly man who still works part-time has assumed, out of necessity, some household duties:

I enjoy my everyday life. I get up early in the morning and do my garden work. My wife is the one who informs me how to do

249

things and I do things in the garden. We have roses and flowers of all kinds. I always get the breakfast in the morning because it is better for her not to be active in the morning. My first interest is taking care of her until she gets going in the morning, and then I go to my business. I have a little tax business—I am glad I did not have to retire. My days are pretty well filled. Many, many of my hours are spent in the yard with my flowers. I don't read much. That is one of my regrets in life. My wife is a very good reader, and I enjoy her reading because she tells me what she reads. I think our evenings with bridge companions are our most enjoyable. I am real happy to help my wife get over some of her rough spots. That is one of my biggest enjoyments I think—to try to help her. She has a hard lot.

Although one begins to get a notion from a description of daily activities of what it is like to experience aging in this community, a question asking residents to identify the most important things in their lives gives us a deeper understanding. Both men's and women's responses almost universally suggested that a concern for their own physical well-being and the well-being of family members occupied their thoughts whatever their daily activities. A widowed housewife said:

My children. My children. That is the most important part in my life. If I hear from them, I am happy. They have been so nice about coming and visiting me now I am so handicapped, and that is my main interest in living right now, is the family.

A married housewife said:

It seems to me without much hesitation it would be the concerns of the family, the grandchildren. The concern that they have necessities and the right kind of lives. That would be just catastrophe to me, if anything happened that was bad in their lives.

Being a grandmother was also important to a widowed housewife:

Being a grandmother. I am very much concerned about the future of the grandchildren. I used to think if I had my own children raised, my worries would be over. The conditions of the world as they are, you just sometimes wonder just what might happen to them.

Another lady said:

My health, if I never accomplish anything, if I can just keep that, I'll make it some way.

250

A retired farmer agrees:

> There isn't really anything. A person at my age just lives from day
> to day. There is no tomorrow for you so there is nothing more
> important than maintaining our good health and enjoying our-
> selves together here.

A man whose wife was quite ill said:

> I believe that my biggest object is to take care of my little gal here
> and do some things that will make me feel that I have done
> something for the town—for the folks whom I love. There are so
> many of them that I do love.

And another gentleman said:

> The welfare of our children and our grandchildren—seeing that
> our children are getting along well and counseling with them
> from time to time.

A few did suggest developing and maintaining a philosophy that would
make each day enjoyable. One 83-year-old lady suggested:

> To grow old beautifully—that is the most important thing. I want to
> grow old and not be an old crank about everything. But I do enjoy
> my life. Now I was raising my children I had to work hard. Every-
> one of my children I had to raise without their father, and I worked.

A retired missionary valued

> Remaining alive. Trying to be useful. Enjoying the friendship of
> people and seeing the beauties in nature and the beauties man
> has created. There is always something interesting to see or hear
> or learn about.

And a widowed housewife discusses changes in her perspectives that
occurred with aging:

> Life is an experience and there is no doubt that if we are living it
> the right kind of way, we learn more about it as we live, and
> things that used to bother me terrifically when I was younger
> don't bother me anymore now. There is a lot of satisfaction in
> getting older even though you do have your handicaps. It just
> seems like each age brings something that is of interest, and I sort
> of look forward to it. When you were younger, things used to stir
> you up and get your blood all heated up when things weren't
> going as you thought they should. In the later part now, you
> come to the more calmer approach to things and you can see the
> whole picture and can spend time on important things instead of

251

some things that are not so important. The thing that has brought me just the most pure satisfaction at all times is my religious life.

There has long been a controversy in social gerontology regarding which variable, health or family, makes the greatest single impact on the satisfaction of the elderly with their lives. Medley's recent study (1976:448–55) concludes that satisfaction with family life weighs more heavily, and at least for these people this would seem to be overriding. Somehow children, grandchildren, and other family members do manage to maintain contact with parents who live in this relatively isolated community. Health status, of course, is important, perhaps masking fears of unwanted dependency and inability to exercise activity choices, but surely also recognizing the unpleasantness of pain and disability.

Residents were asked to comment on the advantages and disadvantages of old age. For the most part, their opinions reflect an acceptance of aging status. For a few, younger years were a happier time, but satisfaction with past accomplishments and the knowledge that "what will be, will be," combine to provide the elderly with a considerable measure of acceptance of old age. Loneliness, ill health, and isolation are, however, major problems intruding upon their everyday existence. The words of a retired farmer, an elderly housewife, a retired missionary, a widow, and a retired janitor are illustrative of residents' acceptance of old age.

When I was younger, strong, and well, life was like an oyster to me. I got a measure of happiness. When I first got sick, I did feel kind of down in the dumps, and I told my wife I would just as well be dead. Afterwards I was ashamed. I don't know as I'd like to turn back the clock. I have lived my life as well as I could, and I think right now that I'm as good an age as any. The best thing about being older is looking back, realizing I've lived this long, got a good name, and nobody can put any blame on me.

I'm pretty well satisfied with everything, try to take things as they come. Because there's not a thing you can do about it, life has storms. What will be, will be, and there's no reason for us to stay up and worry about it. I think I'm just satisfied with the age I am. I don't think I'd want to be any other age. And I don't think I'd want to live my life over. I think I've done a pretty good job. Older people, all they need is to be comfortable and have some place, some pleasures. And we do that.

I get despondent when I live too much in the past. Or when I look forward with apprehension to the billions of underprivileged people who seek more space and opportunity. Work is my salvation. I have enjoyed every year of my life since I was three years old; each stage of development has been delightful to me. I think it is delightful to be 83 years old. But to be decrepit and crippled and blind and deaf, that would not be very enjoyable. The advantages of being this age are the memories and the accumulated knowledge of people and things. It is nice to be kindly treated by people—more now than when I was younger.

I used to cry about everything, and I quit that a long time ago. The worse things about now is not being able to buy anything. Now my earning capacity is over. I never want to go to a nursing home, I'd rather get me a tin bill and go out with the birds than go to a nursing home.

I don't feel lonely very often—only from the standpoint that I do miss my friends that I have worked with—and at the same time I like the independence that there is when you don't need to report to work. You can come and go as you please.

I don't know what the future will bring. Not that we are financially well off, but still it's better than what it looked like years ago. At this age you have time to think back and see what you have done and perhaps feel like you have accomplished something in raising your family. I believe I am happier now than I was, say, twenty years ago.

The minority, who expressed a desire for the satisfactions of earlier days, did so because of personal losses or health problems that are associated with advanced age. An elderly housewife commented:

I get bad spells a little less often than when I was younger because I can understand people and can kind of understand the world a little better. I would like to be younger—I didn't have sickness then.

And a recently widowed housewife said:

It just seems like there is nothing ahead, you can't see nothing ahead. I have been a little that way since my husband is gone. It seems like there is nothing to look forward to. But I just look forward to tomorrow and think, well, maybe tomorrow won't be so bad and it isn't. I like to be just where I am—I won't have so far to go.

Illness, especially, intrudes upon an elderly housewife's happiness:

I have quite a little unhappiness now—especially the days I don't feel like doing anything because of my heart. Sometimes I think you would be better off if you was dead, and did not have to worry about those things.

253

Finally, a very elderly gentleman said:

> There are times when I do have a strong sense of loneliness. I think every old person does that. I try to have enough storing in my home and work that I do that I don't have much time to be lonely, but it comes. It comes sometimes in my bed before I go to sleep, but not often. I wouldn't wish anybody a life over 80. I just feel that way about it, If the Lord gives it to us, we'll accept it and make the best of it, but I don't recommend it to anyone. I'm accepting old age as gracefully as possible, but I'm not advocating it.

The men and women were asked to share their thoughts on what they would be doing five years from now. For most, dramatic changes in everyday existence, where existence is contemplated, are not envisioned. A retired farmer said, for example, "I suppose we will probably be going on pretty much as we are." Some, realistically, knew they would be dead. An elderly widow said:

> I expect I will be resting out in the cemetery. I'm 86 years old now and my family and my brothers and sisters, none of them lives as long as I have now, so I am not counting on many years.

Most, however, hope they will be living about as they are now. None plan to uproot themselves and move to another community: they want to remain in their homes, and in this "dying community."

We return to the original question: What is it like to grow old in a dying community? For the most part, we now have a picture of an easy pace—the press and striving are gone. Household duties are of great importance and are a considerable source of pleasure for the elderly women. Such duties constitute an accustomed routine that does not change with advancing years. The financial "security" afforded by national programs is valued and provides a shield against the waning economic base of the home community. Most suffer some of the health decrements associated with aging—many, nonetheless, have fashioned compensations for their handicaps, and most believe their health, all things considered, is better than that of some other older people they know. The retired men have a rather difficult time. Unlike women, they must find satisfaction in an existence that is totally different from farming, or full-time employment. It is not easy. For the vast majority, television provides entertainment, enlightenment, or a sense of communication with the "outside" world. Community, family, and friends are continued sources of pleasure.

Like their community these people are experiencing terminal decline. They accept the direction, knowing that for them, an irreversible and inevitable personal process is now in full sway. "Terminal drop," the sudden acceleration of decline before death, is feared. A paramount wish is for a happy death, for maintenance of most of one's physical and mental capabilities until death. There is the suggestion in the comments of some that the dying community experiencing "terminal drop" would present a hostile and fracturing environment—that the environmental "time clock" would be "off time" for its elderly residents, many of whom do not have the resources to relocate in another community.

The elderly in this dying community achieved significantly higher life satisfaction scores than their age peers in three other community types in midwestern America: a growing small community; a large metropolitan community; a middle-class suburban community. Several properties of this community, uncharacteristic of thriving communities, seem therefore to reinforce successful aging.

The community houses a very high proportion of elderly. Sheer density alone can produce a subculture, mutually reinforcing and supportive, and united in its claims on society. Indeed, some years ago Arnold Rose predicted the emergence of an aging subculture in America, stimulated by the growing numbers of elderly encountering a societal "agism." From a national perspective, that subculture has yet to crystallize. The elderly as a group continue to vote on critical issues with the same diversity as when younger. But in this small dying community, a high density of elderly and the stability of community residence combine to enable many old people to overcome the loneliness and stigma commonly associated with advanced age. Individual ideology and values, no longer drawn from the productive activities of a younger population, are consonant with those of the community, once thriving but now unable to compete with commercial centers. Two observations suggest that an aging subculture exists in this "dying community."

For the elderly residents, status is accorded by virtue of one's advanced chronological years. This is an age-graded community. The retired banker and the former welfare mother are equally respected and admired for their "helpfulness" to other elderly residents. Both are considered lively and intelligent. The different statuses of earlier years become submerged; many are now receiving the respect and friendship opportunities earlier denied.

255

Second, while professionals may decry the lack of professional services in the dying community, and others may fault the choice constraints imposed by dwindling community resources, the older residents here created a strong and active informal support network, characterized by informality, personal investment, and spontaneity. They give and receive from each other without professional intrusion or bureaucratic organization, whether it be hot meals in times of illness, medical advice, counseling, transportation, or leisure enjoyments in the home. Those who have the resources to go to a physician's office save back a portion of their prescriptions to give to others who exhibit the same symptoms.

Earlier in this chapter it was suggested that to age well in America is not an easy task. To forsake attachment to work and achievement values, to the value of progress, and to accept instead leisure values, which stand in opposition to one's earlier sense of purpose, is difficult at best. But the dying community, also withdrawing from social and economic contribution, exhibits leisurely life-styles, less preoccupation with gainful employment, and more opportunities for a deeper "acquaintanceship with" and acceptable dependence on friends and neighbors, usually also elderly, who remain in the community. If the community has properties that reinforce or complement the social-psychological and biological changes that occur with growing old, then it would seem that that community could provide the continuity, values, and personal friendships cherished by the aging. As a result, an aging subculture arises in which care, when needed, is freely offered by friends and neighbors, and in which the achievement of advanced age obscures the different status labels of earlier years.

11
The Struggle for Community
Can Create Community

HANNAH LEVIN

National Institute For Graduate Studies
Washington, D.C.

DEFINITIONS

Communities have many objective characteristics: natural resources, social structure, demography, economic and capital resources, a history, and institutions. This chapter will focus on the process by which the individual internalizes and experiences community subjectively.

Robert Redfield (1960:30) emphasized this aspect when he wrote: "If one studies the rise of urban communities out of more primitive communities, it is the change in the mental life, in norms and in aspirations in personal character that become the most significant aspect."

The subjective sense of community is not isomorphic with an objective community. When questioned about how they experience community, people most frequently respond in one of the following ways: "It's the place where I live," "It's the group I belong to and trust," or "It's my friends and fellow workers." These three definitions of community—geographic space, community origin, and community interest—all include objective characteristics of the community as well as a subjective, affective relationship.

Sense of Place

When talking about place, an individual includes in his description a feeling about his relationship to it. In the perceiving of the geographic community, the person may be describing the neighbors on each side of his house, in the neighborhood, or in the town.

Irving Howe describes the life of the young Jew in the early twentieth century on the Lower East Side in this fashion: "The streets were ours. . . We learned to operate within the safety of the Lower East Side." (Howe 1976:256– 59)

While walking in a community of four square miles in Brooklyn, I questioned some young unemployed men sitting around on the fringes of a local small park. "What's your neighborhood or community?" I asked.

Two quickly gave the same response: "The street we live on and the two adjoining blocks." When questioned further about why they described such a small area, each responded, "It's the only place where I can trust anyone."

Another determinant of one's geographic sense of community is the area over which one feels a sense of control. And when the sense of control is missing it diminishes the sense of community. These same young men had not voted in the last local election or considered going to see their district political leader about helping them find work. They felt powerless about changing their situation. "What's the use, the politicians only care about themselves." Seeing no possible positive line of action, they felt cut off from the local political apparatus, once a very vital structure in providing a sense of control. In their parents' time, the neighborhood party (democratic) machinery was an all-important cohesive force.

Community of Origin

People experience their community of origin in a very personal fashion. They talk about *their* family, *their* religion, and *their* race. "We're Catholic." "I'm an Italian American." "Black is beautiful." These are all expressions denoting community of origin. And just as a sense of place relates to the need for a protected territory, the community of origin provides one with some kind of historical continuity between the past that one comes from and the future that one moves toward. Often the behavior of people who feel rootless and unaware of any community of origin is amoral.

Community of Interest

Today, most urban dwellers no longer live in small, homogeneous, distinctive, self-sufficient neighborhoods that offer meaningful local roles. Nor is the mood in many cities conducive to community participation. Beyond possibly a few neighbors, city dwellers look to friends, nearby or distant; workplace or professional colleagues; and sometimes relatives for a community of interests. The cafeteria at work, the tennis court, the dinner party, and the telephone all become the grounds for sharing interests and values. This subjective community can provide a rich variety of individual energies and inputs that produce a sense of newly shared interests and ideas.

The Dying Community

But destructive forces are constantly attacking the subjective sense of community. Perhaps the most pernicious is the cyclical economy that has displaced people from their community of work and often forced migration. Some ten million Americans are at present involuntarily unemployed.

They describe how life has lost its meaning and how they feel superfluous and unwanted. Their basic connectedness to the community of work has been severed. Sometimes the nostalgia for what has been lost is expressed when an unemployed person returns to the diner across the street from the factory that laid him off. He has a cup of coffee and talks with whomever—to recall the ties that locate him in a community now denied.

Technology is also a force that can destroy basic linkages. When urban renewal (in the cause of new housing, highways, and commercial development) came to the West End of Boston, as it has to so many other older but coherent communities, people were forced to move. They had to leave a neighborhood they trusted, go through the stressful experience of relocating, and find new social ties to replace years of rootedness and identity.

Technology can often be misused. Even though distances are easier to cover by car and by plane, they do not always bring people closer together. We often use transportation as a means of escape. By constantly moving about we prevent ourselves from developing ties with others. The modern man or woman who is always on the go is not closer to, but more separate from, fellow humans.

War as the most violent of all social upheavals obviously can uproot and destroy people as well as their communities. At the same time, Robert Nisbet points out that war can have a cohesive effect. "However deeply man may continue to hate the devastation and killing and mutilation of war, he cannot being human forget altogether the superior sense of status, the achievement of humanitarian goals, and above all, the warming sense of community that comes with war" (Nisbet 1953:44).

Nisbet appears to be speaking of wars that have general citizen support. If we look at the divisive effects of the Vietnam War, however, community was destroyed both at home and in Vietnam.

Describing the shattered sense of community during the Vietnam War, Herbert Kelman tried to explain how the soldier forced to fight in Vietnam was also robbed of his sense of community:

> In dehumanizing his victims, he loses his capacity to care for them as human beings. He develops a state of psychic numbing (Lifton 1971; 1973) and a sense of detachment (Opton 1971) which sharply reduce his capacity to feel. Insofar as he excludes a whole group of people from his network of shared empathy, his own community becomes more constricted and his sense of involvement in humankind declines . . .
>
> In sum, processes of authorization, routinization and dehumanization of the victim contribute to the weakening of moral restraints, not only directly but also by furthering the dehumanization of the victimizer. As he gradually discards personal responsibility and human empathy, he loses his capacity to act as a moral being. (Kelman 1973:51–52)

The Human Drive for Community

But the human drive for community is not easily stifled. Even in the midst of the most extreme, external, dehumanized conditions in the Nazi concentration camps, a sense of community survived. "The camps were designed to turn prisoners against each other . . . in a multitude of ways men and women persisted in social acts. Fear and privation increased irritability but did not keep inmates from joining in common cause" (Des Pres 1976:136).

Des Pres describes how "prisoners in the concentration camps helped each other." Sometimes this help was given by an individual, sometimes by a group, and always at the risk of one's life.

> A major form of behavior was gift-giving. Inmates were continually giving and sharing little items with each other, and small acts like these were enormously valuable both as morale boosters and often as real aids in the struggle for life. . . . Gift giving, in other words, creates bonds at once spiritual and concrete, social and economic. It is one of the ties which binds. Exchange brings people together and makes them conscious of their worth in each other's eyes. Self-interest turns to good will and the gift relation becomes one of the constitutive structures of social being. (Des Pres 1976:136)

It seemed that prisoners in the concentration camp preserved the sense of community as a method of resisting, maintaining dignity, and surviving. A Treblenka survivor quoted in the Des Pres book said, "In our group we shared everything and the moment one of the group ate something without sharing it, we knew it was the beginning of the end for him" (Des Pres 1976:96).

Thus even when all the forces in a society conspire to destroy an objective community, the most adaptive psychological process may be to struggle to preserve the psychological sense of community.

FUNCTIONS OF COMMUNITY

Community is vital to psychological health. Without a sense of place and trust, individual development is difficult. First the family, and then the larger community, provide positive and negative role models, values, and identity.

By definition, a psychologically healthy person actively masters his environment, shows a certain unity of personality and is able to perceive the world and himself correctly (Jahoda 1950).

Psychological Development: Trust, Structure, Identity, Values, and Social Stimulation

In what way does a community contribute to sound psychological development? In the process of the infant's development to adulthood, the child's initial experience with community occurs in the context of the family. Through the experiences of the first year of life the child

261

begins to learn what is meant by a simple sense of trust of others and a sense of trustworthiness of self. Thus the need for a dependable, predictable environment, inhabited by people who can be trusted and who can depend upon one's own trustworthiness, becomes internalized in this first year.

It is an acceptable psychological principle that humankind has a need for structure. It is the familiar in the environment, as well as the dependability and predictability and trustworthiness of the people who inhabit it, that provides some of the roots that help people to maintain equilibrium in a world of constant flux. Even if we live in a high crime area, we feel more safe and secure if it is our own familiar neighborhood where we know what to expect and whom to trust.

As children move out of their homes and out of the stage of parallel play, their companions are those who live in close proximity. In the developing sense of self, the child's sense of identity is closely associated with the community of origin and the geographic community. In fact, who you are in our society, until one begins working, is directly related to where you live. This includes the status, class, religion, and ethnicity of the neighborhood. If one listens to suburban junior high school students talking, one can quickly pick up the demography of the community. At the top of the hill are the rich Jews or Wasps. In the valley are the hardworking people who just got out of the inner city in time. Then there are the "greasers" or blue-collar youth on the other side of town closer to the city. Often forming a border between the working-class and the old-time residents are the middle-class, professional blacks. The identity one develops from his/her community is reflected in one's interests and values and is often reinforced by the expectations of the teachers in the schools.

The family, the neighbors, the community are all communicators of the norms and values of society. They provide the individual with the internalized rationale for altruistic, humane, and moral behavior. Thus, for example, when urban renewal forced the people of West Boston to move, they reacted with grief over the loss of their homes. People felt a vital portion of themselves had been amputated. "There was an alteration in the world of physically available objects. . . . Continuity was disrupted through the taken for granted framework functioning in a world that has temporal spatial and social dimensions" (Fried 1963:153).

As important as the human need for structure is the need for stimulation. The comings and goings, the family dramas, the liaisons and loves, all of the social relations that make up a community, provide the inhabitants with the possibility for frequent and novel interactions. Turnouts at twenty-fifth and fiftieth high school reunions demonstrate the compelling hold of this basic communal experience. In addition, these social relations and friendships give constant feedback about reality. They also provide the fun and surcease from some of the heavier burdens and worries of daily living.

Young people often identify with the leaders of their communities who can serve as models for appropriate behavior and symbolically give meaning, purpose, and future orientation to their lives. Many prominent people trace much of their early motivation back to a teacher or civic leader. Journalist Bill Moyers credits a high school English teacher with widening his horizons and helping him feel confident of his own abilities.

Ecology and Motivation

Roger Barker, in his fascinating series of studies on behavior settings, described how motives not only exist within individuals but can actually be the consequence of the environmental influence on the individual. Barker was particularly interested in comparing undermanned communities (not enough people to fill all of the formally defined structured roles) with those communities that had more individuals than responsible positions for them. In these comparisons he found that people in undermanned settings worked harder and longer hours, played more different roles, and, therefore, met more people. He also found that underpopulated settings were less sensitive to and less evaluative of differences between people (Barker 1960). Thus, the size of the community can have a real effect on the amount of tensions between ethnic and racial groups. In underpopulated communities, human capability becomes more important than skin color or religion or land of origin. And because every pair of hands and every mind is valued, in turn the individual's sense of responsibility grows. Further, since some level of achievement is almost certain, one's self-esteem is nurtured. These differences between over- and underpopulated communities become particularly significant now as we consider alternatives to the urban densities that contribute to so many of the problems of the megalopolis.

Several years ago, a study group supported by David Rockefeller called for the establishment of a hundred new communities in the less densely populated sections of the nation. Each new city would be planned to reach a maximum size of 250,000.

In the nation's largest, older cities unemployment is generally higher than the national average, services are declining, and there is a growing sense of despair. This tends to erode a communal sense of responsibility, diminish participation, and promote apathy. Should millions of Americans succumb to these feelings, the very fabric of our democratic society would be threatened.

Community and Autonomy

Control over important areas of one's life is a necessary element of sound mental health. Yet, the psychological sense of community seems on the surface to conflict with the notion of individual autonomy.

In the nineteenth century the triumph of secularism and individualism was attained by an emancipation from the values, classes, statuses, and membership in communities. The new freedoms brought an emphasis on the individual at the expense of the social and symbolic relationships that humans need. Nisbet wrote "that the traditional primary relationship of men has become functionally irrelevant to our State and economy and meaningless to the moral aspirations of individuals. . . . Birth, death, courtship, marriage, employment, infirmity and old age were met through these groups [kinship and localism]" (Nisbet 1953:49). But now Nisbet feels that these primary social relationships are without function and almost irrelevant. He describes as a result of all this the quest for community as a conservative search resulting from "personal alienation and cultural disintegration" (Nisbet 1953:45–74).

What is the relation of community to autonomy? Are they polar opposites on the same continuum or are they two separate orthagonal dimensions?

The psychological sense of community cannot be considered separately from the human need for autonomy. But the existence of one does not preclude the existence of the other in the same person. Although the historical development of autonomy and individualism arose in opposition to the power and meaning of community, the two

264

describe different dimensions and different psychological states that may interact in such a way that each can either limit or facilitate the full experiencing of the other.

Japanese society is an example of the totally communalized approach. Dependency on the group is encouraged. The family and work group are the definers of one's behavior, feelings, and values. This has become so strong an influence that the government is reportedly modifying the school curricula to stimulate more individualism. But the present system certainly is adaptive. Many of the indices of pathology are low: little crime, low divorce rate, almost no juvenile delinquency. Still, it has proven to be a varied, productive, and creative society.

In the United States we extol independence. Group ties are de facto downgraded. Our culture idolizes the "star," not the team. It promotes the bootstrap notion, and applauds rugged individualism. It does not blame itself for failing to provide a supportive developmental environment, but holds the individual responsible. And thus in the dying community each individual is made to feel his own inadequacy.

In questioning unemployed people in New York City in 1975, 90 percent felt it was their fault that they were unemployed (Levin 1975). These new unemployed are both victims of an economy over which they have no control, and victims of an internalized American myth that makes them feel at fault. It is not just that the society blames the victim, but the emphasis on individualism leads the victims to blame themselves.

The Power of Community

Just as being reared in a family can either lay the firm basis, through trust and loving relationships, for the development of an autonomous mature person, this same family group, by frustrating and twisting the satisfaction of the child's needs, can lead to a dependent impotent doubting adult.

Families are powerful institutions that can cripple or lay the basis for autonomous growth. So, too, is the community a source of power, one that can either bind humans to the past and limit their ability to change or it can lay the meaningful and secure foundations for humankind to venture forth creatively into the future.

265

THE DYING COMMUNITY: MALADAPTIVE RESPONSES

In the dying community, people are made to feel hopeless, useless, and vulnerable, which exascerbates the process of community deterioration.

In 1966, the Logue Report described the social conditions of some dying communities:

> The most troubled portions of New York are its three major slum and blighted areas—Harlem, South Bronx and Central Brooklyn. A variety of housing and renewal programs have been put into effect for these areas, yet the problem of the ghettoes is worsening. Nor is the problem confined to housing; community facilities are grossly inadequate. These three areas have the highest incidence of poverty-stricken families and welfare, and the greatest sense of alienation. These three areas have the highest incidence of unemployment in the city and the most severe social problems. (Logue 1966:20)

The most neglected area of the South Bronx, Hunts Point, was described this way by the *New York Times:*

> In basic ways portions of the Hunts Point section of the southeast Bronx have ceased to be a part of New York City. Many city services, such as police protection, garbage collection, water supply—and citizen obligations, such as payment of taxes, decent maintenance of property, some semblance of civil order—do not occur with any degree of predictability in Hunts Point. Repeated visits to Hunts Point uncover so much that is not supposed to be American in 1969 that the visitor wonders if he has suddenly entered a time machine and been transported back to frontier days. Nearly everything seems touched by lawlessness. On three of the worst streets, residents have a less than 1 to 20 chance of dying a natural death.
>
> Drug addiction is a major cause of what is wrong in Hunts Point. But the frequently heard argument that blight conditions may be creating the addicts, rather than the other way around, is both reasonable and meaningless at this point. Although former addicts agree that the area's physical condition probably contributes significantly to the mental state of the people who resort to heroin, such reasonable explanations are small comfort to residents, who are literally living in a state of siege. (Severo 1969)

Marc Fried uses the metaphor of death in "Grieving for a Lost Home," his study of the reactions of families who had been moved from the West End of Boston as a part of an urban renewal plan. He concluded that

> for the majority it seems quite precise to speak of their reactions as expressions of grief. These are manifest in the feelings of painful loss, the continued longing, the general depressive tone, frequent symptoms of psychological or social or somatic distress, the active work required in adapting to the altered situation, the sense of helplessness, the occasional expressions of both direct and displaced anger and the tendencies to idealize the lost place. At their most extreme, these reactions of grief are intense, deeply felt and at times overwhelming. (Fried 1963:151)

The previous descriptions catalog some of the possible human responses to the dying community.

Loss of community is experienced similarly to the death of a beloved person. It marks a disruption in the structure and predictability of our lives. The grief reaction following death represents the struggle to retrieve this lost sense of meaning. The will to adapt to change has to overcome an equally strong desire to restore the past. What becomes of a widow, a displaced family, a bankrupt business depends on how these conflicting impulses work themselves out within an individual and within groups. Since resistance to change is a basic human trait, the first responses to the crisis of community are defensive.

Defensive Responses

One response to the threat to one's community is characterized by a solidifying of bonds. Groups pull away from the foreign and the big, and toward the small and the familiar. There is a strong resistance to change. The impulse is to preserve the predictability of the environment by maintaining continuity with all the good old values. Throughout the country, people are drawing together to prevent encroachments from outsiders.

The people of Oregon have adopted a program of disinviting would-be immigrants. In suburban Belle Terre, Long Island, the local residents fought the rental of a large home to unmarried college students up to the United States Supreme Court. The Court ruled in their favor, holding that unmarried adults destroy the quality of a sanctuary that a residential community provides. The national antibusing movement maintains that its purpose is the protection of the neighborhood school.

267

And vigilante groups are forming to protect the streets from roaming gangs of youth.

In the face of the crisis of community, people not only return to old and trusted group ties but tend to regress to more childlike behavior patterns that express helplessness and powerlessness. This kind of negative response is seen in the decline in voter participation. There have been low turnouts in local as well as national elections and when questioned, people say, "Why vote, what difference does it make?"

This feeling of being impotent to effect change has led to low participation in unions and voluntary organizations. But most dramatic has been the decline in church membership and attendance at religious services.

Institutional Responses

The various institutional responses to the dying community succeeded best in the 1960s, when enormous resources went to communities in ferment and helped develop new cadres of local leaders.

But today the institutional responses are totally inadequate and self-defeating. The people sense they have been abandoned and even the best-intentioned, would-be helpers give up in despair. A young physician, Dr. Richard Carlson, in giving his reasons for leaving the new Lincoln Hospital in the South Bronx, said:

> "It is a 'given' that patients die needlessly all the time. When I have worked as medical chief resident, I have often taken people out of the intensive care unit to die."
>
> Describing the case of a young girl suffering from seizures, who after five hours in the emergency room could still not be admitted until somebody died because all the beds in the hospitals were full, Dr. Carlson said, "I spent the whole night running back and forth asking if one comatose patient had died. And finally when he died, we gave the family a few minutes of grief. Then rushed them out to make room for the girl.
>
> "That kind of powerlessness. I almost cried.
>
> ". . .while some good people are hanging on, many more people like me are leaving—not out of a lack of commitment, because many have simply gone to clinics or poverty areas elsewhere.
>
> "Good people will continue to leave, and the place will become a place where people will die without being noticed." (New York Times, August 16, 1976)

Many of the voluntary human service agencies also move out as the ethnic constituency of the community changes. Those institutions that remain can do little but bind the wounds. Healing is impossible.

Certainly the local welfare office is not the place one goes to receive humane service. Clients are given the message of their lowered status and reduced number of rights and privileges as they stand on line, answer questions, and submit to home visits.

"Redlining," the withholding of bank credit from "risky" areas, is a pervasive policy that also hastens the decay of community. "Banks and conventional sources of lending usually refrain from making loans to tenement houses. Then comes ruination financed by shadow world money and then selection of the area by the Planning Commission as a candidate for cataclysmic use of government money to finance renewal clearance" (Jacobs 1961:303).

Although police behavior has become increasingly professionalized, the escalating urban crisis gives the dying portion of the community lowest priority in terms of police attention. Crime that confines itself to slums and ghettoes is often ignored. The criminal justice system seems to swing between two extremes: totally ignoring the problems of the community and its residents, and sporadically being extremely repressive.

Group Responses

One result of this neglect has been the return of the warring youth gangs, a phenomenon that Mobilization for Youth and other 1960s programs tried to control. But the need of the young for identity, leaders, and an outlet for their hostility cannot be suppressed, so gangs are rumbling again.

The growth of gangs has been particularly rapid in Detroit.

Indeed, no one in Detroit had seen it like this. In recent weeks, gangs of black youths have roamed the city's East Side, terrorizing shopkeepers, pedestrians and motorists, both black and white. The aged are favorite targets.

Now, the violence has spread downtown, with hit-and-run attacks on buses and stores and, Sunday night, the invasion of a rock concert in Cobo Hall by several hundred gang members.

By midnight, when violence ended, one woman had been raped, another had been molested and dozens had been robbed, according to the police. There were 47 arrests.

Beyond the violence of gang activities and the large number of participants—the police estimate that there are nine gangs with a total of 300 to 400 members—officials are alarmed by what they see as a new level of sophistication in Detroit's gangs. . . .Members achieve status in the gang by showing heart, usually evidenced by an act of violence against a victim or a rival gang member. (Salpukas 1976:1)

The gangs of Detroit, in using terror tactics, seem to be reacting against their "invisible man" status and demanding recognition. The more horrified people are by their acts, the more their existence is affirmed.

Others living in dying communities turn their aggression inwards. Alcohol and drugs are the tools of self-destruction. They also provide an escape from the anxiety that structureless environment produces.

The main defense of Boston West Enders when faced with losing their homes was either a regression into helplessness, a denial of what was happening through a tendency to idealize their lost home, or repression that produced somatic and psychological symptoms.

Unemployment has cut many people off from their community of interest. And some of the comments of those who lost their jobs reflect a sense of helplessness combined with anger. A man who worked for an insurance company for twenty-three years summed up his feelings this way: "What can one man do, I'm a drop in the bucket, just a number on the government chart. I have the highest qualifications. What good is a degree? I sacrificed my entire social life to go through school. And now I'm on the same unemployment line as a high school drop-out factory worker" (Levin 1975).

When police in New York City were laid off, many of the younger ones, who were attracted by the notion of being a respected helper and authority figure, said things like: "I've had it. If they think I'm ever gonna risk my neck again, they got another think coming." Other civil servants, who thought they had won security, now look at their jobs as a way to get even with the system.

In industry, widespread layoffs produce a bitterness that results in lowered productivity, refusal of workers to share their good ideas with management, theft, and an even more stubborn commitment to featherbedding as a way of saving jobs. Layoffs also produce physiological stress, reflected in poorer physical and mental health on and off the job.

270

The Struggle for Community Can Create Community

The one community that grows during unemployment periods is that of our institutional population. Criminal jailings in 1975 were at an all-time high. And state mental hospitalization rates have increased as employment decreased (Brenner 1973).

Growth of Pseudo-Communities

In response to the dying sense of community, people are creating illusory ties with each other. Consumerism is fast becoming the epoxy for friendships. We share products, commercial jingles, and pride of possession. People who drive VWs on the highway honk their horns at each other, signalling a group tie. There are the audiophiles whose relationship is based on their sharing information about speaker systems and amplifiers. There are 10-speed bike aficionados and yogurt eaters who compete verbally about whose brand is purer or healthier. Wearing old blue jeans is the badge of membership in an international fraternity of youth. One of the most treasured items that Soviet black marketeers try to buy from western tourists are their old blue jeans. It is the symbolic ticket to the western world.

This artificial collegiality is a substitute for real human relations. People feel connected without the emotional risk and responsibility of real community.

Probably the most powerful pseudo-community has been created by television. Marshall McLuhan saw the media creating a "global village." We all become electronic brothers and sisters during prime time. And we spend hours at work discussing what happened to Mary Hartman last night, neglecting the human drama and desperate needs of our neighbors and friends. Our participation and involvement in the unreal lives on the screen allow us to express strong feelings of empathy without ever having to make any behavioral commitment. A community without responsibility is illusory.

The Lou Harris poll says Walter Cronkite of CBS is the most trusted man in America, but nobody knows what he believes, or who he really is.

A major response to these false communities is a new tone in politics. Reflecting the shared need to get back to smallness, and running against the depersonalization that flows from bigness, Jimmy Carter is the new symbol of this trend. He was presented to us as the farmer, the archetypical little guy we could trust. Whether this new politics is delivering the possibilities for participation and control on the community level or is simply the empty rhetoric of another pseudo-community is a question on the minds of many Americans.

ADAPTIVE RESPONSES TO THE DYING COMMUNITY

It seems that the loss of community is adapted to not by ceasing to care for what was good and meaningful in past relationships but by abstracting what was fundamentally important in the lost community of interest, of origin, or of place and reintegrating it to meet the needs of the present and the future. This has led to the rediscovery of the importance of sense of community in one's life.

Group Responses

There are numerous examples of people getting together and trying to regain control of their lives. This is the fertile soil from which community will grow.

At Coop City in the Bronx, tenants, after refusing to pay their rent, took over management of the entire project. Urban homesteaders, block associations, and neighborhood clean-up groups are forming to rebuild the deteriorated housing of the neighborhood. Many middle-class blacks are buying homes in Harlem and moving back with their families. One such family head, Mr. Benjamin Grant, expressed the basic philosophy that underlies his investing in this decaying area:

"We thought if we moved in, then we could turn some of our other friends on to the good things that are available here. We wanted to show people, especially the young kids, that Harlem does have a future; that there are some positive influences here, if only blacks would take advantage of them." (L. Williams 1976)

Another black community that has changed its attitudes and hopes to rebuild itself is Detroit. At the same time that this city, through a decline in services and property values, has seen the negative growth of gang influence, the black community is saying, "Detroit's ours now. Let's rebuild it." This is a fundamental change that is taking place in the character, the psyche, the atmosphere of Detroit. In the last three years Detroit "tipped": its population became majority black, making it the biggest such city in the country. Blacks dominate the social scene.

272

Blacks have assumed much of the city's governmental leadership from the mayor's office and the executive branch to the school board to the city council to the courts.

This leadership has generated fresh hopes, and a new spirit of self-reliance in pursuing those hopes, and a new impatience with those, including other blacks, who would frustrate them.

Mayor Coleman Young told a group of Baptist ministers recently, "If we are not willing to help ourselves, no one else is going to help us" (*New York Times*, July 25, 1976).

It was out of this realization that no one else was going to help them, that community residents in areas of our cities all over the country raised the demand for community control of human services. Frustrated with the inadequate, insensitive delivery of services, they asked for a role in administering the delivery of services, making agency policy, and controlling the budget and hiring personnel. Although the concept of community participation and control is not a new one in America (it harks back to the colonists' demand for self-determination), the 1960s movement for community control was opposed by many professionals and their institutional base.

Nevertheless, the struggle for community participation and control has led to the growth of indigenous-run health centers, urban development corporations, manpower programs, and schools. Through these new settings the alienated and powerless residents of these areas have begun to develop a political power base, develop administrative skills, develop local leadership, provide opportunities for meaningful participation, and make their human service agency accountable and relevant to the clients. The growing movement for self-determination was both a reaction to the dying community and a force shaping the future of new communities. As such it was picked up by labor, management, city governments, and informal groups. In Jamestown and Dunkirk, two small New York towns, newly formed labor management committees have had remarkable success in revitalizing what were literally dead economic communities. In New York City the new charter has given local community boards the power to allocate their own budgets.

For some people the loss of community cannot be regained in their present geographic location. And thus we are witnessing the return of immigrants to the continent for retirement. Many blacks are going back South. And the reverse migration of Puerto Ricans to their homeland is often accompanied by a self-consciousness of nationalism and a demand for independence. We also have job-hungry Americans moving to the Southwest and space-hungry youths going West—all in search of a place to live, a purpose, a small group of people to whom one can belong and feel responsible.

Corporate Responses

When we talk of human service institutions we usually think of public sector, health, education, and welfare organizations. We overlook industry, which may have a most significant role to play in responding to the dying community.

While American management may not be as paternalistic and all-embracing in its relations with employees as Japanese management, there is still plenty of energy and thought going into building and maintaining "company spirit" in the United States. The reason is self-evident: when people feel they are part of a "team" they perform with commitment.

The techniques for building corporate community spirit involve economic and psychological strategies. They range from the company picnic and softball game to slick in-house publications, and creating better working conditions than the competition; they include T-Group and sensitivity training to help managers relate better to each other and the work force.

But in the present period, because of economic vicissitudes, changing value systems, and a loss of confidence in business as an honest institution, wherever there has been a corporate sense of community it has undergone considerable dilution. There is more and more executive job hunting and less and less company loyalty. At the rank-and-file level, especially during the recent economic slump, anticompany attitudes have become rampant, and are reflected in absenteeism, labor turnover, sabotage, strikes, and slowdowns.

All of this has generated a new concern in corporate America for what is called "the quality of working life." Foundations, social-science think tanks, and industrial psychologists and engineers are zeroing in on what can be done to overcome the ever escalating level of conflict and suspicion in the workplace and to reestablish a community of interests.

274

Of course, in a unionized workplace, some employees identify with the trade union and its purposes, and this provides them with a sense of community. But most labor organizations are too remote and bureaucratic to win the full trust of their members, and there is hardly a sense of the "house of labor" as there might have been in the CIO organizing days of the 1930s, or earlier, when the union movement was first beginning.

To improve the quality of working life, most major corporations are now going well beyond what the work theoretician Herzberg calls "cosmetics": improving fringe benefits, cafeteria menus, recreational facilities, equipment, even pay scales. These all have only a temporary booster effect on morale. Some companies are even modifying procedures in the workplace itself, to give employees more decision-making powers.

At the Rushton coal mine in Phillipsburg, Pennsylvania, management was plagued for years by wildcat strikes, endless union grievances, poor productivity, and a high accident rate. The owner invited in work experts, who suggested that the solution might be the creation of autonomous work groups—allowing the nine-man coal digging teams to work without foremen and to be totally responsible for themselves. The young miners wanted to try autonomy while the older miners suspected a company plot. Little by little, however, the older men followed the younger into autonomous work groups.

Today, after two and a half years, the entire mining industry is carefully studying the Rushton model, which has boosted production, virtually eliminated grievances, and most important, given the miners a new sense of respect and confidence. Industrial literature reports many similar successes where decision-making powers are shared.

The community on the job is tremendously important because work is the central interest in most adults' lives. It takes up a large part of the worker's time and effort and is a major source of income. It provides for the individual a chief means of contact with society and has a major influence in shaping his self-concept and self-identity. Studies have also demonstrated that those who receive the most satisfaction in their jobs participate most in community activities. Perhaps these experiments on work enrichment will produce one of the vital links in the chain between healthy psyches and healthy communities.

Alternative Responses

Some people have attempted to cope with the dying community by creating alternative structures. Fearing that the power of economic and political forces might limit their imagination, their quest for community attempted a more individualized approach.

Values once only held by middle-class college kids of the 1960s now permeate working-class youth, who reject old models and beliefs, and are joining what is developing as a universal, youth-culture community, producing an alternative life-style. Included in this group are: Black Muslim communities, gay communities, organic farming enclaves, Paolo Soleri groups, Small is Beautiful experiments, consciousness-raising groups, Ralph Nader PIRGS, groups demanding access to public and cable television, and artists' cooperatives. Another alternative being explored is the participatory economic community. Workers own a newspaper in Hammond, Indiana, an asbestos company in Vermont, and an insurance company in Washington, D.C.

All these experiments have rejected old structural forms and organizational relations for an emphasis on individual responsibility and increased dependence on the creativity and resourcefulness of the individual.

Even the new form of therapeutic intervention and network eschews the role of the professional. Using the tribe as its model, the network process tries to put into motion the energies and talents of a total social network for mutual self-help.

Perhaps these self-help groups that have chosen alternative means of dealing with the problem of the dying community have a better chance of recovering the sense of communtiy. They have managed to keep their scale small and their style personal. They have rejected the model of a hierarchical organization and its alienating roles of leader/follower, professional/client. Because economic reward is not the primary motive for participation, there is a need and a demand for anyone who is willing to participate. This makes people feel important. It also gives people an opportunity to be part of an organization with a broad social mission, whether it be women's liberation, the protection of the environment, the belief in the perfectibility of man, worker control, or personal growth.

Although utopian communities and self-sustaining, alternate innovative, human-service organizations do not have a record of great

276

longevity, they do serve an important purpose. As an antidote to cynicism they serve as models, reassuring us that a sense of community can exist.

The Problem

The problem for human adaptation is first to perceive accurately the signs of a dying community: neither to deny, nor defend against these signs, which threaten the continuity of meaning of our lives. We must, rather, mobilize ourselves and struggle to preserve the remembered sense of community and integrate it into future attempts at change.

In moving society forward, many different communities may be destroyed or die, but for the survival of mankind we must not capitulate to the concept that the sense of community is dead. The most binding, vital, and healthy sense of community may be generated through this struggle.

References

ABBOTT, SUSAN
1974   "Full-Time Farmers and Week-End Wives: Change and Stress Among Rural Kikuyu Women" (Ph.D. diss., University of North Carolina).

AD.·.MS, BERT N.
1969   "The Small Trade Center: Processes and Perceptions of Growth and Decline," in *The Community: A Comparative Perspective*, ed. R. M. French (Itasca, Ill.: F. E. Peacock Publishers).

ADAMS, RICHARD E. W.
1973   "The Collapse of Maya Civlization: A Review of Previous Theories," in *The Classic Maya Collapse*, ed. T. P. Culbert (Albuquerque: University of New Mexico Press, School of American Research Advanced Seminar Series).

ADAMS, ROBERT McC.
1965   *Land Behind Baghdad* (Chicago: University of Chicago Press).

ADAMS, WILLIAM Y.
1961   "The Christian Potteries at Faras," *Kush* 9:30–43.
1962   "Pottery Kiln Excavations," *Kush* 10:62–75.
1964a   "Post-Pharaonic Nubia in the Light of Archaeology, I," *Journal of Egyptian Archaeology* 50:102–20.
1964b   "Sudan Antiquities Service Excavations in Nubia: Fourth Season, 1962-63," *Kush* 12:216–50.
1965   "Sudan Antiquities Service Excavations at Meinarti, 1963–64," *Kush* 13:148–76.
1968a   "Invasion, Diffusion, Evolution?" *Antiquity* 42:194–215.
1968b   "Settlement Pattern in Microcosm: The Changing Aspect of a Nubian Village During Twelve Centuries," in *Settlement Archaeology*, ed. K. C. Chang (Palo Alto, Calif.: National Press.Books).
1970   "The Evolution of Christian Nubian Pottery," in *Kunst und Geschichte Nubiens in Christlicher Zeit*, ed. E. Dinkler (Recklinghausen: Aurel Bongers).
1973   "The Archaeologist as Detective," in *Variation in Anthropology*, ed. D. W. Lathrap and J. Douglas (Urbana: Illinois Archaeological Survey).

279

1976   *Meroitic North and South,* Meroitica no. 2 (Humboldt-Universität zu Berlin, Bereich Ägyptologie und Sudenarchäologie).

ALARCÃO, JORGE

1970   "On the Westernmost Road of the Roman Empire, Part II," *Archaeology* 23:44–48.

ALEXANDER, W. W.

1940   "Overcrowded Farms," in *Farmers in a Changing World,* ed. G. Hambidge (Washington, D.C.: U.S. Department of Agriculture).

ALLEN, FREDERICK LEWIS

1946   *Only Yesterday* (New York: Bantam Books).

AMORY, CLEVELAND

1952   *The Last Resorts* (New York: Harper & Row, Publishers).

ANDERSON, ROBERT T., AND BARBARA G. ANDERSON

1964   *The Vanishing Village* (Seattle: University of Washington Press).

ANDREWS, E. WYLLYS IV

1968   "Dzibilchaltun, a Northern Maya Metropolis," *Archaeology* 21:36–47.

ANNAS, CARL E.

1970   "Problems and Advantages of Rural Locations by Labor-Intensive Industries," in *Rural Development: Problems and Advantages of Rural Locations for Industrial Plants* (Raleigh: Agricultural Policy Institute, North Carolina State University).

ARENSBERG, CONRAD M.

1954   "The Community Study Method," *American Journal of Sociology* 60:109–27.

1955   "American Communities," *American Anthropologist* 57:1143–62.

ARENSBERG, CONRAD M., AND SOLON T. KIMBALL

1940   *Family and Community in Ireland* (Cambridge, Mass.: Harvard University Press).

1965   *Culture and Community* (New York: Harcourt, Brace & World).

BACON, EDWARD, ED.

1963   *Vanished Civilizations* (London: Thames and Hudson).

BANKS, VERA J., ROBERT C. SPEAKER, AND RICHARD L. FORSTALL

1975   *Farm Population of the United States: 1974,* Current Population Reports, U.S. Department of Commerce (Washington, D.C.: Bureau of the Census).

BARKER, R. G.

1960   "Ecology and Motivation," in *Nebraska Symposium on Motivation,* ed. M. R. Jones (Lincoln: University of Nebraska Press).

BARNETT, HOMER G.

1953   *Innovation: The Basis of Culture Change* (New York: McGraw-Hill).

BATES, FREDERICK L., AND CLYDE C. HARVEY

1975   *The Structure of Social Systems* (New York: Gardner Press).

BEALE, CALVIN L.

1974   "Qualitative Dimensions of Decline and Stability Among Rural Communities," in *Communities Left Behind: Alternatives for Development,* ed. L. R. Whiting (Ames: Iowa State University Press).

1975   "The Western Aspect of Renewed Nonmetropolitan Population Growth in the United States," in *Economic Research Service, USDA, Special Report to the Western Rural Development Center* (Corvallis: Oregon State University).

BECKER, HOWARD

1950   *Through Values to Social Interpretation* (Durham, N.C.: Duke University Press).

BELL, BARBARA

1971   "The Dark Ages in Ancient History," *American Journal of Archaeology* 75:1–26.

BELL, EARL H.

1934   "Social Stratification in a Small Community," *Scientific Monthly* 38:157–64.

280

References

BENEDICT, RUTH
1938   "Continuities and Discontinuities in Cultural Conditioning," *Psychiatry* 1:161–67.
BENDER, LLOYD D., BERNAL L. GREEN, AND REX CAMPBELL
1971   *Rural Poverty Ghettoization*, mimeo (Bozeman: Montana State University, Department of Agricultural Economics).
BENNETT, CLAUSE F., AND DONALD L. NELSON
1975   *Analyzing Impacts of Community Development* (Mississippi State, Miss.: Southern Rural Development Center).
BENNETT, JOHN W.
1969   *Northern Plainsmen: Adaptive Strategy and Agrarian Life* (Chicago: Aldine Publishing Company).
1976   "Adaptation, Anticipation, and the Concept of Culture in Anthropology," *Science* 192:847–53.
BENNETT, WENDELL C., AND JUNIUS B. BIRD
1964   *Andean Culture History* (New York: Natural History Press).
BENSMAN, JOSEPH, AND ARTHUR J. VIDICH
1975   *Metropolitan Communities* (New York: Franklin Watts).
BERNARD, JESSIE
1973   *The Sociology of Community* (Glenview, Ill.: Scott, Foresman and Co.).
BERTRAND, ALVIN L.
1963   "The Stress-Strain Element of Social Systems: A Micro Theory of Conflict and Change," *Social Forces* 42:1–9.
1967   *Basic Sociology: An Introduction to Theory and Method* (New York: Appleton-Century-Crofts).
1972   *Social Organization: A General Systems and Role Theory Perspective* (Philadelphia: F. A. Davis Co.).
BERTRAND, ALVIN L., AND MARION B. SMITH
1960   *Environmental Factors and School Attendance: A Study in Rural Louisiana*, Louisiana Agricultural Experiment Station Bulletin 533 (Baton Rouge).
BESNER, ARTHUR
1966   "Economic Deprivation and Family Patterns," in *Low-Income Life Styles*, ed. L. M. Irelan (Washington, D.C.: Division of Research, Welfare Administration, U.S. Dept. of Health, Education and Welfare).
BIRD, CAROLINE
1966   *The Invisible Scar* (New York: David McKay Co.).
BLEGEN, CARL W.
1963   *Troy* (New York: Praeger Publishers).
BLOCH, MARC
1953   *The Historian's Craft* (New York: Vintage Books).
BODINE, JOHN J.
1969   "A Tri-Ethnic Trap: The Spanish Americans in Taos," in *The Community: A Comparative Perspective*, ed. R. M. French (Itasca, Ill.: F. E. Peacock Publishers).
BRENNER, M. HARVEY
1973   *Mental Illness and the Economy* (Cambridge, Mass.: Harvard University Press).
BROKENSHA, DAVID, AND PETER HODGE
1969   *Community Development: An Interpretation* (San Francisco: Chandler Publishing Co.).
BROKENSHA, DAVID, AND THAYER SCUDDER
1968   "Resettlement," in *Manmade Lakes in Africa*, ed. N. Rubin and W. Warren (London: Frank Cass).

281

BROWN, CHARLANE BURKE
1973   "The Differential Acceptance of Social Labeling by Middle-Aged and Aged Popula-
        tions with Implications Regarding the Questionable Inevitability of Many Behavioral
        Characteristics Associated with the Aging Process" (Ph.D. diss., University of
        California, Berkeley).
BUBOLZ, MARGARET J.
1974   "Family Adjustment Under Community Decline," in *Communities Left Behind:
        Alternatives for Development*, ed. L. R. Whiting (Ames: Iowa State University Press).
BULTENA, LOUIS
1944   "Rural Churches and Community Integration," *Rural Sociology* 9:257–64.
BULTENA, G. L., AND VIVIAN WOOD
1969   "The American Retirement Community: Bane or Blessing?" *Journal of Gerontology*
        24:209–17.
BURBY, RAYMOND J., III, AND SHIRLEY F. WEISS
1977   *New Communities, U.S.A.* (Lexington, Mass.: D.C. Heath and Co.).
BURCKHARDT, J. L.
1819   *Travels in Nubia* (London: John Murray).
BURGESS, ELAINE M.
1964   *Negro Leadership in a Southern City*, paperback edition (New Haven: College and
        University Press).
BUTZER, KARL W.
1964   *Environment and Archaeology* (Chicago: Aldine Publishing Company).
CAIN, STEVEN
1972   "Urbanization without Modernization," *Ethnohistory* 19:53–62.
CAMPBELL, JOHN C.
1921   *The Southern Highlander and His Homeland* (New York: Russell Sage Foundation).
CARLSSON, GRETA, AND KATRINA CARLSSON
1970   "Age, Cohorts and the Generation of Generations," *American Sociological Review*
        35:710–18.
CARPENTER, RHYS
1968   *Discontinuity in Greek Civilization* (New York: W. W. Norton and Co.).
CHANG, KWANG-CHIH, ED.
1968   *Settlement Archaeology* (Palo Alto, Calif: National Press Books).
CHENG TE-K'UN
1960   *Archaeology in China*, vol. 2, *Shang China* (Cambridge: W. Heffer & Sons).
CHILDE, V. GORDON
1946   *What Happened in History* (New York: Pelican Books).
CLARK, MARGARET, AND B. G. ANDERSON
1967   *Culture and Aging* (Springfield, Ill.: Charles C. Thomas).
CLAWSON, MARION
1975   "Restoration of the Quality of Life in Rural America," in *Externalities in the
        Transformation of Agriculture: Distribution of Benefits and Costs from Development*,
        ed. E. O. Heady and L. R. Whiting (Ames: Iowa State University Press).
CLAWSON, MARION, HANS H. LANDSBERG, AND LYLE T. ALEXANDER
1969   "Desalted Seawater for Agriculture: Is It Economic?" *Science* 164:1141–48.
COE, MICHAEL D.
1962   *Mexico* (New York: Praeger Publishers).
COHEN, YEHUDI A.
1968   "Culture as Adaptation," in *Man in Adaptation: The Cultural Present*, ed. Y. A.
        Cohen (Chicago: Aldine Publishing Co.).

282

References

COOPER, JOHN M.
1946   "The Yahgan," in *Handbook of South American Indians, vol. 1, The Marginal Tribes,* ed. J. H. Steward, Bureau of American Ethnology Bulletin 143 (Washington, D.C.).
COTTRELL, LEONARD, ED.
1960   *The Concise Encyclopaedia of Archaeology* (New York: Hawthorn Books).
COTTRELL, W. F.
1951   "Death by Dieselization: A Case Study in the Reaction to Technological Change," *American Sociological Review* 16:358–65.
COWGILL, URSULA, AND G. E. HUTCHINSON
1963   "Sex-Ratio in Childhood and the Depopulation of the Peten, Guatemala," *Human Biology* 35:90–103.
CROSSWHITE, WILLIAM M., ED.
1970   *People in Poverty: Selected Case Studies* (Raleigh: Agricultural Policy Institute, North Carolina State University).
CULBERT, T. PATRICK, ED.
1973a   *The Classic Maya Collapse* (Albuquerque: University of New Mexico Press, School of American Research Advanced Seminar Series).
1973b   "The Maya Downfall at Tikal," in *The Classic Maya Collapse,* ed. T. P. Culbert (Albuquerque: University of New Mexico Press, School of American Research Advanced Seminar Series).
CUMMING, ELAINE, AND HENRY WILLING
1961   *Growing Old* (New York: Basic Books).
DALES, G. F.
1966   "The Decline of the Harappans," *Scientific American* 214(5):92–100.
DEAN, JEFFREY S.
1970   "Aspects of Tsegi Phase Social Organization: A Trial Reconstruction," in *Reconstructing Prehistoric Pueblo Societies,* ed. William A. Longacre (Albuquerque: University of New Mexico Press, School of American Research Advanced Seminar Series).
DEAN, LOIS R.
1967   *Five Towns: A Comparative Community Study* (New York: Random House).
DE ARMOND, DALE
1975   *Raven* (Edmonds, Wash.: Alaska Northwest Publishing Co.).
DES PRES, TERRENCE
1976   *The Survivor* (New York: Oxford University Press).
DEUTSCH, KARL W.
1969   *Nationalism and Its Alternatives* (New York: Alfred A. Knopf).
DEVAMBEZ, PIERRE, ET AL.
1967   *The Praeger Encyclopedia of Ancient Greek Civilization* (New York: Praeger Publishers).
DINKLER, ERICH, ED.
1970   *Kunst und Geschichte Nubiens in Christlicher Zeit* (Recklinghausen: Aurel Bongers).
DIXON, J. R., J. R. CANN, AND COLIN RENFREW
1968   "Obsidian and the Origins of Trade," *Scientific American* 218(3):38–48.
DOEKSEN, GERALD A., JOHN KUEHN, AND JOSEPH SCHMIDT
1974   "Consequences of Decline and Community Adjustments to It," in *Communities Left Behind: Alternatives for Development,* ed. L. R. Whiting (Ames: Iowa State University Press).
DOLLARD, JOHN, AND NEAL E. MILLER
1950   *Personality and Psychotherapy* (New York: McGraw-Hill).

283

DOWNING, THEODORE, AND McGUIRE GIBSON, EDS.
1974   *Irrigation's Impact on Society*, Anthropological Papers of the University of Arizona, no. 25 (Tucson).
DRUCKER, PHILIP, C. R. SMITH, AND E. REEVES
1974   *Displacement of Persons by Major Public Works* (Lexington: University of Kentucky Water Resources Institute).
DURKHEIM, EMILE
1933   *The Division of Labor in Society* (Glencoe, Ill.: Free Press).
EDWARDS, ALLEN D.
1939   "The Sociology of Drought," *Rural Sociology* 4:190–202.
EDWARDS, EVERETT E.
1940   "American Agriculture: The First 300 Years," in *Farmers in a Changing World*, ed. G. Hambidge (Washington, D.C.: U.S. Department of Agriculture).
EDWARDS, I. E. S., C. J. GADD, AND N. G. L. HAMMOND, EDS.
1971   *The Cambridge Ancient History*, 3d ed., vol. 1, part 2 (Cambridge: Cambridge University Press).
EISENSTADT, S. N.
1956   *From Generation to Generation: Age Groups and Social Structure* (Glencoe, Ill.: Free Press).
1963   *The Political Systems of Empires* (New York: Free Press).
ELLENBOGEN, BERT L.
1974   "Service Structure of the Small Community: Problems and Options for Change," in *Communities Left Behind: Alternatives for Development*, ed. L. R. Whiting (Ames: Iowa State University Press).
ENCYCLOPAEDIA BRITANNICA
1929a   "Carthage."
1929b   "Delphi."
1929c   "Olympia."
ERICKSON, EUGENE C.
1974   "Consequences for Leadership and Participation," in *Communities Left Behind: Alternatives for Development*, ed. L. R. Whiting (Ames: Iowa State University Press).
ERICKSON, KENNETH A.
1965   "The Morphology of Lumber Settlements in Western Oregon and Washington" (Ph.D. diss., University of California, Berkeley).
ERIKSON, ERIK H.
1950   *Childhood and Society* (New York: W. W. Norton & Co.).
1963   *Childhood and Society*, 2d ed. (New York: W. W. Norton & Co.).
ERIM, KENAN T.
1967   "Ancient Aphrodisias and Its Marble Treasures," *National Geographic* 132:766–91.
1972   "Aphrodisias, Awakened City of Ancient Art," *National Geographic* 141:766–91.
EVANS-PRITCHARD, E. E.
1940   *The Nuer* (Oxford: Clarendon Press).
FAKHOURI, HANI
1972   *Dafr el-Elow: An Egyptian Village in Transition* (New York: Holt, Rinehart and Winston).
FERMAN, LOUIS A., JOYCE L. KORNBLUH, AND ALAN HABER, EDS.
1965   *Poverty in America* (Ann Arbor: University of Michigan Press).
FINLEY, M. I.
1970   *Early Greece: The Bronze and Archaic Ages* (London: Chatto & Windus).
FORD, ARTHUR M.
1973   *Political Economics of Rural Poverty in the South* (Cambridge, Mass.: Ballinger Publishing Co.).

References

FORD, THOMAS R.
1964a   *Health and Demography in Kentucky* (Lexington: University Press of Kentucky).
1964b   "The Passing of Provincialism," in *The Southern Appalachian Region: A Survey*, ed. T. R. Ford (Lexington: University Press of Kentucky).
1969   "Discussion," in *Poverty: New Interdisciplinary Perspectives*, ed. T. Weaver and A. Magid (San Francisco: Chandler Press).

FORDE, C. DARYLL
1934   *Habitat, Economy and Society: A Geographical Introduction to Ethnology* (New York: E. P. Dutton & Co.).

FOWLER, MELVIN L., ED.
1969   *Explorations in Cahokia Archaeology*, Illinois Archaeological Survey Bulletin no. 7 (Urbana).

FOX, ROBIN
1967   *The Keresan Bridge*, London School of Economics Monographs on Social Anthropology, no. 15.

FRANKFORT, HENRI
1956   *The Birth of Civilization in the Near East* (New York: Doubleday & Co., Anchor Books).

FRENCH, ROBERT MILLS, ED.
1969   *The Community: A Comparative Perspective* (Itasca, Ill.: F. E. Peacock Publishers).

FRIED, MARC
1963   "Grieving for a Lost Home," in *The Urban Condition*, ed. L. J. Duhl (New York: Basic Books).

GALLAHER, ART, JR.
1961   *Plainville Fifteen Years Later* (New York: Columbia University Press).

GALPIN, CHARLES J.
1915   *The Social Anatomy of an Agricultural Community*, Wisconsin Agricultural Experiment Station, Bulletin no. 34.

GEERTZ, CLIFFORD
1968   *Peddlers and Princes: Social Development and Economic Change in Two Indonesian Towns* (Chicago: University of Chicago Press).

GIBSON, McGUIRE
1974   "Violation of Fallow and Engineered Disaster in Mesopotamian Civilization," in *Irrigation's Impact on Society*, ed. T. Downing and McG. Gibson, Anthropological Papers of the University of Arizona, no. 25 (Tucson).

GIST, NOEL, AND CARROLL D. CLARK
1938   "Intelligence as a Selective Factor in Rural-Urban Migrations," *American Journal of Sociology* 44:36–58.

GIST, NOEL, C. T. PIHLBLAD, AND CECIL L. GREGORY
1941   "Selective Aspects of Rural Migrations," *Rural Sociology* 6:3–15.

GOODWIN, D. C., AND P. H. JOHNSTONE
1940   "A Brief Chronology of American Agricultural History," in *Farmers in a Changing world*, ed. G. Hambidge (Washington, D.C.: U.S. Department of Agriculture).

GRIESSMAN, B. EUGENE
1975   *Minorities: A Text with Readings in Intergroup Relations* (Hinsdale, Ill.: Dryden Press).

GROUP FOR THE ADVANCEMENT OF PSYCHIATRY
1966   *Psychopathological Disorders in Childhood: Theoretical Considerations and a Proposed Classification*, Report no. 62.

HAGBERG, ULF E.
1976   "Ancient Oland," *Archaeology* 29:108–17.
HALLGREN, MAURITZ A.
1933   *Seeds of Revolt: A Study of American Life and the Temper of the American People During the Depression* (New York: Alfred A. Knopf).
HALLOWELL, A. IRVINE
1955   *Culture and Experience* (Philadelphia: University of Pennsylvania Press).
HAMMOND, MASON
1972   *The City in the Ancient World* (Cambridge, Mass.: Harvard University Press).
HANDMAN, MAX
1934   "Conflict and Equilibrium in a Border Area," in *Race and Culture Contacts*, ed. E. B. Reuter (New York: McGraw-Hill).
HARCOURT, G. C.
1969   "Some Cambridge Controversies in the Theory of Capital," *Journal of Economic Literature* 7:369–405.
HASAN, YUSUF FADL
1967   *The Arabs and the Sudan* (Edinburgh: University of Edinburgh Press).
HAURY, EMIL W.
1958   "Evidence at Point of Pines for a Prehistoric Migration from Northern Arizona," in *Migrations in New World Culture History*, ed. R. H. Thompson, University of Arizona Social Science Bulletin no. 27 (Tucson).
HAUSWALD, EDWARD L.
1971   "The Economically Distressed Community: A Synoptic Outline of Symptoms, Causes and Solutions," *Journal of Community Development Society* 2:96–105.
HAVIGHURST, ROBERT J., AND RUTH ALBRECHT
1953   *Older People* (New York: Longmans, Green and Co.).
HAVIGHURST, ROBERT J., AND M. GERTHON MORGAN
1951   *The Social History of a Warboom Community* (New York: Longmans, Green and Co.).
HEILBRONER, ROBERT L.
1970   *Between Capitalism and Socialism: Essays in Political Economics* (New York: Random House).
HILL, JAMES N.
1970   *Broken K Pueblo*, Anthropological Papers of the University of Arizona, no. 18 (Tucson).
HOFFER, C. R.
1938   "Cooperation as a Culture Pattern Within a Community," *Rural Sociology* 3:153–58.
HOLLINGSHEAD, A. B.
1937   "The Life Cycle of Nebraska Rural Churches," *Rural Sociology* 2:180–91.
1938   "Changes in Land Ownership as an Index of Succession in Rural Communities," *American Journal of Sociology* 43:764–77.
HOMANS, GEORGE
1950   *The Human Group* (New York: Harcourt, Brace & World).
HOOD, SINCLAIR
1967   *The Home of the Heroes* (New York: McGraw-Hill).
HOWE, IRVING
1976   *World of Our Fathers* (New York: Harcourt Brace Jovanovich).
HUNTINGTON, ELLSWORTH
1924   *Civilization and Climate* (New Haven: Yale University Press).

References

1945   *Mainsprings of Civilization* (New York: John Wiley & Sons).

HUTCHINSON, H. W.
1957   *Village and Plantation Life in Northeastern Brazil* (Seattle: University of Washington Press).

HUTCHISON, R. W.
1962   *Prehistoric Crete* (Baltimore: Pelican Books).

HUNTER, CHARLAYNE
1976   "Young Doctor at Lincoln: Disillusion and Departure," *New York Times*, August 16.

IRELAN, LOLA M., AND ARTHUR BESNER
1966   "Low-Income Outlook on Life," in *Low-Income Life Styles*, ed. L. M. Irelan (Washington, D.C.: Division of Research, Welfare Administration, U.S. Dept. of Health, Education and Welfare).

JACOBS, JANE
1961   *The Death and Life of Great American Cities* (New York: Random House).

JAHODA, M.
1950   "Toward a Social Psychology of Mental Health," in *Symposium on the Healthy Personality*, ed. M. J. E. Senn, Supplement II: Problems of Infancy and Childhood, Transactions of Fourth Conference (New York: Josiah Macy, Jr., Foundation).

JAKOBSON, THORKILD, AND ROBERT McC. ADAMS
1958   "Salt and Silt in Ancient Mesopotamian Agriculture," *Science* 128:1251–58.

JENSEN, VERNON H.
1945   *Lumber and Labor* (New York: Farrar and Rinehart).

JESSER, CLINTON J.
1967   "Community Satisfactional Patterns of Professionals in Rural Areas," *Rural Sociology* 32:56–69.

JOHNSON, JOTHAM
1954   "The Slow Death of a City," *Scientific American* 191(1):66–70.

JUDD, NEIL M.
1954   *The Material Culture of Pueblo Bonito*, Smithsonian Miscellaneous Collections, no. 124 (Washington, D.C.: Smithsonian Institution).

KELMAN, HERBERT C.
1973   "Violence Without Moral Restraint: Reflections on the Dehumanization of Victims and Victimizers," *Journal of Social Issues* 29:25–61.

KENYON, KATHLEEN M.
1960   *Archaeology in the Holy Land* (New York: Praeger Publishers).
1971   "The Archaeological Sites," in *The Cambridge Ancient History*, ed. I. E. S. Edwards, C. J. Gadd, and N. G. L. Hammond, 3d ed., vol. 1, part 2 (Cambridge: Cambridge University Press).

KEPHART, HORACE
1913   *Our Southern Highlanders* (New York: Outing Publishing Co.); paperback reprint 1976 (Knoxville: University of Tennessee Press).

KERCHER, LEONARD C.
1941   "Some Sociological Aspects of Consumers' Cooperation," *Rural Sociology* 6:311–22.

KING, DALE S.
1949   *Nalakihu: Excavations at a Pueblo III Site on Wupatki National Monument, Arizona*, Museum of Northern Arizona Bulletin no. 23 (Flagstaff).

KOMAROVSKY, MIRRA
1940   *The Unemployed Man and His Family–The Effect of Unemployment upon the Status of the Man in 59 Families* (New York: Octagon Books).

KROEBER, A. L.
1923   "What Culture Is," in *Man in Adaptation: The Cultural Present*, ed. Y. Cohen (Chicago: Aldine Publishing Co.).
1944   *Configurations of Cultural Growth* (Berkeley: University of California Press).
KROLL, STEPHAN E.
1972   "Excavations at Bastam, Iran," *Archaeology* 25:292–97.
KUTNER, BERNARD
1962   "The Social Nature of Aging," *The Gerontologist* 2:5–8.
LA BARRE, WESTON
1956   *They Shall Take Up Serpents: The Southern Snake Cult* (Durham, N.C.: Duke University Press).
LAMB, CURT
1975   *Political Power in Poor Neighborhoods* (New York: John Wiley & Sons).
LAMBRICK, H. T.
1967   "The Indus Flood-Plain and the 'Indus' Civilization," *Geographical Journal* 133:483–95
LANDIS, PAUL M.
1935   "Social Change and Social Interaction as Factors in Cultural Change," *American Journal of Sociology* 41:52–58.
LANGER, WILLIAM L.
1964   "The Black Death," *Scientific American* 210(2):114–21.
LANNING, EDWARD P.
1967   *Peru Before the Incas* (Englewood Cliffs, N.J.: Prentice-Hall).
LARCO HOYLE, RAFAEL
1966   *Peru* (Cleveland: World Publishing Co.).
LATHRAP, DONALD W., AND JODY DOUGLAS, EDS.
1973   *Variation in Anthropology* (Urbana: Illinois Archaeological Survey).
LAWTON, M. P.
1970   "Ecology and Aging," in *The Spatial Behavior of Older People*, ed. L. Pastalan and D. Carson (Ann Arbor: Institute of Gerontology, University of Michigan).
LEONE, MARK P., ED.
1972   *Contemporary Archaeology* (Carbondale: Southern Illinois University Press).
LEVIN, HANNAH
1975   "Work: The Staff of Life," paper presented at the Eighty-third Annual Meeting of the American Psychological Association, Chicago, in *Symposium: Unemployment, America's Major Mental Health Problem* (Chicago).
LEWIS, PIERCE F.
1972   "Small Town in Pennsylvania," in *Regions of the United States*, ed. J. F. Hart (New York: Harper and Row Publishers).
LIFTON, R. J.
1971   "Existential Evil," in *Sanctions for Evil: Sources of Social Destructiveness*, ed. N. Sanford, C. Comstock, and Associates (San Francisco: Jossey-Bass).
1973   *Home from War—Vietnam Veterans: Neither Victims nor Executioners* (New York: Simon and Schuster).
LINTON, RALPH
1943   "Nativistic Movements," *American Anthropologist* 45:230–40.
1956   *The Tree of Culture* (New York: Alfred A. Knopf).
LOGUE, EDWARD L.
1966   *Let There Be Commitment: A Housing, Planning and Development Program for New York* (New York: Institute for Public Administration).

288

References

LONG, HUEY B., ROBERT C. ANDERSON, AND JON A. BLUBAUGH
1973   *Approaches to Community Development* (Iowa City: American College Testing Program).

LONGACRE, WILLIAM A., ED.
1970   *Reconstructing Prehistoric Pueblo Societies* (Albuquerque: University of New Mexico Press, School of American Research Advanced Seminar Series).

LOOFF, DAVID H.
1970   "Psychophysiologic and Conversion Reactions in Children: Selective Incidence in Verbal and Nonverbal Families," *Journal of the Academy of Child Psychiatry* 9:318–31.
1971   *Appalachia's Children* (Lexington: University Press of Kentucky).
1976a   "Assisting Appalachian Families," *Psychiatric Annals* 6:15–35.
1976b   *Getting to Know the Troubled Child* (Knoxville: University of Tennessee Press).

LOOMIS, CHARLES P.
1959   "Tentative Types of Directed Social Change Involving Systemic Linkage," *Rural Sociology* 24:383–90.

LYFORD, JOSEPH P.
1965   *The Talk in Vandalia* (New York: Harper & Row, Publishers).

MACADAM, M. F. LAMING
1955   *The Temples of Kawa*, vol. 2 (London: Oxford University Press).

McGREGOR, JOHN C.
1965   *Southwestern Archaeology*, 2d ed. (Urbana: University of Illinois Press).

McMULLEN, ROY
1969   "The Life and Death of Bruges," *Horizon* 11(3):74–90.

MACQUEEN, J. G.
1975   *The Hittites* (London: Thames and Hudson).

MANDELBAUM, DAVID G.
1941   "Culture Change among the Nilgiri Tribes," *American Anthropologist* 43:19–26.

MARIS, PAUL V.
1940   "Farm Tenancy," in *Farmers in a Changing World*, ed. G. Hambidge (Washington, D.C.: U.S. Department of Agriculture).

MARTINDALE, DON, AND R. GALEN HANSON
1969   *Small Town and Nation* (Westport, Conn.: Greenwood Publishing Co.).

MASON, JOHN E.
1940   "Private and Public Costs of Isolated Settlement in the Cut-over Area of Minnesota," *Rural Sociology* 5:206–21.

MATTHEWS, KENNETH D., JR.
1957   *Cities in the Sand* (Philadelphia: University of Pennsylvania Press).

MEDLEY, MORRIS L.
1976   "Satisfaction with Life Among Persons Sixty-Five Years and Older: A Causal Model," *Journal of Gerontology* 31:448–55.

MELLAART, JAMES
1965   *Earliest Civilization of the Near East* (New York: McGraw-Hill).

MELLERSH, H. E. L.
1967   *Minoan Crete* (New York: G. P. Putnam's Sons).

MERTON, ROBERT K., ED.
1973   *The Sociology of Science: Theoretical and Empirical Investigations* (Chicago: University of Chicago Press).

MILLON, RENE
1967   "Teotihuacán," *Scientific American* 216(6):38–48.

289

MOOS, RUDOLF H., AND PAUL M. INSEL, EDS.
1974   *Issues in Social Ecology: Human Milieus* (Palo Alto, Calif.: National Press Books).
MORRISON, PETER A.
1974   "Urban Growth and Decline: San Jose and St. Louis in the 1960's," *Science* 185:757–62.
NASH, MANNING
1974   *Peasant Citizens: Politics, Religion and Modernization in Kelantan, Malaysia*, Ohio University Center for International Studies, Southeast Asia Studies, no. 31 (Athens, Ohio).
NEELY, JAMES A.
1974   "Sassanian and Early Islamic Water-Control and Irrigation Systems on the Deh Luran Plain, Iran," in *Irrigation's Impact on Society*, ed. T. Downing and McG. Gibson, Anthropological Papers of the University of Arizona, no. 25 (Tucson).
NEIL, EDWARD J.
1972   "The Revival of Political Economy," *Social Research* 39:32–52.
NELSON, LOWRY
1943   "Cultural Islands in Adams County, Indiana," *Rural Sociology* 8:188–92.
NEUGARTEN, BERNICE L.
1970   "Adaptations on the Life Cycle," *Journal of Geriatric Psychiatry* 4:71–88.
NEUMANN, FRANZ L.
1968   "Approaches to the Study of Political Power," in *Comparative Politics: Notes and Readings*, ed. R. Macridis and B. Brown, 3d ed. (Homewood, Ill.: Dorsey Press).
NISBET, ROBERT A.
1969   *The Quest for Community* (New York: Oxford University Press). (First published in 1953.)
NORBECK, EDWARD
1959   *Pineapple Town, Hawaii* (Berkeley: University of California Press).
NUTTING, ANTHONY
1964   *The Arabs* (New York: Mentor Books).
ODUM, HOWARD
1936   *Southern Regions of the United States* (Chapel Hill: University of North Carolina Press).
OPTON, E. M., JR.
1971   "It Never Happened and Besides They Deserved It," in *Sanctions for Evil: Sources of Social Destructiveness*, ed. N. Sanford, C. Comstock, and Associates (San Francisco: Jossey-Bass).
ÖZGÜC, TASHIM
1963   "An Assyrian Trading Outpost," *Scientific American* 208(2):96–106.
1967   "Ancient Ararat," *Scientific American* 216(3):38–46.
PADFIELD, HARLAND, AND ROY WILLIAMS
1973   *Stay Where You Were: A Study of Unemployables in Industry* (Philadelphia: J. B. Lippincott Co.).
PADFIELD, HARLAND, AND JOHN A. YOUNG
1977   "Institutional Processing of Human Resources: A Theory of Social Marginalization," in *Rural Poverty and the Policy Crisis*, ed. R. O. Coppedge and C. G. Davis (Ames: Iowa State University Press).
PALMER, LEONARD R.
1965   *Mycenaeans and Minoans*, 2d ed. (New York: Alfred A. Knopf).
PARRY, J. H.
1963   *The Age of Reconnaissance* (New York: Mentor Books).

References

PEARSALL, MARION
1959   *Little Smokey Ridge* (Tuscaloosa: University of Alabama Press).
PECK, ROBERT C.
1956   "Psychological Developments in the Second Half of LIfe," in *Psychological Aspects of Aging*, ed. J. E. Anderson (Washington, D.C.: American Psychological Association).
PFEIFFER, JOHN
1974   "America's First City," *Horizon* 16(2):58–63.
PHILLIPS, E. D.
1963   "The Peoples of the Highland," in *Vanished Civilization*, ed. E. Bacon (London: Thames and Hudson).
PIGGOTT, STUART
1952   *Prehistoric India* (Baltimore: Pelican Books).
PIHLBLAD, C. T., AND CECIL L. GREGORY
1954   "Selective Aspects of Migration Among Missouri High School Graduates," *American Sociological Review* 19:314–24.
PIRENNE, HENRI
1956   *Medieval Cities* (New York: Doubleday & Co., Anchor Books).
PLOG, FRED T.
1974   *The Study of Prehistoric Change* (New York: Academic Press).
POLANSKI, NORMAN A., ROBERT D. BORGMAN, AND CHRISTINE DE SAIX
1972   *Roots of Futility* (San Francisco: Jossey-Bass).
PORTER, JAMES W.
1969   "The Mitchell Site and Prehistoric Exchange Systems at Cahokia," in *Explorations in Cahokia Archaeology*, ed. M. L. Fowler, Illinois Archaeological Survey Bulletin no. 7 (Urbana).
POSENER, GEORGES
1959   *A Dictionary of Egyptian Civilization* (London: Methuen & Co.).
POTTER, DAVID M.
1954   *People of Plenty* (Chicago: University of Chicago Press).
PROSKOURIAKOFF, TATIANA
1955   "The Death of a Civilization," *Scientific American* 192(5):82–88.
PYM, CHRISTOPHER
1963   "The Collapse of the Khmers," in *Vanished Civilizations*, ed. E. Bacon (London: Thames and Hudson).
RADIN, PAUL
1953   *The World of Primitive Man* (New York: Henry Schuman).
RAIKES, ROBERT L.
1964   "The End of the Ancient Cities of the Indus," *American Anthropologist* 66:284–89.
1965   "The Mohenjo-daro Floods," *Antiquity* 39:196–203.
1967   *Water, Weather and Prehistory* (New York: Humanities Press).
RATHJE, WILLIAM L.
1974   "The Garbage Project: A New Way of Looking at the Problems of Archaeology," *Archaeology* 27:236–41.
REDFIELD, ROBERT
1947   "The Folk Society," *American Journal of Sociology* 52:292–308.

291

1953   *The Primitive World and Its Transformation* (Ithaca, N.Y.: Cornell University Press).

1956   *Peasant Society and Culture* (Chicago: University of Chicago Press).

1960   *The Little Community* (Chicago: University of Chicago Press).

REISS, A. J., JR.

1959   "The Sociological Study of Communities," *Rural Sociology* 24:118–30.

ROBERTS, ROY L.

1942   "Population Changes in the Great Plains," *Rural Sociology* 7:40–46.

ROBINSON, JOAN

1971   *Economic Heresies: Some Old-Fashioned Questions in Economic Theory* (New York: Basic Books).

RODGERS, HARRELL R.

1969   *Community Conflict, Public Opinion, and the Law* (Columbus, Ohio: Charles E. Merrill Books).

ROHN, ARTHUR H.

1971   *Mug House*, U.S. National Park Service Archaeological Research Series, no. 7-D.

ROHRER, WAYNE C., AND L. H. DOUGLAS

1969   *The Agrarian Transition in America: Dualism and Change* (New York: Bobbs-Merrill Co.).

ROSE, ARNOLD M.

1962   "The Subcultures of the Aging: A Topic for Sociological Research," *The Gerontologist* 2:123–27.

ROSOW, IRVING

1963   "Adjustment of the Normal Aged," in *Processes of Aging*, vol. 1., ed. R. H. Williams, C. Tibbitts, and W. Donahue (New York: Atherton Press).

1967   *Social Integration of the Aged* (New York: Free Press).

ROTHSCHILD, K. W.

1971   *Power in Economics* (Baltimore: Penguin Books).

RUBIN, MORTON

1951   *Plantation County* (Chapel Hill: University of North Carolina Press).

RUDOFSKY, BERNARD

1971   "Shelter for a Dark Age," *Horizon* 13(2):62–73.

RUSSELL, J. C.

1958   "Late Ancient and Medieval Populations," *Transactions of the American Philosophical Society*, n.s., vol. 48, pt. 3.

RYDER, NORMAN B.

1965   "The Cohort as a Concept in the Study of Social Change," *American Sociological Review* 30:843–61.

SACKETT, L. H., AND M. R. POPHAM

1972   "Lefkandi: A Euboean Town of the Bronze Age and the Early Iron Age," *Archaeology* 25:7–19.

SALPUKAS, AGES

1976   "Youth Gangs Plague Detroit," *New York Times*, August 17, p. 1.

SAMUEL, ALAN E.

1966   *The Mycenaeans in History* (Englewood Cliffs, N.J.: Prentice-Hall).

References

SAPIR, EDWARD
1924   "Culture, Genuine and Spurious," *American Journal of Sociology* 29:401–29.
SAVILLE, MURIEL R.
1970   "Language and the Disadvantaged," in *Readings for the Disadvantaged*, ed. T. D. Horn (New York: Harcourt, Brace & World).
SCHEFOLD, KARL
1968   "The Architecture of Eretria," *Archaeology* 21:272–81.
SCHWARTZ, DOUGLAS W.
1970   "The Postmigration Culture: A Base for Archaeological Inference," in *Reconstructing Prehistoric Pueblo Societies*, ed. W. A. Longacre (Albuquerque: University of New Mexico Press, School of American Research Advanced Seminar Series).
SETTIS, SALVATORE
1972   "Medma, an Ancient Greek City of Southern Italy," *Archaeology* 25:27–34.
SEVERO, RICHARD
1969   "Hunts Point," *New York Times*, September 1.
SHIMKIN, DEMITRI B.
1973   "Models for the Downfall: Some Ecological and Culture-Historical Considerations," in *The Classic Maya Collapse*, ed. T. P. Culbert (Albuquerque: University of New Mexico Press, School of American Research Advanced Seminar Series).
SHINNIE, P. L.
1967   *Meroë* (New York: Praeger Publishers).
SIMON, RITA J., ED.
1967   *As We Saw the Thirties* (Urbana: University of Illinois Press).
SINGH, GURDIP
1971   "The Indus Valley Culture," *Archaeology and Physical Anthropology in Oceania* 6:177–88.
SMITH, GERALD L. K.
1967   "The Huey Long Movement," in *As We Saw the Thirties*, ed. R. J. Simon (Urbana: University of Illinois Press).
SMITH, ROBERT J., AND EDUALDO P. REYES
1957   "Community Interrelations with the Outside World: The Case of a Japanese Agricultural Community," *American Anthropologist* 56:973–1002.
SOROKIN, PITIRIM A.
1962   *Social and Cultural Dynamics*, 4 vols. (New York: Bedminster Press).
1963   *Modern Historical and Social Philosophies* (New York: Dover Publications).
SOWER, CHRISTOPHER, JOHN HOLLAND, KENNETH TIEDKE, AND WALTER FREEMAN
1957   *Community Involvement* (Glencoe, Ill.: Free Press).
SPECK, FRANK G.
1935   *The Naskapi* (Norman: University of Oklahoma Press).
SPENCER, B., AND F. J. GILLEN
1927   *The Arunta* (London: Macmillan and Co.).
SPENGLER, OSWALD
1932   *The Decline of the West*, abr. ed. (New York: Modern Library).
SPICER, EDWARD H.
1958   "Social Structure and Cultural Process in Yaqui Religious Acculturation," *American Anthropologist* 60:433–40.

293

STEEN, CHARLIE R.
1966   *Excavations at Tse-Ta'a, Canyon de Chelly National Monument, Arizona*, U.S. National Park Service Archaeological Research Series, no. 9.

STEIGLITZ, E. J.
1943   *Geriatric Medicine* (Philadelphia: W. B. Saunders Co.).

STEIN, AUREL
1964   *On Ancient Central Asian Tracks* (New York: Pantheon Books).

STEIN, MAURICE
1960   *The Eclipse of Community: An Interpretation of American Studies* (Princeton, N.J.: Princeton University Press).

STEVENS, WILLIAM K.
1976   "Blacks See Detroit as Their Own and Hope to Rebuild It," *New York Times*, July 25, p. 1.

STEWARD, JULIAN H.
1950   *Area Research: Theory and Practice* (New York: Social Science Research Council).
1951   "Levels of Sociocultural Integration: An Operational Concept," *Southwest Journal of Anthropology* 7:374–90.
1955   *Theory of Culture Change* (Urbana: University of Illinois Press).
1956ed. *The People of Puerto Rico* (Urbana: University of Illinois Press).
1967   *Contemporary Change in Traditional Societies*, vol. 1 (Urbana: University of Illinois Press).

STILLMAN, EDWARD
1968   "Before the Fall," *Horizon* 10(4)4–15.

SWANSON, JOHN T.
1975   "The Myth of Trans-Saharan Trade During the Roman Era," *International Journal of African Historical Studies* 8:582–600.

SYKES, PERCY
1930   *A History of Persia*, 3d ed., 2 vols. (London: Macmillan and Co.).

TAIETZ, PHILIP
1975   "Community Complexity and Knowledge of Facilities," *Journal of Gerontology* 16:344–56.

TAX, SOL
1941   "World View and Social Relations in Guatemala," *American Anthropologist* 43:27–42.

TAYLOR, CARL C.
1940   "The Contribution of Sociology to Agriculture," in *Farmers in a Changing World*, ed. G. Hambidge (Washington, D.C.: U.S. Department of Agriculture).

THOMPSON, RAYMOND H., ED.
1958   *Migrations in New World Culture History*, University of Arizona Social Science Bulletin no. 27 (Tucson).

TITIEV, MISCHA
1944   *Old Oraibi*, Papers of the Peabody Museum of American Archaeology and Ethnology, vol. 22, no. 1 (Cambridge, Mass.: Harvard University).

TOBIN, S., AND BERNICE NEUGARTEN
1961   "Life Satisfaction and Social Interaction in the Aging," *Journal of Gerontology* 16:344–56.

TOCQUEVILLE, ALEXIS DE
1947   *Democracy in America* (New York: Oxford University Press, Galaxy Books).

TOENNIES, F.
1955   *Community and Association*, trans. C. P. Loomis (London: Routledge & Kegan Paul).

References

TOYNBEE, ARNOLD
1962   *A Study of History*, 12 vols. (New York: Oxford University Press).

TURNER, FREDERICK JACKSON
1921   *The Frontier in American History* (New York: Holt, Rinehart and Winston).

VAN BEEK, GUS W.
1969   "The Rise and Fall of Arabia Felix," *Scientific American* 221(6):36–46.

VANDER ZANDEN, JAMES W.
1963   *American Minority Relations* (New York: Ronald Press).
1966   *American Minority Relations*, 2d ed. (New York: Ronald Press).

VIDICH, ARTHUR J., AND JOSEPH BENSMAN
1968   *Small Town in Mass Society: Class, Power, and Religion in a Rural Community*, rev.
        ed. (Princeton, N.J.: Princeton University Press).
1975   *Metropolitan Communities: New Forms of Urban Sub-Communities* (New York: New
        Viewpoints, New York Times Books).

WALLACE, ANTHONY
1956   "Revitalization Movements," *American Anthropologist* 58:264–81.
1970   *Culture and Personality* (New York: Random House).

WARNER, W. LLOYD
1953   *American Life: Dream and Reality* (Chicago: University of Chicago Press).

WARREN, ROLAND L.
1963   *The Community in America* (Chicago: Rand McNally & Co.).
1975   "External Forces Affecting Local Communities—Bad News and Good News,"
        Journal of Community Development Society 6:5–13.

WEBB, MALCOLM C.
1973   "The Peten Maya Decline Viewed in the Perspective of State Formation," in *The
        Classic Maya Collapse*, ed. T. P. Culbert (Albuquerque: University of New Mexico
        Press, School of American Research Advanced Seminar Series).

WEBB, WALTER PRESCOTT
1931   *The Great Plains* (Boston: Ginn and Co.).
1951   "Ended: The 400 Year Boom: Reflections on the Age of the Frontier," *Harper's
        Magazine* 203:25–33.

WEED, PERRY L.
1973   *The White Ethnic Movement and Ethnic Politics* (New York: Praeger Publishers).

WELLER, JACK
1965   *Yesterday's People: Life in Contemporary Appalachia* (Lexington: University Press of
        Kentucky).

WEST, JAMES
1945   *Plainville U.S.A.* (New York: Columbia University Press).

WHEELER, MORTIMER
1968   *The Indus Civilization*, 3d ed. (Cambridge: Cambridge University Press).

WILKINSON, KENNETH P.
1974   "Consequences of Decline and Social Adjustment to It," in *Communities Left
        Behind: Alternatives for Development*, ed. L. R. Whiting (Ames: Iowa State University
        Press).

WILLIAMS, ANNE S.
1974   "Leadership Patterns in the Declining Rural Community," *Journal of the Community
        Development Society* 5:98–106.

WILLIAMS, LENA
1976   "Middle-Class Blacks Return to Harlem," *New York Times*, August 21, p. 1.

WILSON, JOHN A.
1951   *The Culture of Ancient Egypt* (Chicago: Phoenix Books).

WINGATE, RONALD
1955   *Wingate of the Sudan* (London: John Murray).

295

WISSLER, CLARK
1914   "The Influence of the Horse in the Development of the Plains Culture," *American Anthropologist* 16:1–25.
WOLF, ERIC R.
1959   *Sons of the Shaking Earth* (Chicago: University of Chicago Press).
WOODWARD, G. W. O.
1972   *The Dissolution of the Monasteries* (London: Pitkin Books).
WOOLLEY, LEONARD
1954   *Excavations at Ur* (London: Ernest Benn).
WORMINGTON, H. M.
1947   *Prehistoric Indians of the Southwest*, Colorado Museum of Natural History Popular Series, no. 7 (Denver).
WRIGLEY, E. A.
1969   *Population and History* (New York: McGraw-Hill).
ZIEGLER, PHILIP
1976   "The Black Death," *Horizon* 18(3):86–96.
ZIMMERMAN, CARLE C., AND T. LYNN SMITH
1930   "Migration to Towns and Cities," *American Journal of Sociology* 36:41–51.
ZINSSER, HANS
1945   *Rats, Lice, and History* (Boston: Little, Brown and Co.).
ZUBROW, EZRA
1972   "Carrying Capacity and Dynamic Equilibrium in the Prehistoric Southwest," in *Contemporary Archaeology*, ed. M. P. Leone (Carbondale: Southern Illinois University Press).

Index

Index

Index

Index

Index